# Business and Scientific Workflows

IEEE Press
445 Hoes Lane
Piscataway, NJ 08854



**Technical Reviewer**

**Professor Xudong He**
**School of Computer and Information Services**
**Florida International University**

# Business and Scientific Workflows

## A Web Service-Oriented Approach

**Wei Tan**
**MengChu Zhou**

IEEE PRESS

WILEY

For general information on our other products and services or for technical support, please contact our Customer Care Department within the United States at (800) 762-2974, outside the United States at (317) 572-3993 or fax (317) 572-4002.

Wiley also publishes its books in a variety of electronic formats. Some content that appears in print may not be available in electronic formats. For more information about Wiley products, visit our web site at www.wiley.com.

***Library of Congress Cataloging-in-Publication Data is available.***

ISBN: 978-1-11-817133-2

10 9 8 7 6 5 4 3 2 1

*From Wei Tan*
*Dedicated to my beloved parents,*
*Mr. Manliang Tan and Mrs. Xiaozhen Lin,*
*for their long-lasting support.*

*From MengChu Zhou*
*In memory of Mr. Shenglong Zhou,*
*my father*
*who had constantly inspired and encouraged*
*me to strive toward a better life,*
*better society, and better world.*

# Contents

**Foreword** xi
**Preface** xiii

**1. Introduction** 1

1.1 Background and Motivations, 1
1.1.1 Web Service and Service-Oriented Architecture, 1
1.1.2 Workflow Technology, 4
1.2 Overview of Standards, 8
1.2.1 Web Service-Related Standards, 8
1.2.2 Workflow-Related Standards, 19
1.3 Workflow Design: State of the Art, 22
1.3.1 Automatic Service Composition, 22
1.3.2 Mediation-Aided Service Composition, 23
1.3.3 Verification of Service-Based Workflows, 24
1.3.4 Decentralized Execution of Workflows, 25
1.3.5 Scientific Workflow Systems, 26
1.4 Contributions, 27

**2. Petri Net Formalism** 29

2.1 Basic Petri Nets, 29
2.2 Workflow Nets, 32
2.3 Colored Petri Nets, 35

**3. Data-Driven Service Composition** 39

3.1 Problem Statement, 40
3.1.1 Domains and Data Relations, 41
3.1.2 Problem Formulation, 43
3.2 Data-Driven Composition Rules, 45
3.2.1 Sequential Composition Rule, 46
3.2.2 Parallel Composition Rule, 46
3.2.3 Choice Composition Rule, 47
3.3 Data-Driven Service Composition, 48
3.3.1 Basic Definitions, 48
3.3.2 Derive AWSP from Service Net, 50

3.4 Effectiveness and Efficiency of the Data-Driven Approach, 55
3.4.1 Solution Effectiveness, 55
3.4.2 Complexity Analysis, 56
3.5 Case Study, 57
3.6 Discussion, 60
3.7 Summary, 61
3.8 Bibliographic Notes, 62

**4. Analysis and Composition of Partially-Compatible Web Services 65**
4.1 Problem Definition and Motivating Scenario, 65
4.1.1 A Motivating Scenario, 68
4.2 Petri Net Formalism for BPEL Service, Mediation, and Compatibility, 70
4.2.1 CPN Formalism for BPEL Process, 70
4.2.2 CPN Formalism for Service Composition, 73
4.2.3 Mediator and Mediation-Aided Service Composition, 75
4.3 Compatibility Analysis via Petri Net Models, 78
4.3.1 Transforming Abstract BPEL Process to SWF-net, 79
4.3.2 Specifying Data Mapping, 80
4.3.3 Mediator Existence Checking, 81
4.3.4 Proof of Theorem 4.1, 85
4.4 Mediator Generation Approach, 88
4.4.1 Types of Mediation, 88
4.4.2 Guided Mediator Generation, 90
4.5 Bibliographic Notes, 94
4.5.1 Web Service Composition, 94
4.5.2 Business Process Integration, 94
4.5.3 Web Service Configuration, 94
4.5.4 Petri Net Model of BPEL Processes, 94
4.5.5 Component/Web Service Mediation, 95

**5. Web Service Configuration with Multiple Quality-of-Service Attributes 99**
5.1 Introduction, 99
5.2 Quality-of-Service Measurements, 104
5.2.1 QoS Attributes, 104
5.2.2 Aggregation, 104
5.2.3 Computation of QoS, 105
5.3 Assembly Petri Nets and Their Properties, 107
5.3.1 Assembly and Disassembly Petri Nets, 107

5.3.2 Definition of Incidence Matrix and State-Shift Equation, 110
5.3.3 Definition of Subgraphs and Solutions, 111
5.4 Optimal Web Service Configuration, 114
5.4.1 Web Service Configuration under Single QoS Objective, 115
5.4.2 Web Service Configuration under Multiple QoS Objectives, 116
5.4.3 Experiments and Performance Analysis, 117
5.5 Implementation, 121
5.6 Summary, 123
5.7 Bibliographic Notes, 124

**6. A Web Service-Based Public-Oriented Personalized Health Care Platform 127**

6.1 Background and Motivation, 127
6.2 System Architecture, 129
6.2.1 The System Architecture of PHISP, 129
6.2.2 Services Encapsulated in PHISP, 131
6.2.3 Composite Service Specifications, 133
6.2.4 User/Domain Preferences, 134
6.3 Web Service Composition with Branch Structures, 137
6.3.1 Basic Ideas and Concepts, 137
6.3.2 Service Composition Planner Supporting Branch Structures, 139
6.3.3 Illustrating Examples, 148
6.4 Web Service Composition with Parallel Structures, 153
6.5 Demonstrations and Results, 155
6.5.1 WSC Example in PHISP, 155
6.5.2 Implementation of PHISP, 158
6.6 Summary, 159

**7. Scientific Workflows Enabling Web-Scale Collaboration 161**

7.1 Service-Oriented Infrastructure for Science, 162
7.1.1 Service-Oriented Scientific Exploration, 162
7.1.2 Case Study: The Cancer Grid (caGrid), 166
7.2 Scientific Workflows in Service-Oriented Science, 167
7.2.1 Scientific Workflow: Old Wine in New Bottle? 167
7.2.2 caGrid Workflow Toolkit, 174
7.2.3 Exemplary caGrid Workflows, 183
7.3 Summary, 188

**8. Network Analysis and Reuse of Scientific Workflows** **189**

8.1 Social Computing Meets Scientific Workflow, 190
8.1.1 Social Network Services for Scientists, 191
8.1.2 Related Research Work, 197
8.2 Network Analysis of myExperiment, 199
8.2.1 Network Model at a Glance, 199
8.2.2 Undirected Network, 200
8.2.3 Directed Graph, 205
8.2.4 Summary of Findings, 206
8.3 ServiceMap: Providing Map and GPS Assisting Service Composition in Bioinformatics, 207
8.3.1 Motivation, 207
8.3.2 ServiceMap Approach, 209
8.3.3 What Do People Who Use These Services Also Use? 210
8.3.4 What is an Operation Chain Between Services/Operations, 212
8.3.5 An Empirical Study, 218
8.4 Summary, 219

**9. Future Perspectives** **221**

9.1 Workflows in Hosting Platforms, 222
9.2 Workflows Empowered by Social Computing, 223
9.3 Workflows Meeting Big Data, 224
9.4 Emergency Workflow Management, 225

**Abbreviations List** **227**

**References** **231**

**Index** **247**

# Foreword

In 2001, as the first high-speed networks were deployed, the inimitable George Gilder observed that "when the network is as fast as the computer's internal links, the machine disintegrates across the net into a set of special purpose appliances." More than a decade later, our networks are faster and more reliable than ever. It is now entirely feasible to decompose not only our computer systems but also our software systems and applications—and then to reconstitute them as services that can be accessed over the network and combined into a myriad of applications. By so doing, we can achieve efficiencies and a flexibility unimaginable when our hardware, software, and data had to be laboriously acquired, integrated, and maintained at a single location.

But just how are we to combine services to build our applications? In this new world, programmers must select and combine services to create workflows that meet specific requirements. But this new world is not more disciplined than the old. Services are defined and operated by many providers who may differentiate themselves according to the services they offer, their implementations of those services, or the price or performance of their implementations. Faced with a choice between different services and service implementations, how should programmers identify service instances that will meet goals for functionality, correctness, performance, and price? How do they combine services without acquiring knowledge of their implementation? How to determine what qualities of services they can expect from the resulting workflows? Without proper answers to these questions, the experience of creating and operating distributed workflows can be more frustrating than liberating.

These are the questions that Tan and Zhou take on in this book. They do not necessarily provide definitive answers—that is not yet a feasible goal. But they provide the reader with the knowledge and tools required to understand the questions, to evaluate new technologies in the rapidly evolving world of service-oriented workflows, and to make sense of results emerging from academic research. Bridging the theoretical and the practical concerns, Tan and Zhou describe methods for reasoning about workflows, methodologies for constructing workflows from services, and substantial applications of these methodologies.

A particularly attractive feature of this book, in my opinion, is its integrated view of services in business and science—two domains with increasingly similar requirements but still far too few connections. It irritates my colleagues in the science community when I talk about capturing and accelerating their *business processes*—by which I mean not their accounting practices, but the data collection, lifecycle management, and other informatics activities that take so much of their time. But in both business and science, automation of the routine activities is a key to competitiveness. Science certainly has much to learn from business in this regard. We should also expect that demanding science applications will motivate new methods and tools that can be useful to business. I hope that this book can contribute to a conversation between these two communities.

As our old computer systems disintegrate around us, to use Gilder's phrasing, an understanding of the service-oriented workflow will become increasingly important to programmers, software engineers, managers, and researchers. For some, the most important element of this understanding will be knowledge of tools, programming methodologies, and technical standards. For others, it will be learning to reason about workflows with a view to establish a formal foundation for the creation of a new type of software system. For yet others, it will be gaining insight into how service-oriented workflows work in practice. This book has something to offer each of these audiences, so read and enjoy.

IAN FOSTER
*Director, Computation Institute,*
*University of Chicago, USA;*

*Arthur Holly Compton Distinguished Service Professor,*
*Department of Computer Science, University of Chicago, USA;*

*Distinguished Fellow, Argonne National Laboratory, USA*

# Preface

This book describes the technologies to build better workflows in the context of services computing, and the applications in both business and scientific domains. Originating from office automation, workflows are the computer models and automation mechanisms of business processes. Nowadays, workflow management is usually an indispensable subsystem in enterprise information systems. In the meanwhile, Web services technology, emerging from the early 2000s, has laid out a new foundation, that is, the service-oriented architecture (SOA), for the componentization, reuse, and interoperability of enterprise software. The interplay of workflow technology and SOA has provided a way to reuse existing services, quickly compose them into workflows, and adapt business processes with evolving requirements. Moreover, workflows themselves can be exposed as new services that can be used and/or composed by others.

However, there is still a big gap between academic research and real applications. This book tries to present the authors' efforts on advancing service composition methods and applying them to both business and scientific software systems, with both theoretical and empirical contributions. Methodology-wise, lightweight and flexible approaches are needed to compose services together, without imposing the need to acquire too much metadata or adapt services' internal workings. Application-wise, research results need to be incorporated into software tools to benefit academic researchers, industrial practitioners, and service users.

This book addresses both methodology and application problems in service-based workflows. We present a lightweight data-driven service composition approach, a mediation-aided approach to analyze and compose services, and a quality-of-service aware Web service functional configuration method. In the application aspect, we present the application of Web service composition techniques in a health care service platform and Web services and scientific workflows in e-Science. In particular, we discuss the network analysis and reuse of scientific workflows and introduce the social network concept into the workflow area.

Compared with the prior state of the art, this book has a salient feature, that is, it covers both research and engineering aspects. Since its first author is from an industry lab and the second author is a university professor, this book provides a unique perspective of business and scientific workflows from both academia and industry.

## ORGANIZATION OF THE BOOK

Chapter 1 provides an overview of the theme of this book, that is, the design of business and scientific workflows under a services computing paradigm. First, it gives an introduction to Web service technology and workflow technology. Then, it presents the industry standards in both areas, that is, services computing and workflow. Afterwards, it surveys five research topics, that is, automatic service composition, mediation-aided service composition, verification of service-based workflows, support for decentralized execution, and scientific workflows.

Chapter 2 provides a preliminary introduction to the formalism of Petri nets, its extensions, and applications to workflow and service composition. We make the Petri net formalism a standalone chapter because it is used in Chapters 3–5 of this book.

Chapter 3 presents a lightweight, data-driven approach for service composition in a Petri net framework. We utilize data relations in both business and service domains, and add data mediation constructs to make the data model in these domains complete and coherent. We devise three composition rules, that is, sequential, parallel, and choice, based on the augmented data model. On the basis of the data relations and composition rules, we propose a formal method to derive all the possible composition candidates, given a service portfolio. A prototype system is developed and an example is given to validate our approach as well as the algorithm.

Chapter 4 addresses how to compose partially compatible services and meet user requirements. Partial compatibility refers to the situation where two (or more) Web services provide complementary functionality and can be linked together in principle; however, their interfaces and interaction patterns do not fit each other as desired. Given two services whose interface invocation constraints are described by Business Process Execution Language (BPEL), we analyze their compatibility and adopt mediation as a lightweight approach to make them compatible without changing their internal logic. We first transform BPEL programs into a service workflow net, which is a type of colored Petri nets. Based on this formalism, we analyze the compatibility of two services and then devise an approach to verify whether there exists any message mediator whose composition does not violate the constraints imposed by either side. The method for mediator generation is finally proposed to assist the automatic composition of partially compatible services.

Chapter 5 deals with the automatic configuration of services under practical constraints. First, all Web services are discovered according to the customized or application-specific functional requirements. Second, by analyzing function decomposition and function selection on the service interface information, a complete service functional dependency configuration net based on Petri nets is built. Third, the quality-of-service (QoS) attributes for the whole configuration are chosen and computed. A transformation method is presented to convert nonlinear aggregation functions to linear ones. Relative importance or value trade offs of different attributes are represented through subjective preference or perception. Fourth, the QoS attribute value for each real Web service is gained. An association algorithm translates and compiles QoS attributes. Finally, the linear programming problem is set and solved based on a Petri net mechanism to identify the best composition.

Chapter 6 presents a Public-oriented Health care Information Service Platform (PHISP). It can provide individuals with health information management, and intelligent and personalized health care services; for some specific diseases, it supports basic remote health care and guardianship. In the platform, most of the functional modules are packaged in the form of services, and in order to realize the personalized customization and active recommendation of intelligent health care services for individuals, several key techniques for service composition are used, which can support branch and parallel control structures in the process models of composite services. The implementation status of the platform is also described.

Chapter 7 focuses on the application of workflow and Web services in e-Science. We start with an introduction to the data deluge phenomenon in science—specifically in biological sciences. Then we introduce the paradigm of service-oriented science (SOS) in which Web services are virtual access points to data and computational resources. We introduce the design and implementation of caGrid (Cancer Grid), which is a service-based data and computation infrastructure. Afterwards we discuss the requirements for developing scientific workflows for caGrid and explain how we fulfill these requirements. The caGrid Workflow Toolkit, an extension to the Taverna workflow system, is designed and implemented to ease building and running caGrid workflows. It provides users with support for various phases in using workflows: service discovery, composition and orchestration, data access, and secure service invocation. We also present real-life and service-based scientific workflows at the end of this chapter.

Chapter 8 takes a step further based on the work in caGrid and the caGrid Workflow Toolkit. The wide adoption of scientific workflows is hampered by the fact that scientists are unaware of the existence of services, and thus, are not able to effectively incorporate the best practices and tailor them in their new experiments. Our solution to this challenge is to introduce the social network concept into scientific workflows. We try to address the issue of network analysis and reuse of scientific workflows in a why-what-how approach. Why: first we review the advances in social network technology and its far-reaching impact on science. What: we then present a network analysis on "myExperiment," an online biological workflow repository. By examining the relationship among workflows and services, we reveal the usage pattern of services in scientific workflows, and how this knowledge can be extracted to facilitate reuse. How: based on a network-based model called ServiceMap, we aim to provide a GPS-like support to (1) help domain scientists better understand various usage patterns of the existing services and (2) provide a system-level support to recommend possible service compositions.

Chapter 9 summarizes the contribution of this book and highlights a few future research directions.

The following figure illustrates the organization of the contents in this book.

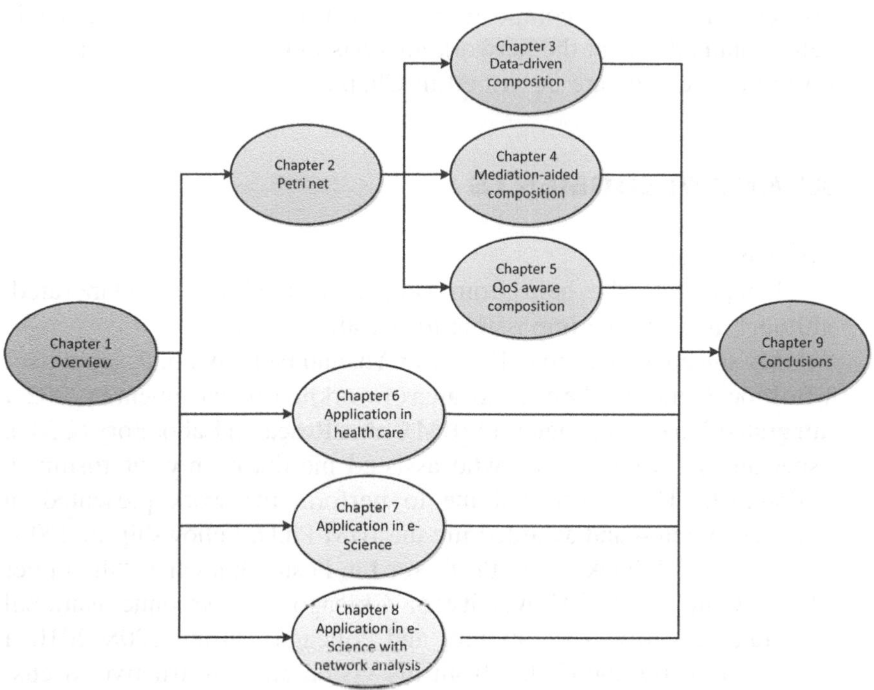


## HOW TO READ THIS BOOK

This book can be used as a reference book for either researchers in areas of business process management and services computing, or engineers who want to develop service-based workflow systems in business, scientific, and medical applications. More broadly, researchers and practitioners in areas such as software engineering, distributed computing, and management information systems (MIS) should find the topics of their interest.

All readers are encouraged to read Chapters 1 and 9, since they introduce the state of the art and point out some future directions, respectively. Chapters 2–5 are for readers who are more interested in service composition methodologies; readers who are familiar with the Petri net formalism can skip Chapter 2 and directly go to Chapters 3, 4, or 5. Chapters 6–8 are for those who are more interested in applications; particularly, Chapter 8 discusses the incorporation of social network concepts into service composition. From Chapter 3, every chapter is self-contained except the network analysis in Chapter 8 which is built on top of the software described in Chapter 7.

## ACKNOWLEDGMENTS

From Wei Tan:

I appreciate the help from people with whom I collaborated, although it would be impossible to list all of them.

My sincere thanks go to Professor Yushun Fan, my Ph.D. supervisor who brought me into the exciting area of workflow management in 2002. I am grateful to my colleagues in IBM China Research Laboratory (CRL), especially Dr. Zhong Tian, who assisted me during my internship in 2005–2006. They motivated me to perform the work presented in Chapters 3 and 4 and awarded me the IBM Ph.D. Fellowship in 2006.

My special thanks go to Professor Ian Foster, known as "the father of the Grid," at the University of Chicago and Argonne National Laboratory, who was my mentor and colleague during 2008–2010. I gained immense knowledge from his vision and constructive discussions with him. I would also like to thank two renowned scholars in the area of e-Science, Professor Carole Goble, at the University of Manchester, and Professor David De Roure, at the University of Oxford, for their collaboration on scientific workflows.

I also thank my colleagues in caBIG project, especially Ravi Madduri, Dinanath Sulakhe, Stian Soiland-Reyes, and Alexandra Nenadic. I enjoyed the collaboration with Professor Jia Zhang at Carnegie Mellon University, Silicon Valley Campus, on the topic of network analysis of scientific workflows. Some of this collaboration is reflected in Chapter 8. The work in Chapters 7 and 8 was funded in part with federal funds from the National Cancer Institute, National Institutes of Health, under Contract No. N01-CO-12400, and the Google Summer of Code program (2009–2010).

I would like to thank my manager at IBM T. J. Watson Research Center, Ms. Liana Fong, who supported me while working on this book. My friends, Dr. Bo Liu, Dr. Yanhua Du, Dr. Jianwu Wang, Mr. Keman Huang, Dr. Zi Ye, Dr. Wei Tang, Dr. Xitong Li, and Ms. Lina Chen helped proofread some parts of the book, which I greatly appreciate.

Finally I would like to thank Professor MengChu Zhou who is my mentor and the coauthor of this book. He is a renowned scholar in Petri nets and discrete event systems, and I really enjoyed our collaboration on the use of Petri nets in various studies on workflow and service composition.

From MengChu Zhou:

There have been numerous collaborations behind this book and its related work. It would have been impossible to achieve without the help of the following collaborators, some of whom are already mentioned in the first author's message.

Dr. Pengcheng Xiong and Professor Yushun Fan collaborated with me for a number of years; we promoted the application of Petri nets to the area of Web composition successfully. We applied the disassembly Petri nets to the optimal configuration of Web services subject to environmental changes by considering multiple QoS measures, and adopted Petri net siphon and related theory for compatibility analysis, and a Petri net approach to the identification and resolution of protocol-level service composition mismatches. Some of our collaborative work is reflected in Chapter 5.

I enjoyed the collaboration with Dr. Pengwei Wang, Dr. Guanjun Liu, Dr. Ping Sun, Dr. Xianfei Tang, Professor Zhijun Ding, and Professor Changjun Jiang at the Key Laboratory of Embedded System and Service Computing, Ministry of Education, Tongji University. In recent years, Professor Changjun Jiang built up and led a world-class research group who made and are still making many important contributions in the areas of Web service theory and applications:

1. development of interactive Web service composition method based on Petri nets;
2. development of automated Web service composition method based on Horn clauses and Petri nets;
3. development of automated Web service composition method supporting both parallel and conditional branch structures;
4. design and implementation of a public-oriented personalized healthcare platform based on service-oriented architectures and Web service composition methods; and
5. invention of interactive Petri nets to describe interacting Web services and workflow systems.

Some of these research results are reflected in Chapter 6.

I have enjoyed the great support from my family for many years. Albert Zhou, my older son, currently a college student, helped proofread some parts of the book, which I greatly appreciated.

The work presented in this book was in part supported by the National Basic Research Program of China (2010CB328101 and 2011CB302804), the National Natural Science Foundation of China (NSFC) (60773001, 61074035, 61173016, and 61034004), and the National Science Foundation under Grant No. **CMMI-1162482**.

Wei Tan
*IBM T. J. Watson Research Center, USA*

MengChu Zhou
*New Jersey Institute of Technology, USA*
*and Tongji University, China*

# CHAPTER 1

# Introduction

With the emergence of service-oriented architecture (SOA), Web services are gaining momentum as key elements in enterprise information systems. Meanwhile, building business and scientific workflows using service composition has become an important method for system integration and process reengineering. Therefore, workflow-driven service composition is now a hot topic in both academia and industry. This book focuses on how to design, analyze, and deploy Web service-based workflows for business, scientific, and medical applications. This chapter discusses the state of the art in both technologies, that is, Web services and workflow management, with a focus on their impact on each other.

## 1.1 BACKGROUND AND MOTIVATIONS

### 1.1.1 Web Service and Service-Oriented Architecture

In a 1996 report, Schulte and Natis of Gartner Inc. first used the term service-oriented architecture (SOA) to describe a style of multitier computing that helped organizations share logic and data among multiple applications and usage modes [1].

Thomas Erl, who is recognized as a major contributor in the area of SOA, describes it as an architecture that is *open, agile, extensible, federated,* and *composable*—one that is composed of *autonomous, QoS-capable, vendor diverse, interoperable, discoverable,* and

*Business and Scientific Workflows: A Web Service-Oriented Approach*, First Edition.
Edited by Wei Tan and MengChu Zhou.

*potentially reusable services* [2]. He further summarizes the following eight principles of SOA [3]:

- *Standardized Service Contract.* Services should expose their interface and their level of service explicitly, in a standard way. That is the only information needed by a user.
- *Service Loose Coupling.* Services may collaborate with each other but their dependencies should be minimized such that in their communication, they only need to know the contract of others.
- *Service Abstraction.* Services should hide their internal workings from the outside world, except the contract. For example, a service should not expose its technical details, such as the programming language, operating system, and database used, to users.
- *Service Reusability.* Services should be designed in a granularity to promote reuse. If a service is only to be used by a single user, then there is no reason to expose it as a service.
- *Service Autonomy.* A service should have control over its behavior and respond to invocation requests. In a service system, a centralized control is not necessary.
- *Service Statelessness.* Services should minimize the state information exposed to peers and other users, to improve the loose coupling and scalability of the architecture. If a service is stateless, the server side does not need to maintain session or state information; more importantly, a request can be routed easily for the load balance purpose.
- *Service Discoverability.* Services are annotated with metadata such that they can be discovered by users.
- *Service Composability.* Services should be able to be composed to fulfill new and more complex requirements. This principle is closely related to reusability, that is, services are composable such that they can be reused in different applications.

Although Schulte and Natis created the term in 1996, the interest in it only revived in 2000s when Web service technology emerged and matured. In W3C's glossary, a *Web service* is a software system for machine-to-machine interaction over a network [4]. A Web service (or service for short) should have an *interface description* and be invoked in a way prescribed by this description and using HTTP (Hypertext Transfer Protocol) related protocols. W3C's recommendation is to use WSDL (Web Service Definition Language) to describe its interface, and SOAP (Simple Object Access Protocol) over HTTP to invoke it. All these specifications (WSDL, SOAP, and other Web-related ones) are XML (Extensible Markup Language)-based and can be understood and processed by computer programs. We introduce these related standards in more detail later.

The term *service* in the original definition [1] is abstract and does not tie in with any concrete technology. It is Web service technology that quickly makes SOA tangible and practical to many users. SOA principles provide guidance to Web service implementations and differentiate it with competing technologies such as CORBA, DCOM, and Java RMI [5]. Although SOA does not necessarily build upon Web services and Web service technology by itself is not equivalent to SOA, there is a tight relation between these two concepts. In this book we consider Web services as the best implementation technology for SOA, and SOA principles are applied in Web service practices. Therefore, from now on we do not explicitly distinguish between *Web service* and *service* unless otherwise mentioned.

The triangle in Figure 1.1 lays the foundation of all Web service technologies, by describing the interplay of *service client*, *service registry*, and *service provider*. Consider the following scenario. Multiple service providers want to offer services but are not aware of their clients. Neither do the clients know where and how to access desired services. In SOA, every provider *registers* its service into a registry by providing its function, quality of service, provider information, and so on. The service registry acts like the yellow pages and search engine for services. It categorizes services based on different criteria such as functions, providers, quality of service, and offers a flexible search mechanism to be used by clients. Service clients *look up* the service they want, and obtain the reference to it from the registry. They then *bind* to the service's reference and *invoke* it. Currently, UDDI (Universal Description, Discovery, and Integration) is the standard designed for service registry. Service providers register service descriptions using WSDL. Once clients obtain the WSDL of a service from the registry, they use SOAP to interact with the service. This book introduces these standards in more detail in Section 1.2.

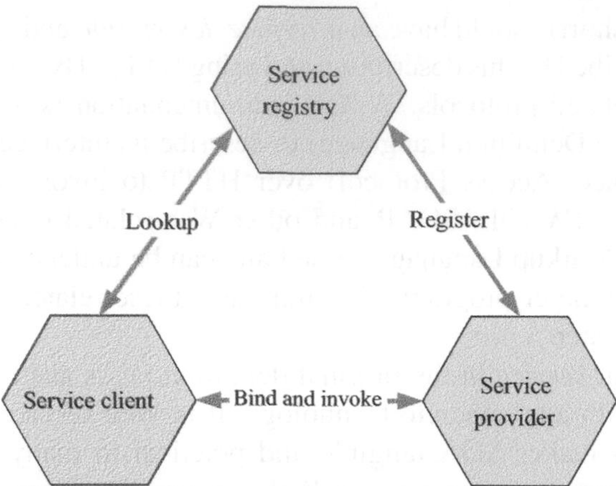


**Figure 1.1** The Web service triangle.

## 1.1.2 Workflow Technology

As defined by Workflow Management Coalition (WfMC), a forerunner in standardizing the workflow technology, workflow is *the computerized facilitation or automation of a business process, in whole or part*. This book focuses on the automation aspect of a business process and thus will not distinguish between a *workflow* and a *business process* unless otherwise mentioned.

The *Workflow Reference Model* [6] published by WfMC in 1995 has laid the foundation in defining a vocabulary and architecture of a workflow system. Despite the drastic technology evolution over the years, this reference model is still applicable to most workflow systems in use today. Here, we use this vocabulary to go over the key concepts in a workflow system and introduce the reference architecture in Section 1.2.2. The reference model defines a common glossary to describe business processes (also known as, workflows) and various artifacts associated with them. It divides the function of a workflow management system into two aspects, that is, *build time* and *run time*. At build time, a *process definition* or *workflow definition* is designed, usually with the help of a modeling tool, as the representation of a business process to be automated. A workflow definition usually contains a set of *activities* and the sequence among them. An activity can be either a *manual activity* that needs human intervention or an *automated workflow activity* that will be executed by a software application. At run time, a *workflow engine* is the computer software that provides the execution environment for workflows. Given a workflow definition, the engine can start multiple *workflow instances*. For example, an order processing workflow definition can have multiple instances, each of which deals with one particular incoming customer order. There can be many concurrent instances in a workflow engine. In a workflow instance, each activity also has its corresponding *activity instance*.

The workflow technology originated from office automation (OA) area and initially handled the documentation flow among multiple persons or applications. In recent years, workflow has been evolved from a pure IT technology for business process automation, to a much broader concept called business process management (BPM) [7]. BPM is a holistic approach to align many aspects of an enterprise, such as organization, rules, resources, and quality management, in a process centric manner so as to optimize overall operational efficiency and customer satisfaction.

Figure 1.2 illustrates the life cycle of BPM. It starts with the *design* phase. In this phase, first the existing processes (also known as, *as-is* processes) inside an organization, both non-automated and automated ones, are identified. Afterward the *to-be* processes, that is, those to be managed by the BPM system are designed with different criteria. The criteria can be customer satisfaction, response time, or quality of service. A process includes not only a sequenced series of tasks, but also the *organizational unit* responsible for tasks and processes, the

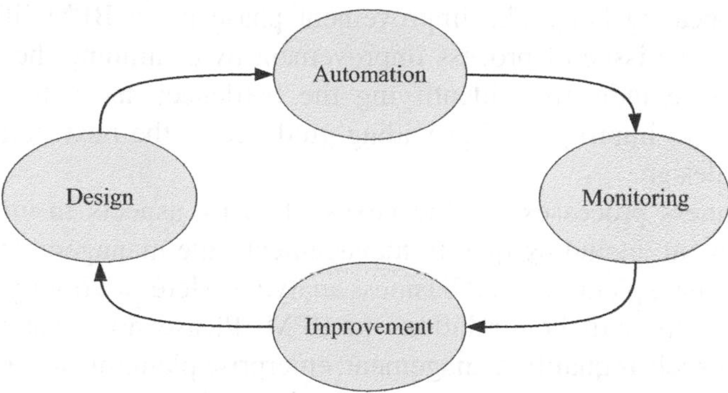


**Figure 1.2** The life cycle of BPM.

*resources* needed, and the *business rules* to control the behavior of tasks or processes.

Second, in the *automation* phase, the business processes designed are translated into a format that can be understood by the underlying process engine (also known as, workflow engine) and become operational in a BPM system (BPMS). Through the BPMS backbone, a process in execution can invoke computer applications, command organizational units, and consume resources to achieve the goal defined in the previous design phase. Nowadays many BPMSs are based on SOA infrastructure. Business processes are translated into BPEL [8] and Web services are adopted as the communication interfaces among processes, applications, and even organizational units.

The designed and later automated processes are monitored in the *monitoring* phase. Usually in a BPMS, the status of running processes and activities are traced, the performance indicators measured, and anomalies reported. Besides the real-time aspect of business process monitoring, the historical data collected in this phase can be used in the subsequent improvement phase.

In the fourth phase, that is, *improvement*, the process model from the design and automation phases, as well as the performance indicator accumulated from the monitoring phase, are put together to provide a retrospect to a process. In 1990s, business process reengineering (BPR) [9,10] emerged. It states that managers need to fundamentally rethink their processes and change them in a dramatic way so as to offer processes with improved customer satisfaction and reduced operational cost. Later when business processes were better managed, a less radical approach compared to BPR, i.e., business process improvement (BPI), became more appealing [11]. The improvement phase in a BPM life cycle addresses the issue of process improvement by examining the process performance indicators, identifying the bottleneck as well as other potentials to improve, and providing guidance to the next iteration of process design.

Business processes are the nexus of many aspects in enterprise management, including quality management, rule management, enterprise resource planning, and business analytics. Here, we briefly discuss these aspects and their relations to BPM. Please note that because concepts such as quality management, enterprise planning, and business analytics are by themselves complex and evolving, we do not mean to make a comprehensive survey.

Six Sigma [12] and total quality management (TQM) [13] are two approaches to identify defects in production processes and improve the quality of process output. Since products are the main output of business processes, processes with associated applications and persons should be responsible for their quality. BPMS can enforce the quality control methodology into the process engine and continuously monitor the process output.

A business rule management system (BRMS) [14] is a software system to define the decision logic of an enterprise, and to provide the result of this decision logic to other enterprise applications at run-time. For example, a business rule may be defined as *if a customer has bought a vitamin product, issue him/her a coupon of the same brand at checkout*. Then at run-time when the checkout system asks the rule engine, it should check the customer's purchase and decide whether or not to issue a coupon. The combination of BPMS and BRMS has two advantages. First of all, business rules can take the responsibility to model the complex decision logic inside a process and drive the decision point at run-time. This separation can make the process model more compact and more adaptive to changes of business requirements. Second, BPMS can record the rules that have been applied and the rule evaluation results. These statistics provides insights into how the rules have governed the operation of a business.

Computer-supported cooperative work (CSCW) addresses how computer systems can support group activities involving multiple people and their coordination [15]. Typical CSCW systems include digital whiteboard, video conferencing, groupware, wiki, and version control software. Since designing a business process is an approach to model how tasks are routed among people, BPMS can be seen as a kind of CSCW systems in terms of its capability to coordinate multiple tasks that involve multiple organizational units. However, typical CSCW systems can better support *ad hoc* coordination or processes compared with BPMS.

Enterprise resource planning (ERP) [16] attempts to integrate all the operations across an enterprise in a single computer system that can serve all departments' essential needs, such as finance, accounting, manufacturing, sales and service, and customer relationship management. Since most enterprise operations are conducted through business processes, BPMS can be cross-department glue to compose multiple individual ERP components into a meaningful business function. Moreover, BPMS can make an ERP system more flexible and responsive to business needs, by dynamically reengineering business processes and reorganizing the ERP components associated with them.

Business analytics (BA) [17] uses quantitative methods to understand what happened and why (descriptive), and what will happen next (predictive) in business. Business analytics is closely related to multiple BPM phases in Figure 1.2: data needed in analytics are collected in the monitoring phase while the results of such analytics are used as guidance in the improvement phase and eventually reflected in the design phase.

## 1.2 OVERVIEW OF STANDARDS

### 1.2.1 Web Service-Related Standards

Figure 1.3 is a layered architecture of Web service-related standards. From bottom to top, it consists of different layers such as message,

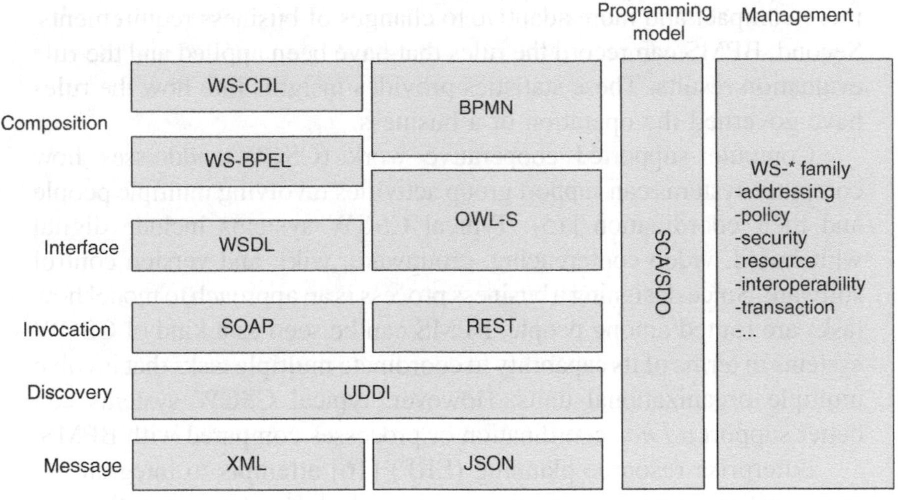


**Figure 1.3** Web service-related standards. XML, Extensible Markup Language; JSON, JavaScript Object Notation; UDDI, Universal Description, Discovery, and Integration; SOAP, Simple Object Access Protocol; REST, Representational State Transfer; WSDL, Web Service Definition Language; OWL-S, Web Ontology Language-Service; WS-BPEL, Web Services Business Process Execution Language; BPMN, Business Process Modeling Notation; WS-CDL, Web Services Choreography Description Language; SCA, Service Component Architecture; and SDO, Service Data Objects.

discovery, invocation, interface, and composition. The message layer is about the format of messages exchanged between Web services, and between services and clients. XML [18] and JSON [20] are two major industry standards in this layer. The discovery layer is about how services are advertised and registered such that users can find them. UDDI [21] serves this purpose. The invocation layer defines the protocol specification when services are invoked. Currently, SOAP [22] and RESTful API [23] are the two major protocols where API stands for application programming interface. The interface layer is about the service interface specification that describes how a service can be called, what data structure it expects, and what it returns. WSDL [24] is the standard in this layer and OWL-S [25] offers a semantics-enhanced option. As we mentioned earlier, service composability is an important principle of SOA, and therefore service composition has been a major focus of research by both academia and industry. Among many specifications in this layer, WS-BPEL [8] is the *de facto* industry standard to compose multiple Web services into a business process and to expose this process also as a (composite) service. OWL-S offers semantics-enabled composite service description. WS-CDL [26], from a higher level, defines the peer-to-peer collaborations of services by specifying the ordered message exchanges between them. BPMN [31] is a popular business process modeling specification, and has a tight relation with service composition.

In Figure 1.3, there are also two cross-layer categories, that is, programming model and management. The programming model, which is independent of any specific programming language, defines how to abstract functions as components and use them as building blocks to assemble SOA solutions. Currently, Service Component Architecture (SCA) is a popular SOA programming model; while Service Data Object (SDO) is its data model. Service management involves many cross-cutting and nonfunctional specifications, such as addressing, policy, security, resource, interoperability, and transaction.

### Message

XML (Extensible Markup Language) [18] is often used as the message exchange format for interfacing Web services, though this is not required. JSON (JavaScript Object Notation) [20] is also becoming increasingly common. Here, we briefly introduce both languages.

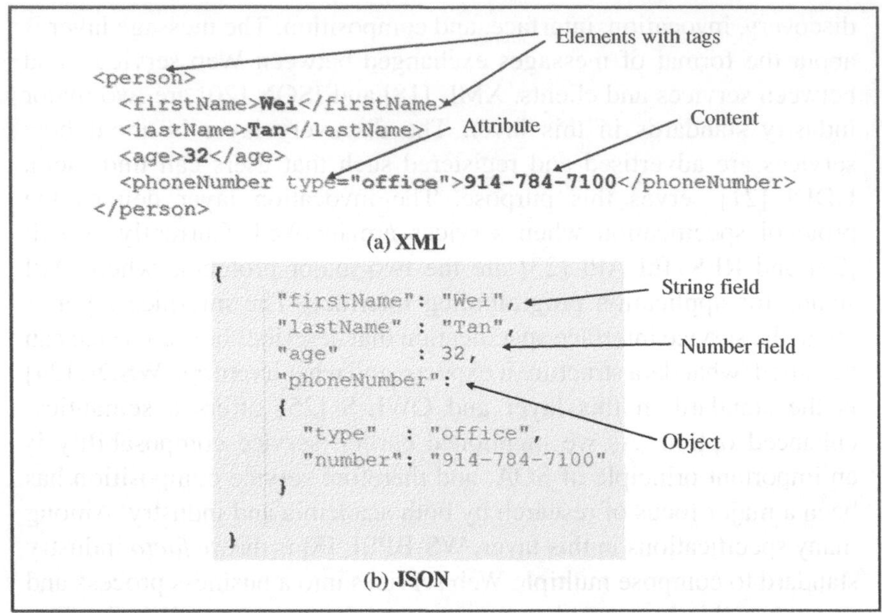


**Figure 1.4** (a) XML and (b) JSON presentations of a person.

XML is a text format designed to carry and store data. It uses tags to organize elements, associated contents and attributes. Figure 1.4a shows the XML representation of a piece of information that describes a person, regarding its name, age, and phone number. Element <person> contains nested elements such as <firstName>, <lastName>, <age>, and <phoneNumber>; <firstName> contains content *Wei*; <phoneNumber> also contains attribute "type" that specifies the type of the phone number is *office*.

Compared to XML, JSON, which is based on a subset of the JavaScript programming language, is a lightweight data-interchange format. JSON is built on two structures, that is, a collection of name/value pairs and an ordered list of values. Figure 1.4b shows the JSON representation of the same person we have just illustrated with XML in Figure 1.4a. The object has two string fields for first name and last name, respectively, a number field for age, and a nested object storing the phone number.

## Discovery

UDDI (Universal Description, Discovery, and Integration) [27], as a specification language, defines a universal method for enterprises to dynamically discover and invoke Web services. UDDI was originally designed as a registry and brokerage system that helped users locate services needed in a dynamic way. For example, assume that the hotel industry adopted UDDI standard for hotel room rate checking and reservation. Hotels could then register their services into a central UDDI directory. Individual travelers or travel agencies could then search the UDDI directory to find any hotel's reservation interface. When an interface is found, users would be able to communicate with the service directly.

A UDDI business registry consists of three components:

- *White Pages.* They give information about the business providing the service. Using white pages, users can look for services based on providers.
- *Yellow Pages.* They provide a classification of the service or business, based on standard taxonomies.
- *Green Pages.* They describe how to access a Web service, including the interface, parameters, and address of the service.

WSDL, SOAP, and UDDI were originally designed to be the three pillars of Web services. However, UDDI does not enjoy as much popularity as WSDL and SOAP do.

### Interface

WSDL [24] (Web Services Description Language) is an XML-based interface definition specification for describing Web services and how to access them. WSDL describes a Web service, along with the message format and protocol details for it.

Figure 1.5 shows a skeleton of a WSDL document.[1] Such a document describes a Web service by using the following major elements:

- <types>: *Types* section defines the data types used by the service. Types will be referred by the *message* section.

[1] Here we use WSDL 1.1 specification as an example. This is because that, although WSDL 2.0 specification has been released since 2007, we found many public available Web services are written in WSDL 1.1. For a comparison of WSDL 1.1 and 2.0, please see Reference [28] W3C. "Web Services Description Language (WSDL) Version 2.0 Part 1: Core Language." Retrieved January 7, 2012, from http://www.w3.org/TR/wsdl20/.

```
<definitions>

<types>
  definition of data types used in message
</types>

<message>
  definition of messages used by operation as input/output
</message>

<portType>
  A portType contains one or more operations,
  each operation has an input and optionally an output message
    <operation>
        <input message="refer-to-message"/>
        <output message="refer-to-message"/>
    </operation>
</portType>

<binding>
  A binding binds a portType to a communication protocol,
  such as SOAP, HTTP Get, and HTTP Post
</binding>

<service>
  A service contains one or more ports, each port assigns a URL to a binding;
  service requests can be sent to this URL w/ protocols defined in binding
    <port name="..." binding="refer-to-binding">
        <address location="URL to send service request"/>
    </port>
</service>

</definitions>
```

**Figure 1.5** Skeleton of a WSDL document.

- <message>: *Messages* are to be referred as the input and output of *operations*.
- <portType>: A *portType* contains a collection of *operations*. Each operation has an input message and optionally an output one. Both input and output messages are defined in the *message* section.
- <binding>: A *binding* binds a *portType* to a specific communication protocol, such as SOAP, HTTP Get, and HTTP Post. By this means a client knows which protocol to use when communicating with the service.
- <service>: A *service*, as a concrete entity to be accessed by clients, contains one or more *ports*, and each port assigns a URL to a *binding*. To access a given port, requests should be sent to its URL, by using the protocols (e.g., SOAP, HTTP Get/Post) defined in the corresponding *binding* element.

```
<Envelope>

<Header>
  application-specific information such as authentication, payment,
  intermediary processing about this message
</Header>

<Body>
  contains the actual SOAP message intended for the endpoint of the message
    <Fault>
      contains error messages for this invocation
    </Fault>
</Body>

</Envelope>
```

**Figure 1.6** Skeleton of a SOAP message.

## *Invocation*

SOAP [22] (Simple Object Access Protocol) is an XML-based protocol to let applications exchange information over HTTP or other methods such as Simple Mail Transfer Protocol (SMTP). As we have seen in the WSDL specification, SOAP is a binding method to enable the message exchange with a service.

Figure 1.6 shows a skeleton of a SOAP document that contains the following major elements:

- <header>: The *header* section defines the application-specific information such as authentication, payment, and how an intermediary node should process this message.
- <body>: The *body* section contains the actual SOAP message for the endpoint of the message. The format of the actual SOAP message is defined in the WSDL document of the service.
- <fault>: The *fault* section contains error messages for this invocation. The fault can be from the client side, for example, the message is incorrectly formed by the client; or from the server side, for example, the server cannot process the message because it is too busy.

Here we use a real Web service example to illustrate a SOAP request and its response. We use the *NASDAQ Analytics Web Service*[2]

[2] http://www.nasdaqdod.com/NASDAQAnalytics.asmx?v=xOperations

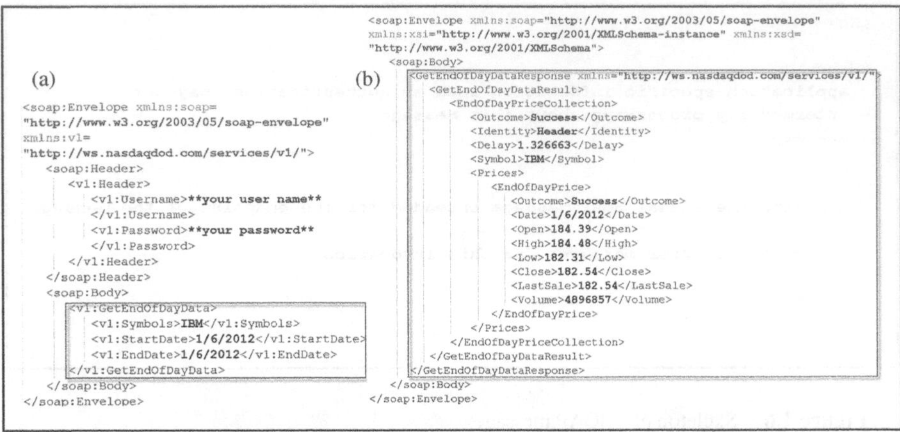


**Figure 1.7** The SOAP request (a) and response (b) of the *GetEndOfDayData* operation in the *NASDAQ Analytics Web Service*. The actual SOAP bodies are highlighted in rectangles. Here we ask the end-of-date data for IBM of January 6, 2012.

that offers historical stock quote data. Figure 1.7 illustrates the actual SOAP request and response of the *GetEndOfDayData* operation.[3] In the SOAP body, we ask the end-of-date stock data, by giving a symbol (IBM), and start and end date on January 6, 2012. In the SOAP header we need to give the user name and password[4] for an authentication purpose. The SOAP response includes *Outcome* (Success), authentication *identity* (from Header of the SOAP request), and *open*, *close*, *high*, and *low* price of the IBM stock, as well as the *volume*.

REST (Representational State Transfer) is a lightweight alternative to WSDL/SOAP based Web services. While WSDL/SOAP is still dominant in enterprise applications, REST services are becoming more popular on the Web. For example, companies such as Yahoo, Google, and Facebook have all adopted REST as their service model, while deprecating many of the WSDL/SOAP counterparts. Key architectural features of REST services include the following:

- *Use URI to Organize Web Resources*. In the REST paradigm, every piece of data (also known as, resource) users can access is exposed using a URI (uniform resource identifier). For example,

[3] http://www.nasdaqdod.com/NASDAQAnalytics.asmx?op=GetEndOfDayData

[4] An account with limited free access to this service can be obtained by registration at the Nasdaq data on demand Web site: https://www.nasdaqdod.com/.

http://en.wikipedia.org/wiki/URI is the URI of the article "uniform resource identifier" in Wikipedia.

- *Use HTTP Methods to Access Resources.* Use PUT to create new resources, use GET to obtain resource properties, use POST to update a resource, and DELETE to remove it. For example, you can use the Wikipedia REST API [29] to obtain, create, update, and delete resources, i.e., Wikipedia articles.
- *Make Interactions Stateless.* By "statelessness," we here mean that, a request is self-contained and does not require the server to retrieve or maintain state information for it. Statelessness of a service makes it easy to use and allow the server for easy load-balancing during run time.

The aforementioned *NASDAQ Analytics Web Service* also provides a REST interface, and the end-of-day data for IBM on January 6, 2012 can be obtained by using the HTTP GET method shown below:

```
GET http://ws.nasdaqdod.com/v1/NASDAQAnalytics
.asmx/GetEndOfDayData?
Symbols=IBM&StartDate=1/6/2012&EndDate=1/6/
2012&MarketCenters=Q,B5
```

### Service Composition

The following discussions focus on service composition specifications including Web Services Business Process Execution Language (WS-BPEL), Web Services Choreography Description Language (WS-CDL), Ontology Web Language – Service (OWL-S), and Business Process Model and Notation (BPMN).

**Web Services Business Process Execution Language (WS-BPEL).** Among service composition specifications, WS-BPEL [8] is a dominant one because it is not only approved by OASIS (Organization for the Advancement of Structured Information Standards) as an industry standard, but also execution-oriented and supported by major software vendors as well as the open source community. WS-BPEL stands for Web Services Business Process Execution Language, called BPEL for short.

[5] To use this REST API you need an account with limited free access. It can be obtained by registration at the Nasdaq data on demand Web site: https://www.nasdaqdod.com/.

BPEL defines a meta-model and an XML-based grammar to describe the behavior of a business process that is composed of Web services as well as exposed as a Web service. A BPEL process defines the execution structure on how multiple Web service invocations are coordinated to achieve a business goal. The main constructs and their functions are listed below while a reader may refer to [8] for a comprehensive description.

- <partnerLinks>: It refers to the communication channels between a process and partners. The process can invoke a partner and/or be invoked by a partner.
- <variables>: It defines the variables used by the process; <assign> activity is used to manipulate these variables and, in turn, change the state of the process.
- <receive>: It is used to receive messages from an external partner.
- <reply>: It is used to respond to an external partner with messages. Typically, a <reply> activity is associated with a <receive> one to implement a WSDL request-response operation on a particular partner link. By this means, a BPEL process exposes a WSDL operation to be invoked by others.
- <invoke>: It is used to call a WSDL operation of a Web service.
- Structural constructs such as <sequence>, <if-else>, <while>, <repeatUntil>, <forEach>, and <flow> define the sequential (<sequence>), conditional (<if-else>), repetitive (<repeatUntil> and <forEach>), and parallel (<flow>) execution of the activities contained in them.
- <faultHandlers>: It is used to handle exceptions and faults in a process.

As seen in the description above, another feature that makes BPEL favorable is that it is tightly integrated with many XML specifications such as XML Schema, WSDL, XPath (XML Path language), and XSLT (Extensible Stylesheet Language Transformation). XML Schemas are used as data type definitions; XPath and XSLT provide the support for data assignment; and WSDL is used to model partner services as well as the interface exposed by a BPEL process.

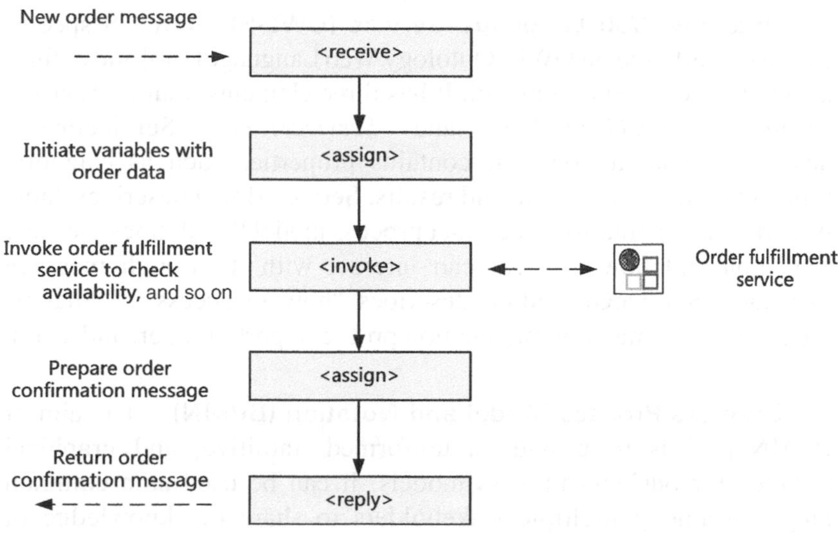


**Figure 1.8** An online book selling process in BPEL.

Think of an online book selling application that is implemented in BPEL, as illustrated in Figure 1.8. A customer (through either a Web interface or software application) sends a new order message to the <receive> activity. The process initiates internal variables with the order received in the first <assign> activity, and then invokes the order fulfillment Web service (through the <invoke> activity) to determine the availability of the book, payment status, and so on. When the order fulfillment service returns a result, an order confirmation message is prepared in the second <assign> and the process responds to the customer regarding the status of the order, that is, successful or not.

**Web Services Choreography Description Language (WS-CDL).** Different from BPEL, WS-CDL [26] is not targeted at describing one executable workflow. From a global viewpoint, it defines the peer-to-peer collaboration of services by specifying the ordered message exchanges between them. That is to say, it abstractly describes the global observable behavior of multiple parties in a collaboration. While BPEL is called a service orchestration language, WS-CDL is usually referred to as a service choreography language.

**Ontology Web Language-Service (OWL-S).** OWL-S specification [25] is based on OWL (Ontology Web Language) [30] and defines an ontology of a service model. It has three elements, that is, *Service-Profile*, *ServiceGrounding*, and *ServiceModel*. ServiceProfile describes "what it does." It contains properties such as category, input, output, precondition, and results. ServiceModel describes "how it works," and contains an abstract process model that defines the state transition and how a client can interact with it through message exchange. ServiceGrounding describes "how to access it," that is, the message format, communication protocol, port number, and so on.

**Business Process Model and Notation (BPMN).** The aim of BPMN [31] is to provide a uniformed, intuitive, and graphical notation for business process models. It can be used as a common language among multiple stakeholders to share the knowledge of business processes: business analysts can use it to express the business goal and function to be achieved; IT experts can use it to implement a workflow that automates the process; managers can use it to monitor the execution and examine the performance of business. Although not originally designed for SOA, it is closely related to the concepts in it. For a few examples, it has a model element called a service task to depict a service. BPMN to BPEL mapping is also a part of its specification. It also contains a collaboration model to describe process choreographies.

### *Programming Model*

Service Component Architecture (SCA) [32] is an industry standard proposed by major software vendors such as IBM, Oracle, and SAP for a generic, language-independent programming model for SOA. Using SCA, users can specify what interfaces a component exposes (i.e., the services to be used by others), what interfaces a component needs to invoke (i.e., the services to be referenced), how a component is implemented (Java, BPEL, etc.), and how many components are wired to compose a larger one. Service Data Object (SDO) defines a data model in SCA and its mapping to Java objects, XML schema, and so on. SCA and SDO are currently supported by software products such as IBM Business Process Manager [33] and Oracle SOA Suite [34].

### Management

There are many standards addressing the management and non-functional aspects of Web services. Here, we only list some from W3C's *Web Service Activity Statement* [35]. For a more comprehensive list, please refer to [3,35–37].

- *WS-Policy* describes the policies (security, quality of service, etc.) of entities in a Web services-based system.
- *WS-Addressing* specifies how to describe an endpoint reference of a Web service, and policies to transmit and route messages among endpoints.
- *WS-Transfer* defines a SOAP-based protocol to create, update, and delete Web service-based resources.
- *WS-Enumeration* defines a SOAP-based protocol to enumerate a sequence of XML elements in large data sets, such as logs, event streams, and message queues.

## 1.2.2 Workflow-Related Standards

In Section 1.2.1, we have discussed Web service-related standards. Some of them, such as BPMN and BPEL, are related to workflow. As the theme of the book is Web service-based workflow, next we introduce workflow-related standards. Among them, the most important one is WfMC's Workflow Reference Model [6], which has laid the foundation in defining the structure of a workflow system. The reference model first defines a general glossary to be used in workflow systems, and we have used this glossary when we introduce workflow technology. The reference model also includes a reference architecture of a workflow system. In this architecture, the core component of a workflow system is one or more workflow engines, and each engine has five interfaces interacting with other major components in the system. Figure 1.9 illustrates the WfMC Workflow Reference Model. Now we introduce what a workflow engine is and how it interacts with other components via five interfaces.

A workflow engine is the software to create, execute, and manage workflow instances, and facilitate their interactions with human and automated applications. A workflow system mainly consists of one or more workflow engines that form *workflow enactment services.*

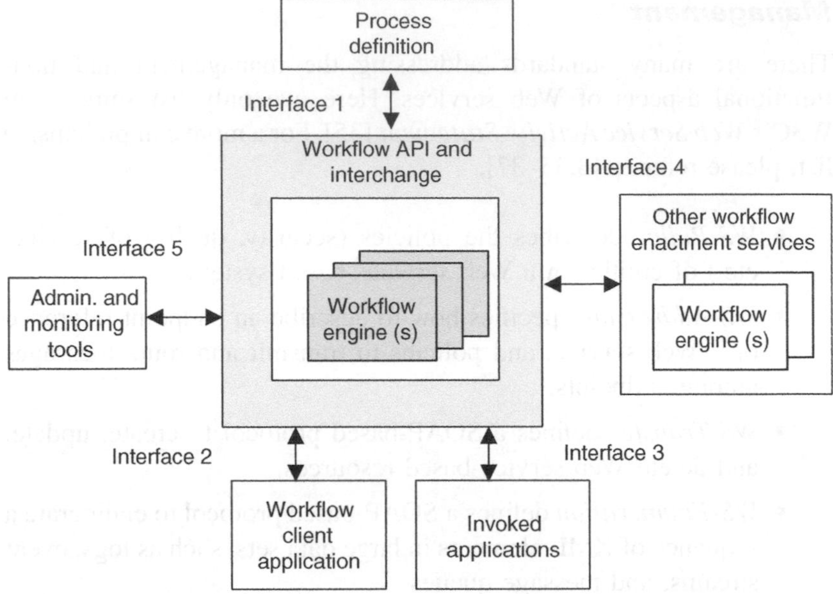


**Figure 1.9** The WfMC Workflow Reference Model. *Source*: Reproduced from Reference [6].

A workflow enactment service interacts with other five components via five interfaces as illustrated in Figure 1.9.

### *Interface 1: Process Definition*

Interface 1 defines the interchange format for a process definition, and the API to get it. It is the logic separation between workflow build-time and run-time. Users may use any tool to build a process definition that can be fetched by an enactment service via Interface 1 by means of file transfer or API. To facilitate the exchange of process definitions, in Interface 1, WfMC also defines a meta-model and process definition specification, that is, XML Process Definition Language (XPDL) [38]. XPDL is similar to BPEL and BPMN in various aspects but has its own features. Its meta-model for a process includes the following elements:

- *Activity*, its start and end *events*, and *participants* and *applications* to perform it.
- *Gateways*, such as AND/OR split or join structures.

- *Swimlanes* to lay out a process according to different participants.
- *Workflow relevant data* that are used in each workflow instance at run-time.

### Interface 2: Workflow Client Application

Interface 2 is the way to deal with manual activities in a workflow. The client application interface allows participants to retrieve the tasks together with the related data, finish the task, and submit the execution results.

### Interface 3: Invoked Applications

Interface 3 is the way to deal with an automated activity in a workflow. This interface allows the engine to invoke an application when a workflow instance reaches an automated activity. There are various protocols to invoke a remote application and a Web service interface is becoming a predominant one among them.

### Interface 4: Other Workflow Enactment Services

Workflows in different systems may need to communicate with one another. For example, an order processing workflow of an online merchant like Amazon, may need to talk to a payment workflow of a payment provider like PayPal. Therefore there is a need to define an interface for multiple workflow enactment services to collaborate. Interface 4 defines how two enactment services can set up communication, transfer a process definition, delegate the execution of a subprocess, and transfer data between them.

### Interface 5: Administration and Monitoring Tools

Interface 5 defines the administration and monitoring interfaces such as user management, auditing, and resource control.

There exist other standards in workflow and BPM. However, BPEL, BPMN, and XPDL represent the most influential ones. For a more comprehensive discussion about workflow-related standards, please refer to [7,39].

## 1.3 WORKFLOW DESIGN: STATE OF THE ART

This book focuses on the design (i.e., build-time) aspect of service-based workflow systems. This section surveys the related work and categorizes them into five areas, that is, automatic service composition, mediation-aided service composition, verification of service-based workflows, support for decentralized execution, and scientific workflows. This categorization does not imply that the first four areas are related to business workflows and the last one to scientific ones. Instead, it reflects the fact that the research on business workflows has a longer history and more comprehensive literature coverage. Many of the studies in the first four categories are applicable to both business and scientific workflows, although most of them were originally targeted at business workflows. On the other hand, we have a separate subsection for scientific workflows to discuss their specific topics.

### 1.3.1 Automatic Service Composition

Composability and reusability are among the eight principles of SOA, as proposed by Erl [3]. Services need to be reusable to make sense for their presence, and need to be composable so as to be reusable. Methods to compose services in a full or semiautomatic way play an important role in SOA, due to the large number of candidate services and the complexity that is required to perform such a composition. Manual composition can be tedious, error-prone, and more importantly, not able to yield satisfactory solutions in a timely manner. Automatic service composition means that given a goal or an abstract process, a desired composite service that consists of the existing services is constructed in an algorithmic way.

Automatic service composition methods can be classified into two categories, that is, planning based [95] and optimization based [43,44]. The former transforms the service composition problem into an AI-planning method, in which the goal state of the composition is given and a chain of service invocations is constructed from the initial state to reach it. They mainly concern the behavior, that is, the sequence of service invocations, of a composite service.

The optimization-based methods mainly concern the nonfunctional aspect, that is, QoS of a composite service [44] after the desired function is fulfilled. QoS constraints include cost, time, availability, and reliability. Optimization methods such as linear programming [43] and genetic algorithm [44] are used to solve the QoS constraints and yield the optimal solution(s).

Automatic composition attracts the most attention in SOA research because of its importance. However, most of the approaches are theory-oriented and usually require a substantial effort to build a model for each candidate service first. For example, planning-based approaches require an IOPE (Input, Output, Precondition, and Effect) structure for each service operation; optimization-based ones usually require the QoS attributes of each operation as input to the optimization problem. Such a prerequisite affects the applicability of these theoretically sound but heavyweight approaches, and also calls for more lightweight ones.

## 1.3.2 Mediation-Aided Service Composition

The service orchestration and choreography specifications, and most of the automatic service composition methods, assume the direct composition among services. This is possible under the following assumptions:

1. Services in a composition consent to the same vocabulary in message exchange.
2. The incoming messages of one service are the exact ones provided by its partner(s); the outgoing messages of one service are the exact ones consumed by its partner(s).
3. Services in a composition consent to message exchange sequences.

Services may become partially compatible if any one of the above assumptions no longer holds. Dealing with such cases leads to two major methods, that is, configuration [46] and mediation [47,48], to make partially compatible services work with each other. The former is a heavyweight approach that equips a service with additional variable points such that it can work smoothly with more partners.

Configuration-based approaches require the modification of service implementation. On the other hand, mediation-based approaches are lightweight and less intrusive than the former. The basic idea behind it is that, if two services cannot be directly composed with each other, an adaptor is developed to mediate the mismatch on message formats and/or sequences. Benatallah et al. [49] provide a summary of the mismatch patterns in service composition. Based on the work in

[49], Kongdenfha et al. [50] propose the use of an aspect-oriented programming (AOP) approach to weave adaptor code into services. Brogi and Popescu [51] present a method to automatically generate a mediator between two BPEL services. Nezhad et al. [52,53] propose an automata-based method to synthesize partial compatible services.

### 1.3.3 Verification of Service-Based Workflows

The issue of verification is not a new topic in workflow research [54]. However, in an SOA paradigm, this problem has unique features to be explored. First, the model elements in specifications such as BPEL are much more complicated than those in traditional workflow specifications such as XPDL. BPEL concepts such as correlation set, dead path elimination, compensation, and fault handling are unique, which brings complexity in verification. Second, because service-based workflows usually interact with each other by message exchange, the correctness of a workflow relies on not only its internal logic, but also how its partners collaborate with it. Even if a workflow is correct from a single-process point of view, its composition with another one may still fail because these two workflows do not agree on their interactions.

Based on the formal methods used, the researches in this area can be classified into several categories, that is, Petri net, automata, and process algebra-based ones.

#### *Petri Net-Based Verification*

Ouyang et al. [55] propose a comprehensive Petri net formalism for various BPEL model elements, including basic activities, structured activities, event handler, control link, and fault handling. Martens et al. [56] try to verify the choreography of multiple BPEL processes. Hinz et al. [57] transform BPEL into Petri nets, and then use CTL (Computational Tree Logic) and a model-checking tool to verify various temporal properties.

#### *Automata-Based Verification*

Su et al. [58,59] focus on the automaton model for services and apply model checking via LTL (linear temporal logic). A special contribution of their research is a technique called synchronizability analysis to tackle the problem of state space explosion brought about by asynchronous messaging. Their result shows that, if a composite Web service is synchronizable, its conversation set remains the same when asynchronous communication is replaced with synchronous communication. Thus, a synchronous communication model can be used in LTL model checking. Kazhamiakin et al. [60] develop a set of parametric communication models in service composition. These models range from synchronous communications to asynchronous ones with complex buffer structures. In addition, they develop a technique to associate a service composition with the most adequate communication model that is sufficient to capture all the behaviors of the composition. Using this model, the analysis before the actual verification can speed up the verification.

#### *Process Algebra-Based Verification*

Process algebra [61] is an algebraic approach to the modeling and analysis of concurrent processes. Its advantage is that it provides not only temporal logic model checking, but also bisimulation analysis through which whether two processes have equivalent behaviors can be determined. Foster et al. transform BPEL into a kind of process algebra called a finite state process (FSP), and then use a model checking tool to verify properties like whether the implementation satisfies the abstract design specifications [62], whether two services are compatible [63], and whether the composition of BPEL services satisfies the properties defined in WS-CDL [64]. A formal BPEL model based on $\pi$-calculus (a kind of process algebra based on Calculus of Communicating Systems) can be found in [65]; a $\pi$-calculus-based technique to analyze the behavioral substitution of Web services is proposed in [66].

### 1.3.4 Decentralized Execution of Workflows

Workflow systems are often built on a client/server architecture in which a single engine takes the responsibility for the operation of a whole process. In many circumstances, this sort of centralized systems may not fully meet the requirements when a workflow is across organizations or security boundaries. Partitioning an integrated workflow into small fragments, each of which is orchestrated by one engine, is a preliminary requirement for its decentralized execution. A team from IBM India Research Lab has conducted a series of studies in the decentralized execution of composite BPEL services [67–70]. They have investigated how to partition a BPEL program into multiple parts, especially the partitioning of fault-handling code; they model partition policies to improve execution performance; and they consider how to partition the model when dataflow is constrained. Recently, a process-mining-based model fragmentation technique has been proposed for distributed workflow execution [71].

### 1.3.5 Scientific Workflow Systems

Besides the business community, the scientific community has shown growing interest in workflow technology and has exploited its power in Grid computing, scientific investigation, and job flow management [72,73]. Essentially, a *scientific workflow* is a specialized workflow orchestrating computation and data manipulation tasks into a process of scientific value. A scientific workflow system becomes prominent with the arising interest in *data-intensive science*, or *e-Science* [74]. In e-Science, scientists are facing an enormous increase in raw data from various resources, such as telescopes, instruments, sensor networks, accelerators, and supercomputers. For example, in high-energy physics, the main detectors at the Large Hadron Collider (LHC) produced 13 petabytes of data [75] in 2010. In bioinformatics, 1330 molecular biology databases [76] were reported in 2011. Among them, *GenBank*, the US NIH DNA sequence database, contains more than 286 billion entries for more than 380,000 organisms [77]. To conduct any nontrivial analysis using large amounts of data, scientists need the help of a workflow system.

There are many scientific workflow systems available and the edited book [72] provides a good summary of them. Each of them provides a graph-based interface for service composition, with an underlying workflow metamodel. The workflow metamodels used by these service-based systems are either adopted from industry standard or homegrown.

GPEL and OMII-UK have adopted BPEL. Adopting BPEL can bring advantages such as rigorously defined model syntax and semantics, readily available software tools, and portability of workflow specifications. However, scientific workflows have a particular focus on data flow (versus control flow in business workflows) and parallelism (versus the complex logic in business workflows), and are tightly integrated with the underlying computation infrastructure. To deal with these unique features of scientific workflows, many systems have their own workflow metamodels.

## 1.4 CONTRIBUTIONS

Besides this chapter, Chapter 2, which introduces the Petri net formalism, and Chapter 9, which provides a summary, the remaining six chapters can be categorized into methodologies and applications (Table 1.1).

Chapters 3–5 cover methodologies. Many service composition approaches are heavyweight, that is, they require much input such as semantic notation. This book presents a lightweight approach, by making the best use of the data structure and relations embedded in service descriptions, and designing a data-driven composition method. It is also observed that in real-life scenarios, services do not exactly match one another. Hence, this book presents a method to analyze this

**Table 1.1** Contributions of This Book

| Chapter | Problem | Contribution | Category |
|---|---|---|---|
| 3 | A lightweight service composition approach | Data driven service composition | Methodology |
| 4 | Compose partial compatible services | An mediation-aided approach to analyze and compose services | Methodology |
| 5 | Web service selection under QoS constraint | QoS aware Web service functional configuration | Methodology |
| 6 | Application in healthcare | Web service composition techniques in a healthcare service platform | Application |
| 7 | Application in e-Science | Web services and scientific workflows in e-Science | Application |
| 8 | Social network meets services computing | Network analysis and reuse of scientific workflows | Application |

phenomenon and to add a mediator to glue partially compatible services. Finally, there may be many configurations providing identical functionality with different QoS; this book gives a Web service functional configuration model using Petri nets and uses a novel linear programming formulation to find the configuration with the best QoS.

Chapters 6–8 cover applications. There is a strong demand to compose various health services for the creation of personalized healthcare service systems. This book presents our experience in building a public healthcare information service platform and in applying service composition in such a platform. This book also discusses the wide application of Web services and workflows in the e-Science domain. Specifically, it introduces the design and implementation of caGrid Workflow Toolkit that supports service discovery, composition, and orchestration in the cancer Biomedical Informatics Grid (caBIG). Finally, the proliferation of social network services has started to impact services computing, especially in the e-Science domain. This book presents a network analysis on myExperiment, an online biological workflow repository, and reveals the usage pattern of services in scientific workflows. Based on this network model, we develop a GPS-like system that provides guidance and recommendations to domain scientists when they perform service composition to fulfill their research needs.

CHAPTER 2

# Petri Net Formalism

## 2.1 BASIC PETRI NETS

To make this book self-contained and help readers understand subsequent chapters more easily (especially Chapters 3–5), in this chapter, we give an introduction to a Petri net formalism and its extensions. We start with the definition of Petri nets, and then discuss a special form of Petri nets, that is, the workflow net that is widely used in the modeling and analysis of workflow and Web service composition. We also introduce another extension of Petri nets, that is, colored Petri net (CPN) that is capable of describing different data types in a compact way. We assume that readers have a basic understanding of set theory, matrix, and graph theory.

Petri nets [78–80] are a graphical and mathematical modeling and analysis tool for many systems, especially those with nondeterministic, distributed, asynchronous, and concurrent behavior. Workflows and service compositions can be viewed as such type of systems. Many researchers in the field of workflow and service composition have used Petri nets as a powerful framework to study various issues.

**Definition 2.1. (Petri Nets)** A Petri net is a five-tuple, $PN=(P, T, F, W, M_0)$, where,

$P=\{p_1, p_2, \ldots, p_m\}$ is a finite set of places,

$T=\{t_1, t_2, \ldots, t_n\}$ is a finite set of transitions with $P \cap T=\varnothing$ and $P \cup T \neq \varnothing$,

*Business and Scientific Workflows: A Web Service-Oriented Approach*, First Edition.
Edited by Wei Tan and MengChu Zhou.

$F \subseteq (P \times T) \cup (T \times P)$ is a set of arcs (flow relation),

$W$: $F \rightarrow \{1, 2, 3, \ldots\}$ is a weight function,

$M_0$: $P \rightarrow \{0, 1, 2, 3, \ldots\}$ is an initial marking.

A Petri net $N = (P, T, F, W)$ without any specific initial marking is denoted by $N$.

A Petri net with a given initial marking $M_0$ is denoted by $(N, M_0)$.

The meaning of Definition 2.1 is explained intuitively as follows. A Petri net is a bipartite graph that consists of two disjoint set of nodes, that is, *places* and *transitions*. Place nodes represent conditions or resources, and transition nodes represent events that change conditions, or consume/generate resources. In this bipartite graph, the *flow* relation defines the directed arcs connecting places and transitions. If there is an arc from a place $p$ to a transition $t$, $p$ is called an input place of $t$; if there is an arc from a transition $t$ to a place $p$, $p$ is called an output place of $t$. We use ${}^{\bullet}t$ and $t^{\bullet}$ to denote the sets of input and output places for a transition $t$, respectively. Likewise, ${}^{\bullet}p$ and $p^{\bullet}$ are the sets of input and output transitions of place $p$, respectively. Such a notation can be extended to a set $S \in P \cup T$, ${}^{\bullet}S = \cup_{x \in S} x_{\bullet}$ and $S^{\bullet} = \cup_{x \in S} x_{\bullet}$.

Each arc has a *weight* that is a positive natural number. A Petri net is called *ordinary* if each of the arc weights is one. When a place is assigned a nonnegative integer $n$, we say that the place is holding or marked with $n$ tokens; when each place in a Petri net is assigned a nonnegative integer, we say that the net is in a *marking* designated by this token assignment. In Definition 2.1 of Petri nets, tokens in all places are identical. Later we will see extensions of this definition in which tokens belong to different types and thus are different.

The behavior of a Petri net is governed by its transition enabling and firing rules, called execution rules for short. A transition of a Petri net is *enabled* and may *fire* when every of its input place has sufficient tokens, that is, the number of tokens in it is not less than the weight of the connecting arc. When a transition fires, it consumes tokens from each of its input places and deposits tokens to all of its output places. The numbers of consumed and deposited tokens are equal to the weight of the corresponding arcs. Firing of a transition is atomic, that is, a single noninterruptible step.

The firings of transitions are *nondeterministic* and *concurrent*. When multiple transitions are enabled in some marking, any one of them may fire, but does not have to. Simultaneous firing of multiple enabled transitions is not allowed in the original Petri net definition. This semantics make Petri nets well-suited to model the concurrent behavior of distributed systems. Here we give the formal definition of the execution rules of Petri nets.

**Definition 2.2. (Execution Rule of a Petri Net)**

1. A transition $t$ is said to be *enabled* if each of its input place is marked with at least $W(p, t)$ tokens, where $W(p, t)$ is the weight of the arc from $p$ to $t$. Mathematically, $\forall p \in P$, $M(p) \geq W(p, t)$.
2. An enabled transition may or may not fire in a given state transition step.
3. A firing of an enabled transition $t$ removes $W(p, t)$ tokens from each input place $p$ of $t$, and adds $W(t, p)$ tokens to each output place $p$ of $t$, where $W(t, p)$ is the weight of the arc from $t$ to $p$. Mathematically, $M'(p) = M(p) - W(p, t) + W(t, p)$, for any $p$ in $P$.

Typical properties one might analyze by using Petri nets are illustrated as follows. For brevity we only give an intuitive explanation; please refer to [78–80] for formal definitions and more details.

- *Reachability.* Starting from an initial marking, firing transitions will lead a Petri net to different markings. This property considers, given an initial marking, whether or not a target marking can be reached, after a sequence of firings. All markings given a Petri net and initial marking $M_0$ constitute the reachability set denoted by $R(\mathrm{N}, M_0)$ and sometimes $R(M_0)$.
- *Boundedness.* This property considers whether or not the number of tokens in each place does not exceed a finite number, in any reachable marking.
- *Liveness.* This property considers whether or not a given transition, or any transition, can be fired ultimately, given any marking in $R(\mathrm{PN}, M_0)$.

There are mainly three types of analysis approaches [78], that is, reachability graph, matrix equation, and reduction and decomposition. The reachability graph method relies on building the state space (i.e., all the possible markings of the net). It is a very powerful method and capable of analyzing most of the properties, but it is subject to the state explosion problem. The matrix equation method describes the state transition using matrix calculation, but it is only applicable to certain circumstances. Reduction and decomposition method tries to reduce a complex net into simpler ones, or decompose a large net into smaller ones, while preserving certain properties. It has the same weakness of the matrix-equation method, that is, it is only applicable to certain subclasses of Petri nets.

## 2.2 WORKFLOW NETS

Petri nets are widely used to model and analyze workflows. When they are used to describe workflows, places usually represent conditions or resources to execute activities, and transitions represent activities. Aalst [54] proposed *Workflow Net* as the Petri net model of a workflow definition.

**Definition 2.3. (Workflow Net)** [81] An ordinary Petri net $PN=(P, T, F)$ is a WF-net (WorkFlow net) if and only if

1. *PN* has two special places: $i$ and $o$. Place $i$ is a source place: $^\bullet i=\varnothing$; Place $o$ is a sink place: $o^\bullet=\varnothing$ and
2. If we add a transition $t^*$ to *PN* that connects place $o$ with $i$ (i.e., $^\bullet t^*=\{o\}$ and $t^{*\bullet}=\{i\}$), then the resulting Petri net is strongly connected.

Compared to an ordinary Petri net, a WF-net (1) has an input place as the start of a workflow and an output one as the end; and (2) has no dangling activities. Figure 2.1 illustrates the basic workflow structures expressed with Petri nets. In structure *sequence*, activities $t_1$ and $t_2$ execute sequentially, that is, $t_2$ starts after the completion of $t_1$. In *AND-split-and-join*, after the completion of $t_1$, both $t_2$ and $t_3$ are enabled and are executed in parallel; only after $t_2$ and $t_3$ both complete can $t_4$ start. In this case $t_1$ is called an AND-split and $t_4$ an AND-join. In *OR-split-and-join*, after the firing of $t_1$, either $t_2$ or $t_3$ is enabled and only one of the two can fire; when $t_2$ or $t_3$ completes its firing, $t_4$ will start. In this case $t_1$ is called an OR-split and $t_4$ an OR-join. Structure *iteration* describes an

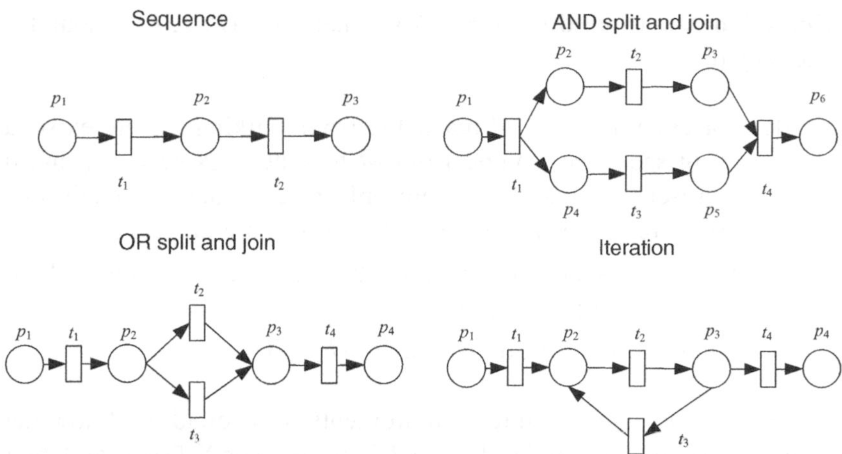


**Figure 2.1** Basic workflow structures expressed in Petri nets.

iteration that is a special case of OR split and join. First $t_1$ and $t_2$ are fired in sequence; when $t_2$ completes its firing, either $t_3$ or $t_4$ is executed; if $t_3$ executes, $t_2$ will fire afterward, which achieves an iteration of $t_2$; otherwise $t_4$ fires and the iteration is completed.

In a Petri net model of a workflow, the aforementioned reachability, boundedness, and liveness properties have the following practical meanings. Consider an order processing workflow of an online merchant, for example, Amazon.com. Reachability concerns whether some state of processing can be reached. For example, a customer order should eventually be put into either *completed* or *canceled* state. Boundedness usually concerns whether or not some activity will be executed more than expected. For example, the place that enables a payment activity should never have more than one token such that the payment only carries through once. Liveness concerns the absence of deadlock and possibility to execute an arbitrary activity involved in a workflow. For example, regardless of the execution sequence, the order processing should end properly and does not hang in the middle (absence of deadlock). Also, for an arbitrary activity in a workflow, it should be able to be executed in some circumstances. That is to say, if there is an activity that is not able to execute in any situation, then it makes no sense to include it in the workflow. To address the aforementioned concerns, Aalst further defined *soundness* as the property of a correct WF-net.

**Definition 2.4. (Soundness)** [81] A WF-net *PN*=(*P*, *T*, *F*) is sound if and only if

1. For every marking *M* reachable from marking *i*, there exists a firing sequence leading from *M* to state *o*. Note that *i* and *o* represent the marking where only places *i* and *o* contain one token, respectively, and all other places are empty;
2. Marking *o* is the only one reachable from marking *i* with at least one token in place *o*; and
3. There are no dead transitions in (*PN*, *i*).

Here we explain the three requirements of a sound workflow net using some simple examples. Figure 2.2 shows some WF-nets and their *i* and *o* places are explicitly highlighted.

Requirement 1 says that once a workflow starts from initial state *i*, no matter which intermediate state it goes to, it is always possible to reach a final state *o*. Figure 2.2a illustrates a workflow net that does not fulfill this requirement. Let us think about a travel request approval process in some company. A request needs to be approved by either the line manager (activity $t_1$) or the comptroller (activity $t_2$), and then archived for later reference (activity $t_3$). The WF-net in

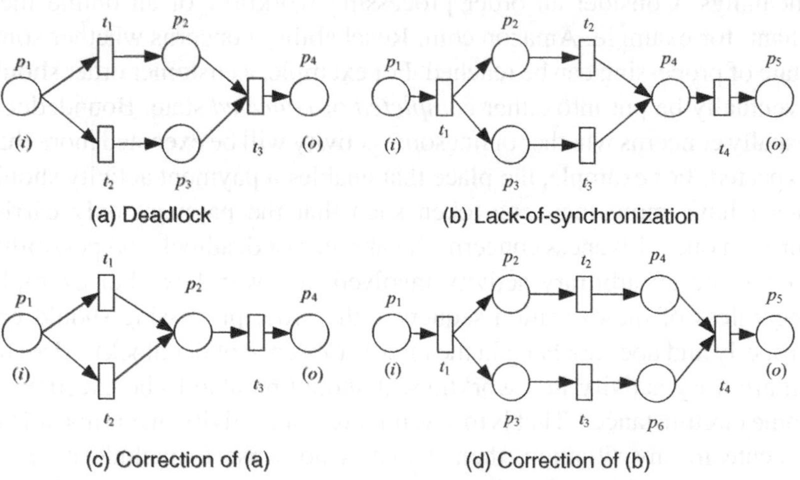


**Figure 2.2** Two workflow nets that are not sound and their corrections.

Figure 2.2a is not sound because starting from $i$, either $t_1$ or $t_2$ can fire and therefore either $p_2$ or $p_3$ contains a token. Then $t_3$ is never enabled because it needs tokens in both $p_2$ and $p_3$, and therefore state $o$ is not reachable. This is called a *deadlock* when no transition can fire after either $t_1$ or $t_2$ fires. A sound implementation is shown in Figure 2.2c where the firing of either $t_1$ or $t_2$ can enable $t_3$ and the deadlock is eliminated.

Requirement 2 says when a workflow reaches a final state $o$, all other places should not contain any token. Figure 2.2b illustrates a workflow net that does not fulfill this requirement. Let us think about a modified version of the travel request approval process in which a request needs to be approved by both line manager (activity $t_2$) and comptroller (activity $t_3$), and then archived for later reference (activity $t_4$). The WF-net in Figure 2.2b is not sound because starting from $i$, after $t_1$ (an activity to split a task and send to two subsequent tasks) fires, both $t_2$ and $t_3$ are enabled since each of $p_2$ and $p_3$ contains a token. Later $t_2$ can fire and $p_4$ contains a token, which in turn enables $t_4$. When $t_4$ fires, $p_5$ (i.e., place $o$) contains a token. However, in the meanwhile $p_3$ still contains a token, which violates requirement 2. This is called *lack-of-synchronization* where two or more activities should be synchronized but actually not. A sound implementation is shown in Figure 2.2d where $t_4$ is enabled only after both $t_2$ and $t_3$ fire.

## 2.3 COLORED PETRI NETS

As we mentioned earlier, places usually represent messages or resources in workflows. Therefore, by introducing types to tokens, one can distinguish messages or resources in a workflow. In basic Petri nets the tokens in different places are indistinguishable. The formalism of colored Petri nets, as an extension to the basic Petri nets, was stimulated by the idea that each token should have a *type* assigned to it.

Before we define colored Petri nets, we first need to define *multiset*, which is the extension of the set concept. $N$ denotes the set of all nonnegative integers.

**Definition 2.5. (Multiset)** A multiset $m$, over a nonempty set $S$, is a function $m$: $S \rightarrow N$ that we represent as a formal sum, $\sum_{s \in S} m(s)'s$

By $S_{MS}$ we denote the set of all multisets over $S$. The nonnegative integers $\{m(s) \mid s \in S\}$ are the coefficients of the multiset. $s \in m$ if $m(s) \neq 0$.

Suppose $S$ is the set of fruits sold by a supermarket, that is,

$S = \{apple, banana, orange\}$

If there is a shopping bag that contains two apples, one banana, and three oranges, then this bag can be represented as a multiset over $S$, that is,

$m_1 = \{2'apple, 1'banana, 3'orange\} \in S_{MS}$

In $m_1$, the coefficients of apple, banana, and orange are two, one, and three, respectively. We often write

$m_1 = 2\ apple + 1\ banana + 3\ orange$

Let us assume that there is another shopping bag that contains one apple and two oranges. Then this bag can be represented as another multiset over $S$, that is,

$m_2 = \{1'apple, 2'orange\} \in S_{MS}$

In $m_2$ the coefficients of *apple*, *banana*, and *orange* are 1, 0, and 2, respectively. $banana \notin m_2$ because $m_2(banana) = 0$.

Here we introduce the formal definition of colored Petri nets following Reference [82]. We deliberately omit the lengthy introduction of concepts such as *expression* and *type*. Instead, we briefly explain them in the remarks right after the definition. For more details on them, and the firing rule and analysis of CPN, please refer to Reference [82].

**Definition 2.6. (Colored Petri Nets)** A colored Petri net is a nine-tuple $CPN = (P, T, F, \Sigma, V, C, G, E, I)$, where

1. $P$ is a finite set of places;
2. $T$ is a finite set of transitions, $P \cap T = \emptyset$ and $P \cup T \neq \emptyset$;
3. $F$ is a finite set of arcs and $F \subseteq (P \times T) \cup (T \times P)$;
4. $\Sigma$ is a finite set of nonempty types, or color sets;
5. $C: P \rightarrow \Sigma$ is a color set function that assigns a color set to each place;

6. $V$ is a finite set of typed variables such that $Type[v] \in \Sigma$ for all variables $v \in V$;
7. $G$: $T \rightarrow EXPR_V$ is a guard function that assigns a guard to each transition $t$ such that $Type[G(t)] = Bool$;
8. $E$: $F \rightarrow EXPR_V$ is an arc expression function that assigns an arc expression to each arc $f \in F$ such that $Type[E(f)] = C(p)_{MS}$, where $p$ is the place connected to the arc $f$; and
9. $I$: $P \rightarrow EXPR_{\varnothing}$ is an initialization function that assigns an initialization expression to each place $p$ such that $Type[I(p)] = C(p)_{MS}$.

**Remarks:**

(1)–(3) ($P$, $T$, $F$) is a Petri net structure as defined earlier.

(4) The set of *types* each of which is a set of values. A type is also referred to as a *color set* and each value belonging to it is referred to as a *color*. We assume that each type has at least one value (i.e., color).

(5) Function $C$ maps each place $p$ to a type $C(p)$. That is, each token in place $p$ must have a data value that belongs to $C(p)$.

(6) $V$ is a finite set of typed variables. Each variable belongs to a type defined in $\Sigma$. This set of variables is to be used in expressions in (7)–(8).

(7) The guard function $G$ maps each transition $t$, into a Boolean expression where all variables are from $V$. At runtime the Boolean expression is evaluated to be *true* or *false* depending on the values of variables. Only when $G(t)$ is *true* a transition may fire. Guard expressions that are always evaluated to be *true* are omitted.

(8) The arc expression function $E$ maps each arc $f$ into an expression of type $C(p)_{MS}$. That is, each arc expression must be evaluated to multisets over the type of the connected place $p$, and it indicates the tokens to take from or yield to $p$ when the associated transition fires.

(9) The initialization function $I$ maps each place $p$ into an expression without any variable and must be of type $C(p)_{MS}$. Initialization expressions that are evaluated to be empty set ($\varnothing$) are omitted.

**Table 2.1** A Comparison of Basic Petri Nets and Colored Petri Nets

| | | Colored Petri nets (Definition 2.6) | Petri nets (Definition 2.1) |
|---|---|---|---|
| *Place* | *Type of tokens* | Color set (specifying the type of tokens that may reside in a place) | N/A (tokens in all places are nondistinguishable) |
| | *Initial marking of a place* | A multiset of token colors | A nonnegative integer |
| *Transition* | *Firing conditions* | When its guard function (Boolean expression containing some variables) evaluates to true | N/A (a transition can fire when its input places have sufficient tokens) |
| *Arc* | *Tokens to consume and produce* | Arc expression (containing some variables) evaluates to a multiset of token colors | Each arc has a weight that is a nonnegative integer |

To help understand the enhancement of colored Petri nets over prior-defined Petri nets, Table 2.1 gives the comparison results for them.

In Chapters 3 and 4 we use colored Petri nets to model different data types and messages used by service workflows. Other types of Petri net extensions, such as hierarchical Petri nets, timed Petri nets and stochastic Petri nets, are also relevant in the analysis of workflow and service composition. In this book we do not specifically use them and readers are referred to References [83–85] for various Petri net extensions.

CHAPTER 3

# Data-Driven Service Composition

Automatic Web service composition is considered to be a key technology in stimulating the Web evolving from an information-delivering center to a function-offering platform to better support the wide use of existing services. It is of great importance in service-oriented architecture (SOA) because reusability is a key feature in SOA to ensure the scalability and productivity. When new business requirements emerge, solution designers should devise a composite process that makes the best use of existing services, and SOA provides a way to glue all components together with the least augmentation or modification. Service composition techniques provide ways to devise a composition of services that fulfills the requirement. There are a number of studies on automatic Web service composition, but there is not much on the linkage between requirements and services.

This chapter presents a data-based approach to provide guidance for service (or process) composition with a given service portfolio in mind. The data relations between business domain and service domain are explored, and data mediation constructs are added to bridge the existing artifacts. We use colored Petri nets as a formalism to represent the data relations. Based on this formalism, three composition rules, sequential, parallel, and choice composition rules, are proposed. Then,

---

*Business and Scientific Workflows: A Web Service-Oriented Approach*, First Edition.
Edited by Wei Tan and MengChu Zhou.

we present a formal method to derive service compositions that satisfy the requirement with respect to the input/output data types. This method is based on a Petri net decomposition technique. A prototype system is developed to test the validity of the proposed approach. It well utilizes the data relation in business/service portfolio to derive composite services.

## 3.1 PROBLEM STATEMENT

In software tools such as IBM Business Process Manager [32], composite services can be directly derived from business processes. It seems that business requirements represented by business processes can be directly transformed to refined processes realized by available services. In practice, however, some gaps remain.

First, the model elements of a business process and a service composition are not identical. In practice, there are various kinds of specifications, languages, and notations to model a business process and a service composition [86]. Second, the data model in business and service domains are heterogeneous. Therefore, direct or indirect mappings between them are required to give an integrated and coherent view of the two domains. The third reason is more critical. Without proper guidance from the service domain, there is no guarantee that the refined process model can be implemented by available services. Hence, it is highly desired that we generate certain operational guidance from the existing service portfolio to help refine a business domain process into a customized process that can be implemented by existing services to a greater extent.

On one hand, the difficulties mentioned above hamper the effective and efficient utilization of available services. On the other hand, a service portfolio contains abundant information to be further investigated. For example, WSDL files contain the input/output data type of operations, and WSDL files with associated data definition schemas contain the relations among these data types, such as aggregation and generalization. From these data relations, much guidance can be derived to help perform better service composition.

In this section, we present how to drive data structures from WSDL files, how to model data structures in two domains, and how to formulate service compositions based on them.

### 3.1.1 Domains and Data Relations

Various languages exist for modeling. Thus, we utilize one that is common to represent the artifacts we are working on. Colored Petri nets [87] capture both control and data aspects of a process. In this chapter, we use them as a common model for both business processes and services.

There are two domains involved in the scenario of service composition: *business* and *service*. Business domain is also known as the requirement specification domain in which requirements are represented by business processes consisting of abstract activities with input/output data. Service domain is also known as the implementation domain in which a service is modeled by a set of operations with input/output data modeled as messages in WSDL.

We borrow some ideas from the UML class diagram and type definition in the XML schema. Two kinds of relations, in-domain relation and cross-domain relation, are of our concern. From now on, the data types in the business domain are denoted with uppercase strings, while those in the service domain with lowercase strings.

Before we start to define data relations, we need to emphasize the difference between *data* and *data type*. A *data type* defines a set of values that a *data* element can take. Since this chapter is about service composition at build-time (instead of at runtime), we focus on "data type" instead of "data." Therefore, except those otherwise noted, the term *data* also refers to *data type* throughout this chapter. For example, when we talk about "data relations," we mean the relations between two data types. We believe that this can simplify the expression and readers can easily catch the exact meaning through the context.

#### *In-Domain Relations*

We need to use the following in-domain relations:

**Aggregation**: *has-a* relation;

**Generalization**: *is-a* relation; and

**Generation**: The relation between input and output data types of a business activity or service operation.

Consider a real-life example, that is, an ADSL Order Processing Service (AOPS) provided by a telecommunication company. Note that this example is taken from a real customer case in IBM SOA solution

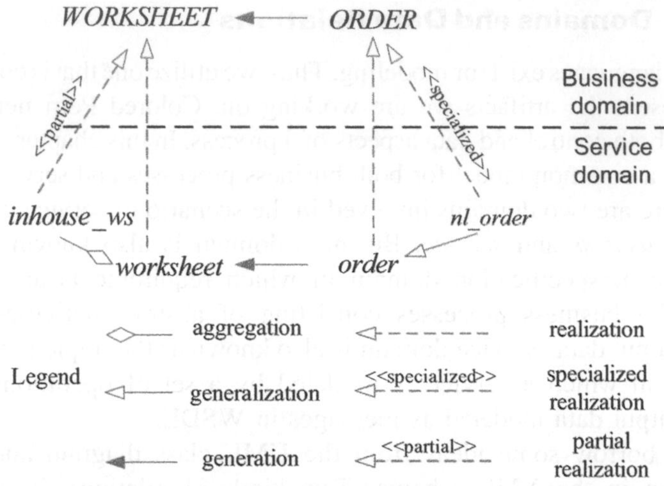


**Figure 3.1** Domains and data relations.

in telecommunication industry. In Figure 3.1, the lower part is a segment extracted from a WSDL file. Operation *generate_worksheet* receives ADSL application order (data type *order*) and **generates** a worksheet (data type *worksheet*). Data type *worksheet* represents the work items to fulfill the order. It **aggregates** *inhouse_ws* that represents the work items undertaken in a customer's house. Data type *order* is the **generalization** of *nl_order* that represents new-telephone-line-plus-ADSL business.

With this information, the data structure in the service domain is derived and illustrated in the lower part of Figure 3.1. In a business domain, there are two data types *ORDER* and *WORKSHEET*; and a business requirement is expressed as *ORDER* that generates *WORKSHEET* (*ORDER* → *WORKSHEET*).

### Cross-Domain Relations

Since we intend to make the best use of existing services to meet the needs of business requirements, ideally data types in a service domain should be the implementation of those in a business domain. We note that *realization* is defined as a primitive in UML 2.0 specification, and it signifies the specification–implementation relation between two model elements. Thus, here we use *realization* as a cross-domain relation to signify that one data type in a service domain directly implements one data type in a business domain. For example, in Figure 3.1, data type *order* in the service domain is the realization of data type *ORDER* in the business one. In the following sections of this chapter, a pair of data types, one's name in the lower case and the other's in the upper case, has the realization relation between them.

Given that the granularity of business data is usually coarser than that of service data, a complete realization relation between them is not guaranteed. To model an incomplete realization relation between them, we use two stereotypes to extend the realization relation: *partial* and *specialized* realizations.

1. Partial realization describes the situation that service data realize a part of business data. For example, in Figure 3.1, data type *inhouse_ws* is a part of *worksheet*, which realizes *WORKSHEET*. Thus, we define *inhouse_ws* as the *partial realization* of *WORKSHEET*.
2. Specialized realization describes the situation that service data realize a special kind of business data. For example, in Figure 3.1, data type *nl_order* is a special class of data type *order*, which realizes *ORDER*. Thus, we define *nl_order* as the *specialized realization* of *ORDER*.

Figure 3.1 illustrates all the data relations we have discussed and gives the notations to model these relations. For simplicity, we only present the UML model while the actual data definition in XML is omitted.

### 3.1.2 Problem Formulation

In Section 3.1.1, we use UML notation to express data relations. To save some space, we show only the graph presentation of UML class diagrams, and in this subsection, we show their corresponding Petri net constructs.

To align with the requirement of process composition, we use colored Petri nets to represent all the data relations in a service domain, as illustrated in Figure 3.2. In Figure 3.2, the notation of a place (e.g., *order*) represents the color set attached to it. The color set in turn represents a data type associated with this place. A hollow transition represents the generation relation between two data types (*order* can

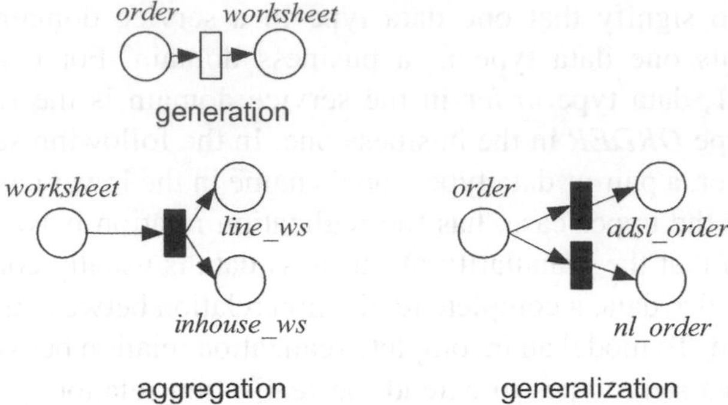


**Figure 3.2** CPN representation of generation, aggregation, and generalization relations.

generate *worksheet*); a solid transition represents the generation/aggregation relations (*worksheet* is the aggregation of *inhouse_ws* and *line_ws*, and *order* is the generalization of *adsl_order* and *nl_order*). For simplicity, we omit the arc expressions that represent the token consuming relation when a connecting transition fires. In our model, each arc will either consume exactly one token of the input place's data type or yield one token of the output place's data type, when a connecting transition fires.

To address the challenge of service composition from the perspective of data, first we define the property that a composite service should satisfy. Since a composite service is represented by a colored Petri net, we define data coherency on the latter.

**Definition 3.1. (Data Coherency)** A colored Petri net *N* is data-coherent with respect to a given business/service portfolio, if every transition in *N* either represents an operation in the service portfolio and transforms an input data type into an output data type or represents the aggregation or generalization relationship among data types.

**Remarks:** *N* is data-coherent if every transition *t* in *N* represents a kind of data relation as shown in Figure 3.2.

Based on the formalization of a process and data, we have the following problem statement (Figure 3.3).

Requirement is expressed as a colored Petri net with a single transition *t*. The data types of the input and output places of *t* are denoted

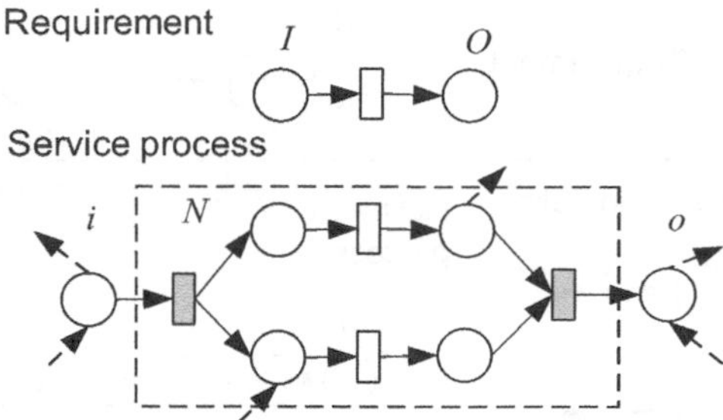


**Figure 3.3** Service composition: problem formulation.

as $I$ and $O$, respectively. Thus, the requirement can be simply expressed as $I \rightarrow O$. Operations in a service portfolio can also be expressed as $i \rightarrow o$, that is, the operation consumes one instance of data type $i$ and yields one instance of data type $o$.

Our goal is to find a collection of operations in a large service portfolio. These operations are connected to form a colored Petri net $N$. As shown in Figure 3.3, the data type attached to one place is denoted as an italic string.

We declare that $N$ is a valid composition of the requirement $I \rightarrow O$ if

1. $N$ takes $i$ as its only input and $o$ as its only output;
2. $N$ is data-coherent; and
3. $N$ has some additional properties to be discussed later in Section 3.3.2.

Before addressing the problem of service composition, we introduce in the next section data-driven composition rules used to refine processes in a business domain into processes in a service domain.

## 3.2 DATA-DRIVEN COMPOSITION RULES

The composition and transformation rules in this chapter are all expressed with a graph transformation formalism. We believe that this formalism is intuitive and thus easy to understand; more details on graph transformation can be found in [88]. The sequential, parallel, and choice composition rules correspond to the sequential, parallel, and conditional routes given in a Workflow Net [81].

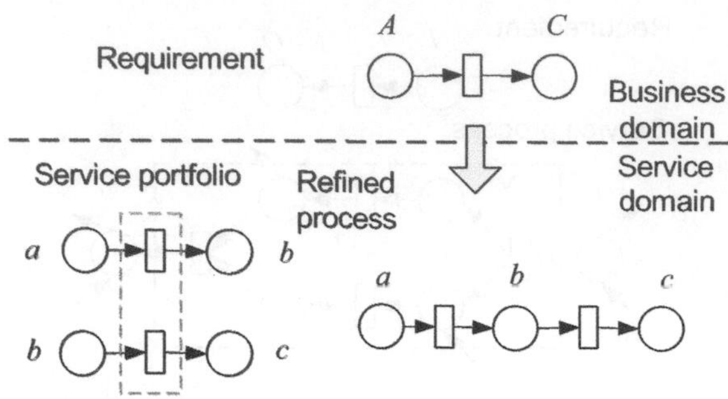


**Figure 3.4** Sequential composition rule.

### 3.2.1 Sequential Composition Rule

The sequential composition rule is illustrated in Figure 3.4. For a business requirement $A \rightarrow C$, if there are two operations in service portfolio, $a \rightarrow b$ and $b \rightarrow c$, we can refine the business requirement into a process realized by existing services, that is, $a \rightarrow b \rightarrow c$.

### 3.2.2 Parallel Composition Rule

We explain this rule through an example in Figure 3.5. If $a = a_1 \times a_2$, $b = b_1 \times b_2$, and we have two operations $\{a_1 \rightarrow b_1, a_2 \rightarrow b_2\}$, the requirement $A \rightarrow B$ can be realized by the AND collection of $\{a_1 \rightarrow b_1, a_2 \rightarrow b_2\}$, with two additional mediation transitions as

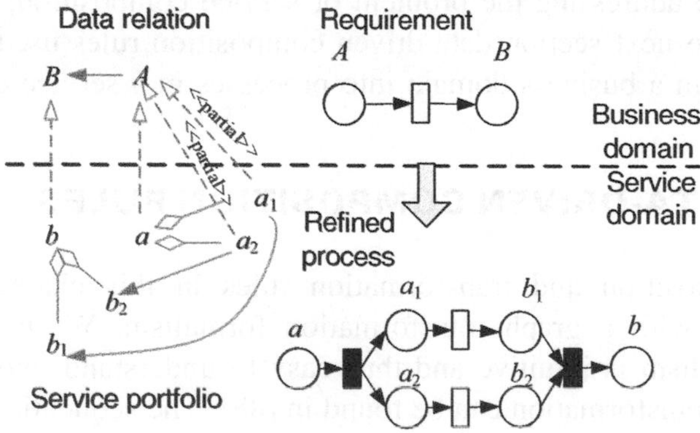


**Figure 3.5** Parallel composition rule.

represented by black rectangles. With mediation transitions, $a$ is decomposed to $a_1$ and $a_2$, and $b$ is decomposed to $b_1$ and $b_2$.

### 3.2.3 Choice Composition Rule

This rule is related to data generalization as explained via Figure 3.6. In a business domain, we have a requirement $A \rightarrow B$, while in a service domain, we have two operations $\{a_1 \rightarrow b, a_2 \rightarrow b\}$ $(a = a_1 \cup a_2, a_1 \cap a_2 = \varnothing)$. Then, requirement $A \rightarrow B$ can be realized by the XOR (exclusive OR) collection of $\{a_1 \rightarrow b, a_2 \rightarrow b\}$, with two additional mediation transitions as represented by black rectangles. With mediation transitions, data type $a$ is specified to either $a_1$ or $a_2$.

As shown in the composition rules we illustrate in this section, there are direct mappings between business data and service data. Nevertheless, usually there is no existing service data that realize some business data. Hence, we need to add newly created service data to make the data structure coherent. These newly created service data can be regarded as a *virtual* data type to facilitate service composition. For example, in Figure 3.5, if there is no service data type $a(b)$ that directly realizes $A(B)$, we should create virtual data type $a$ and $b$ from the partial realization data types of $A$ and $B$, s.t. $a = a_1 \times a_2$, $b = b_1 \times b_2$, and then refine $A \rightarrow B$ to the AND collection of $\{a_1 \rightarrow b_1, a_2 \rightarrow b_2\}$. Another circumstance is that, if $a$, $b$, $a_1$, and $b_1$ exist, but $a_2$ and $b_2$ do not exist in the service portfolio, we should manually add $a_2$ and $b_2$ as virtual data types in the service domain to indicate that there is a missing operation $a_2 \rightarrow b_2$ in the service portfolio to fulfill the requirement $a \rightarrow b$. A virtual data type can be a powerful

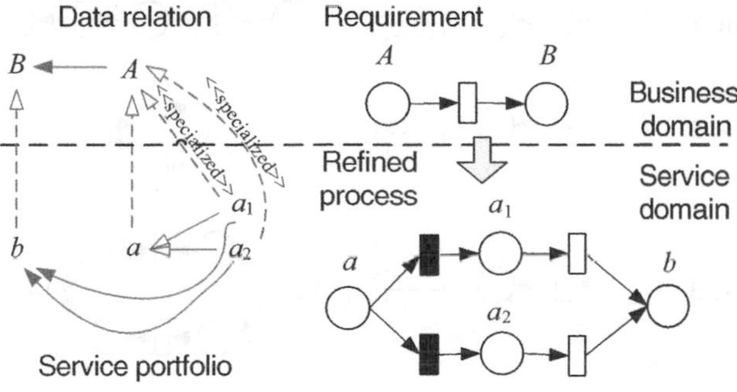


**Figure 3.6** Choice composition rule.

tool to better combine business data and service data and further combine business requirements and service operations. In the remaining sections of this chapter, we concentrate on the approach and algorithm for data-driven service composition while leaving the issue of virtual data for future exploration.

## 3.3 DATA-DRIVEN SERVICE COMPOSITION

Based on the data relations and composition rules, we are now ready to solve the problem formulated in Section 3.1.2. That is, if a business requirement is represented as $I \rightarrow O$, find a service composition from a service portfolio to realize this requirement.

### 3.3.1 Basic Definitions

Here, some definitions to be used later are given.

**Definition 3.2. (Acyclic Well-Structured Process, AWSP)** An *Acyclic Well-Structured Process* is defined as follows:

1. A transition with one single input place and one single output place is an AWSP.
2. All Petri nets obtained by using transformation rules 1–3 in Figure 3.7 are AWSPs.

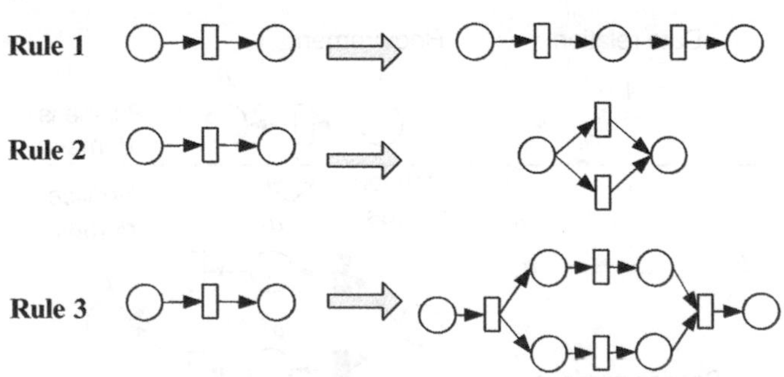

Rule 1

Rule 2

Rule 3

**Figure 3.7** Generation rules for AWSP.

Based on the composition rules we have given in Section 3.2, we give the definition of a service net and the method to derive it given a service portfolio.

**Definition 3.3. (Service Net, SN)** A service net $N_S$ with respect to a service portfolio and data mediation is a colored Petri net $CPN = (P, T, F, \Sigma, V, C, G, E, I)$, where

1. $P$ is a finite set of places.
2. $T$ is a finite set of transitions, $T = T_O \cup T_M$ where $T_O$ is the set of operation transitions, and $T_M$ is the set of mediation ones.
3. $F$ is a finite set of arcs.
4. $\sum$ is a finite set of data types modeled as color sets.
5. $C$ is a color function defined from $P$ into $\Sigma$. $C$ is *injective*, that is, $C(p_1) = C(p_2) \Rightarrow p_1 = p_2$.
6. $V$ is a finite set of typed variables such that $Type[v] \in \Sigma$ for all variables $v \in V$.
7. $G$: $T \rightarrow EXPR_V$ is a guard function that assigns a guard to each transition $t$ such that $Type[G(t)] = Bool$.
8. $E$: $F \rightarrow EXPR_V$ is an arc expression function that assigns an arc expression to each arc $f \in F$ such that $Type[E(f)] = C(p)_{MS}$, where $p$ is the place connected to the arc $f$.
9. $I$: $P \rightarrow EXPR_\varnothing$ is an initialization function that assigns an initialization expression to each place $p$ such that $Type[I(p)] = C(p)_{MS}$.

This chapter focuses on the *structural* decomposition of service nets guided by data types of places. Therefore, for simplicity, we will use $(P, T, F, \Sigma, C)$ or $(P, T, F)$ to represent a net later.

A service net can be constructed in the following ways:

1. Data relations and mediations are modeled with mediation transitions.
2. Service operations are modeled with operation transitions.
3. Places attached with an identical data type are merged into a single one.

**Remarks:**

1. A service net $N_S$ is data-coherent since transitions represent data mediation or transformation. Any well-formed subnet of $N_S$ is also data-coherent.
2. An SN after any refinement process in Figs. 3.4 to 3.6 is still an SN.

**Definition 3.4. (Conflict Place)** Given a service net $N_S = (P, T, F)$ with $T = T_O \cup T_M$, $P_C \subset P$ is a set of conflict places if $p \in P_C$ satisfying that $p^{\bullet} > 1$ and $\exists t \in p^{\bullet}$, s.t. $t \in T_O$.

An SN is *conflict-free* if it does not contain any conflict places, that is, $P_C = \emptyset$.

**Definition 3.5. (Reachability)** In a Petri net $(P, T, F)$, we define relation **R** as the reachability relation between two nodes. $n_1, n_j \in P \cup T$, $\mathbf{R}(n_1, n_j)$ is true if there is a path $C$ from $n_1$ to $n_j < n_1, n_2, \ldots, n_j >$ such that $(n_i, n_{i+1}) \in F$ for $1 \leq i \leq j-1$, and for any two nodes $n_p$ and $n_q$ in $C$, $p \neq q \Rightarrow n_p \neq n_q$. By default, $\mathbf{R}(n_i, n_i) = true, \forall n_i \in P \cup T$.

### 3.3.2 Derive AWSP from Service Net

With the definitions given in Section 3.3.1, the problem raised in Section 3.1.2 can be interpreted more formally.

**Definition 3.6. (Feasible Solution)** Given a service portfolio, and service composition requirement $I \rightarrow O$, $N$ is a feasible solution of requirement $I \rightarrow O$ if

1. $N$ takes $i$ as its only input and $o$ as its only output;
2. $N$ is data-coherent with respect to the given service portfolio and
3. $N$ is an AWSP and is conflict-free.

**Remarks:** Why are these requirements imposed on a feasible solution?

1. The solution should consume data $i$ and yield data $o$, given the requirement $I \rightarrow O$.

2. *Data coherency*. Because we are addressing the service composition problem from the perspective of data, the composite process should represent the data relations in the given service portfolio.
3. Well-structuredness and conflict-freeness are favorable properties of business processes. We also require the solution to be acyclic because a cyclic structure represents the iterative processing of the same type of data. Therefore, for computational simplicity, we generate acyclic solutions, but in an execution phase, the process can be cyclic.

First, we define the concept of a reduced service net before we outline the solution steps.

**Definition 3.7. (Reduced Service Net, RSN)** A reduced service net $N_R = (P_R, T_R, F_R)$ of service net $N_S = (P, T, F)$ with respect to input data type $i$ and output data type $o$, or $N_R(N_S, i, o)$, is a subgraph of $N_S$, s.t., $\forall n \in P \cup T, n \in P_R \cup T_R$ if in $N_S$, $\mathbf{R}(i,n) = \mathbf{R}(n,o) = \mathit{true}$.

**Remarks:** When $N_S$ is reduced to $N_R$, any operations, data mediations, and data types that are not on a path from data type $i$ to data type $o$ are eliminated. We reduce a service net in order to remove the unrelated parts, and the reduction process can be done by slightly modifying the graph traverse algorithm [89].

Now, we can generate a feasible solution.

**Input:**

$I \rightarrow O$.

**Output:**

An AWSP, data-coherent $N$, which is a subgraph of service net $N_S$, with $i$ as its input and $o$ as its output, and contains no conflict place.

**Step 1**. Construct a service net $N_S$ given a service portfolio and data mediations in both business and service domains. The method is given in Definition 3.3.

**Step 2**. Derive a reduced service net $N_R$ from $N_S$.

**Step 3**. Decompose $N_R$ into subnets, each of which contains no conflict place.

**Step 4**. Check each of the decomposed net derived from Step 3 to decide whether it is a feasible solution.

The following discussions focus on the decomposition procedure of Step 3.

The branches after each conflict place represent options from which we can choose for data processing. A snippet of RSN is shown in Figure 3.8. Place $p_1$ is a conflict place. Hence, data type $a$ attached to $p_1$ can be processed by operation $t_1$ or $t_2$, or the XOR join of operations $\{t_{31}, t_{32}\}$.

An RSN must be decomposed into a set of subnets that do not contain any conflict places. Simply speaking, each time a conflict place is encountered, one branch is selected as the active one, and the other branches are removed. As Figure 3.8 illustrates, three subnets are generated because $p_1$ has three succeeding transitions ($t_{31}$ and $t_{32}$ are grouped and treated as one single branch).

When there are more than one conflict place in an RSN, the decomposition is more complicated. If there are $n$ conflict places each with $m$ branches, possibly we have $m^n$ distinctive subnets. This clearly shows the exponential growth of subnets, which is the worst-case scenario. We use *selection tuple* to decide which branch to choose for each conflict place. One selection tuple corresponds to one situation of decomposition, and we use *Decomposition Algorithm* to obtain one subnet for each evaluation. Now, we give function definitions before a decomposition algorithm is given.

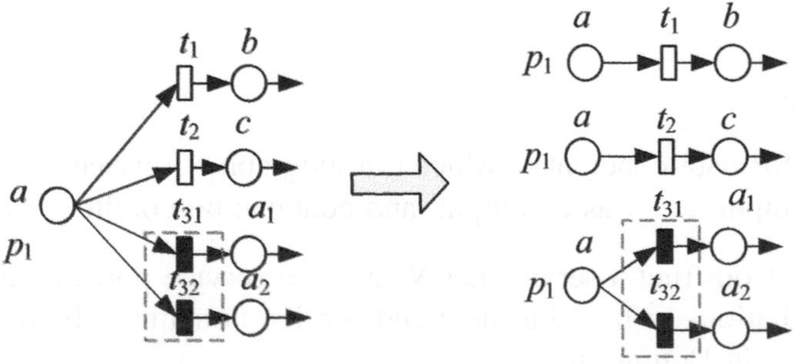


**Figure 3.8** Illustration of the decomposition algorithm.

Given a reduced service net,

1. $\forall p \in P_R$, $p$ is a *source place* if $p \neq p_i \wedge {}^{\bullet}p = \varnothing$.
2. $\forall p \in P_R$, function $\mathrm{S}(p)$ is a Boolean function. $\mathrm{S}(p)$ returns true if $p$ is a source place. Each source place is initially marked to be *nondead.*
3. $\forall p \in P$, function $\mathrm{D}_S(p)$ is a Boolean function. $\mathrm{D}_S(p)$ returns true if $p$ is a source place and is explicitly marked to be *dead.*

Given a net $N = (P, T, F)$, $p \in P$, $t \in T$, $p \in {}^{\bullet}t$,

Function $\mathrm{M}\,(p,\ t,\ p',\ N)$ modifies the structure of $N$ by redirecting $(p, t)$ to $(p', t)$, or

$$P = P \cup \{p'\}; \quad F = (F - \{(p, t)\}) \cup \{(p', t)\}$$

Given a net $N = (P,\ T,\ F)$, $n \in P \cup T$,

Function $\mathrm{D}(n, N)$ modifies the structure of $N$ by deleting $n$ and the arcs leading and ending at $n$, that is,

If $n \in P$

$$P = P - \{n\}$$
$$F = F - \{(n,\ x) | x \in T \wedge (n,\ x) \in F\} \cup \{(y,\ n) | y \in T \wedge (y,\ n) \in F\}$$

If $n \in T$

$$T = T - \{n\}$$
$$F = F - \{(n,\ x) | x \in P \wedge (n,\ x) \in F\} \cup \{(y,\ n) | y \in P \wedge (y,\ n) \in F\}$$

If $N' \subseteq P \cup T$, $\mathrm{D}(N', N)$ modifies the structure of $N$ by invoking $\mathrm{D}(n, N)$ sequentially for all $n \in N'$.

**Definition 3.8. (Selection Tuple)** Given a reduced service net $N_R = (P, T, F)$ with $P_C = \{p_1, p_2, \ldots, p_n\} \subset P$, and $p_i^{\bullet} = \{t_{i1}, t_{i2}, \ldots, t_{ik_i}\}$ $(1 \leq i \leq n)$,

$\Theta(P_C)$ is a finite set of $n$-tuples. Each tuple $h$ in $\Theta(P_C)$ is an ordered list of transitions, and each transition is an output transition of a conflict place, that is,

$$\Theta(P_C) = \{(t_{1m_1}, t_{2m_2}, \ldots, t_{nm_n}) | m_i \in \{1, 2, \ldots, k_i\}, i \in \{1, 2, \ldots, n\}\}$$

Each $h = (t_{1q_1}, t_{2q_2}, \ldots, t_{nq_n}) \in \Theta(P_C)$ is a *selection tuple* (or $h$ tuple) with respect to conflict place set $P_C$.

For $h = (t_{1q_1}, t_{2q_2}, \ldots, t_{nq_n}) \in \Theta(P_C)$, we define

$$\prod\nolimits_h (p_i) = t_{iq_i}$$

For example, in Figure 3.8, $P_C = \{p_1\}$, then

$$\Theta(P_C) = \{(t_1), (t_2), (t_{31}), (t_{32})\}$$

If we define $h_1 = (t_{31}), h_2 = (t_{32}) \in \Theta(P_C)$, then

$$\prod\nolimits_{h_1} (p_1) = t_{31}, \prod\nolimits_{h_2} (p_1) = t_{32}$$

We also define the $\approx$ relation among transitions, $t_i \approx t_j$ if $i = j$, or $t_i$ and $t_j$ belong to the same group of a mediation transition. For example, in Figure 3.8, $t_{31} \approx t_{32}$. We use it later in the following decomposition algorithm such that mediation transitions are treated as one group.

**Algorithm 3.1. (Decomposition Algorithm)**

**Input:**

$$N_R = (P, T, F); \quad P_C = \{p_1, p_2, \ldots, p_n\} \subset P$$
$$h = (t_{1q_1}, t_{2q_2}, \ldots, t_{nq_n}) \in \Theta(P_C)$$

**Output:**

$$R_i = (P_i, T_i, F_i)$$

```
Ri =NR
ForEach pn ∈PC
    ForEach tk s.t. tk∈ pn• ∧¬∏h(pn) ≈ tk
        M(pn, tk, pnk, .Ri)
    EndFor
EndFor

While (∃s∈Pi s.t. S(s) ∧¬DS(s))
    t = s•
    If•t={s}
        D(s, Ri)
        D(t, Ri)
    ElseIf•t ⊃{s}∧∃s′ ∈•t −{s}s.t.¬DS(s′)
        Mark s as dead
    ElseIf•t ⊃{s}∧∀s′ ∈•t −{s} ⇒ DS(s′)
        D(•t, Ri)
        D(t, Ri)
    EndIf
    ForEach pm ∈Pi s.t. S(pm) ∧| pm•|>1
            ForEach tj ∈ pm•
            M(pm, tj, pmj, Ri)
                EndFor
    EndFor
EndWhile
```

The decomposition algorithm is intuitively explained as follows. For each conflict place, it removes all the unwanted branches according to a given selection tuple. First, for each conflict place, the branches not selected are isolated (the first *ForEach* procedure). Afterwards, all the source places in the net are examined; they are deleted with their succeeding transitions or marked as *dead*, until no new node can be removed/marked (the *While* procedure).

## 3.4 EFFECTIVENESS AND EFFICIENCY OF THE DATA-DRIVEN APPROACH

### 3.4.1 Solution Effectiveness

**Theorem 3.1. (Solution Effectiveness)** *Given a service net $N_S$ and a requirement $I \rightarrow O$, if there is a feasible solution* with respect to *requirement $I \rightarrow O$, the decomposition algorithm can find it.*

*Proof:* Suppose that there is a feasible solution $\chi$. Then, $\chi$ must be a subnet of $N_S$ because $N_S$ contains all the data relations in this service portfolio. Our decomposition algorithm finds all ASWP and conflict-free subnets of $N_S$ by iterating on all possible selection tuples, and we denote the derived subnets set as $\Omega(N_S)$. Because $\chi$ is also ASWP and conflict-free, $\chi \in \Omega(N_S)$ and that is, if there is a feasible solution, our decomposition algorithm can find it.

□

### 3.4.2 Complexity Analysis

The complexity of each run of the decomposition algorithm equals the complexity of traversing the reduced service net, that is, $O(|V| + |E|)$ where $V$ and $E$ are the vertex and edge sets of the reduced service net, respectively. If *RSN* contains $n$ OR-split places, each with $m$ branches, we have $m^n$ selection tuples. In the worst case, from each tuple, we run the decomposition algorithm and obtain one distinctive subnet. Thus, we can have $m^n$ subnets altogether. In the worst case, the computational complexity is $O((|V| + |E|) \times m^n)$, that is, $O(m^n)$.

In practice, $m$ and $n$ are usually not large. Moreover, it is observed that some selection tuples may derive nonfeasible subnets, and some different tuples derive identical subnets. By detecting these circumstances, many selection tuples can be simply ignored. One circumstance is *dead path elimination*, that is, to detect whether different selection tuples lead to the same decomposition.

As shown in Figure 3.9a, if $h = (t_1, *, *)$ ($*$ stands for arbitrary value), when we apply the decomposition algorithm on the net, $p_{c3}$ is removed. We can conclude that once $p_{c1}$ selects $t_1$, the selection value of $p_{c3}$, that is, $\prod_h(p_{c3})$, does not make a difference in terms of the result. Thus, many different selection tuples will lead to the same decomposition result, and by using this fact, we do not have to run the decomposition algorithm for each selection tuple.

The other circumstance is *lack-of-synchronization detection*, that is, to detect whether one valuation will derive nonfeasible subnets. When we run the decomposition algorithm, if $\exists t, |{}^\bullet t| > 1 \wedge (\exists p \in {}^\bullet t, p$ is a dead source place) $\wedge$ ($\exists p \in {}^\bullet t$ such that any path from $i$ to $p$ does not contain any conflict place), then this subnet must be the one with lack-of-synchronization. At this point, the algorithm can stop and we conclude that no feasible solution can be derived from this selection tuple. In Figure 3.9b, $|{}^\bullet t_d| > 1, p_1 \in {}^\bullet t_d$ and $p_1$ is a dead source place;

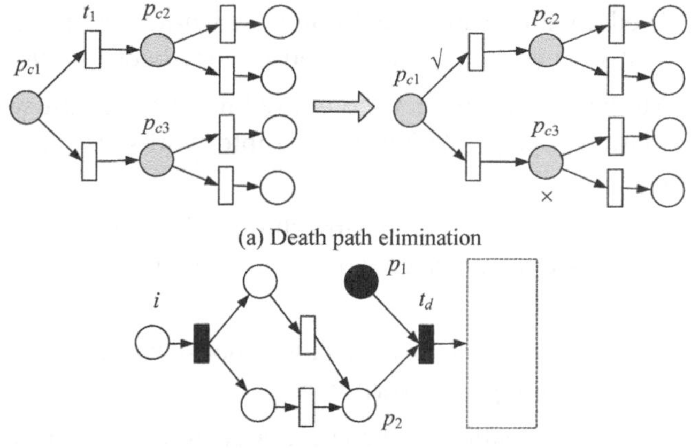


**Figure 3.9** Methods to reduce computation complexity.

$p_2 \in {}^\bullet t_d$, and all paths from $i$ to $p_2$ do not contain any conflict place. Therefore, lack-of-synchronization is detected and we can conclude that this $h$ tuple does not yield any feasible solution.

## 3.5 CASE STUDY

Based on the proposed concepts and algorithms, we have developed a prototype system called *DDSCS* (Data-Driven Service Composition System) [90]. We take the AOPS example mentioned in Section 3.1 to illustrate the validity of the proposed approach. The service portfolio and data relations in AOPS are shown in Figure 3.10. For simplicity, we omit the unrelated data/relations such that in the next step RSN equals SN. The operation and mediation transitions are explained as follows:

$mt_{11}$, $mt_{12}$: Mediation transition, to classify *order* into two subtypes: ADSL order (*adsl_order*) and new-telephone-line order (*nl_order*).

$t_2$: Operation transition, to search a corresponding worksheet according to an order. The worksheet has to be already generated before the search can return a meaningful result.

$t_3$/$t_4$: Operation transition, to generate a worksheet based on an ADSL/new-telephone-line order.

$mt_{21}$: Mediation transition, to decompose *worksheet* into two parts: line worksheet (*line_ws*) and in-house worksheet (*inhouse_ws*).

$mt_{22}$: Mediation transition, to compose line and in-house worksheet confirmation (*line_con*/*inhouse_con*) into worksheet confirmation (*ws_con*).

$t_5/t_7$: Operation transition, to carry through line/in-house construction work based on the given worksheet and return a corresponding confirmation form.

$t_6$: Operation transition, to search an in-house worksheet according to its corresponding line worksheet.

$t_8$: Operation transition, to generate a customer receipt (*cus_rec*) based on a worksheet confirmation (*ws_con*).

The requirement is *ORDER* → *CUS_REC* (given an ADSL business order, do all the necessary operations and return a customer receipt).

As shown in Figure 3.10, given this portfolio in which service operations are modeled as operation transitions and data relations modeled with mediation transitions, an SN is easily obtained by merging the places attached with an identical data type into a single one. We use two eclipses to group places labeled with *order* and *worksheet*, respectively, to demonstrate the merge of places. Figure 3.11 illustrates the RSN (same as SN, in this case) and decomposed nets displayed in Petri Net Kernel. The uppermost net is the RSN.

From top to bottom, the second to fourth nets in Figure 3.11 illustrate three subnets decomposed from RSN. The second net corresponds to $h$ tuples ($mt_{11}$, $t_5$) or ($mt_{12}$, $t_5$). The third net corresponds to $h$ tuple

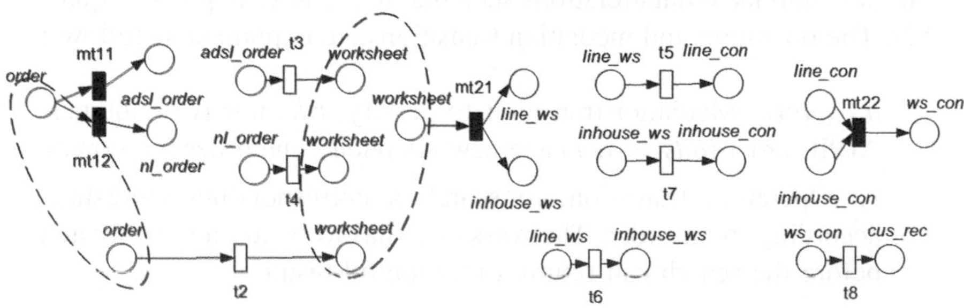


**Figure 3.10** The service portfolio with data relations.

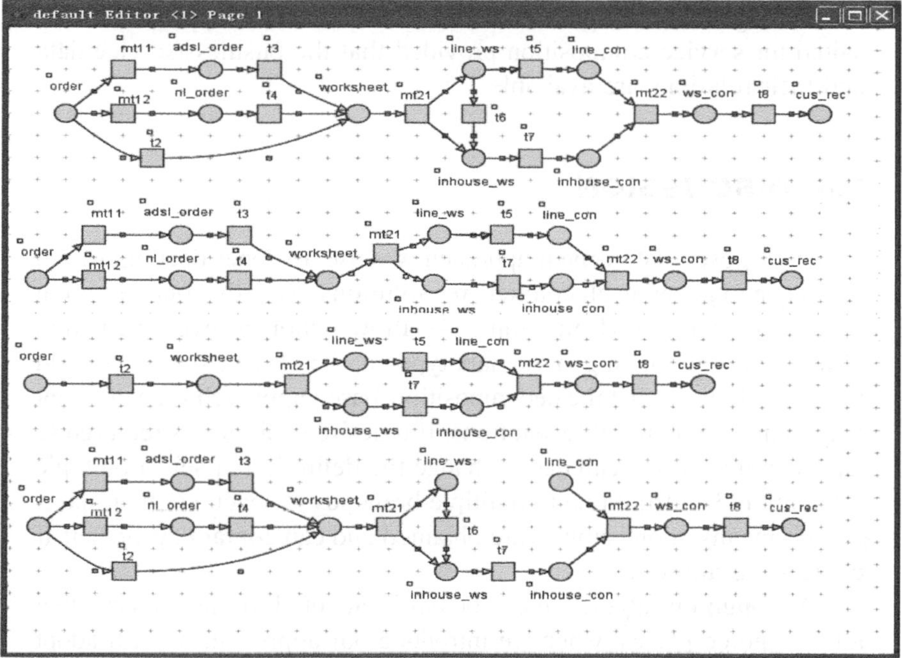


**Figure 3.11** The reduced service net and decomposition results of AOPS (in Petri net kernel).

($t_2$, $t_5$). They are both feasible service composition candidates. The fourth net corresponds to *h* tuples ($*$, $t_6$). In the fourth net, lack-of-synchronization is encountered, and therefore, it cannot generate any feasible solution. Now, we obtain two feasible solutions (the second and the third nets in Figure 3.11) based on the proposed data-driven approach.

In the mean time, we find that the second net is a satisfactory solution. The result for service composition is made up of three steps: *Apply*, *Construct,* and *Offering*. In step *Apply*, AOPS receives customer's ADSL order and generates a worksheet according to the type of business; in step *Construct*, AOPS undertakes required construction work according to the worksheets' content and generates confirmation forms; in step *Offering*, AOPS delivers a receipt to the customer.

Later on, if we manually check the third net, we find that it does not fulfill the requirement since operation $t_2$ does a search job instead of a worksheet generation job. Therefore, it is not a satisfactory solution, although from the perspective of data flow it is a feasible one.

Through this example, we can see that data-driven approach is well suited for service composition provided that the business/service data and their relations are available.

## 3.6 DISCUSSION

In the proposed data-driven approach, we use a subnet decomposition technique to generate all conflict-free solutions. Note that our definition of conflict-freeness (Definition 3.4) allows choices over mediation transitions such that a generic data type can be classified into its child types. We believe that the decomposition-based approach is an efficient way to find some feasible solutions. If a desired solution is required to have conflicts, users can easily change the definition of selection tuple (Definition 3.8) from one to multiple branches for each conflict place. By this means, more subnets are obtained and can contain cyclic nets if choices are allowed.

Although our algorithm can be easily adapted to this scenario that allows choice places, when we introduce our approach, we still adopt the conflict-free option because of the following reasons:

1. *Less Computation Complexity*. Allowing arbitrary combination of choices among branches will increase the computation complexity from $O(m^n)$ to $O[(2^m)^n]$, that is, $O(2^{mn})$.
2. *Compactness and Intuitiveness to Users*. When each choice place selects multiple branches, many meaningless solutions will result. For example, in the AOPS example in Section 3.5, if we allow choice places, then the RSN (see the upmost net in Figure 3.11) itself is a candidate solution, but obviously, this net is an undesired one.

Although the candidate solutions generated by the conflict-freeness constraint do not contain loop and choice (again, it may contain choice over subtypes of data), they offer the "backbones" that can be further refined (e.g., by adding choice branches or loop) by users. This assumption is realistic since (1) choice branches occur in different candidate solutions we give and it is easy to combine them; (2) as for a choice or loop, which branches to select and the start/termination of looping is beyond the scope that can be handled from services' signature. Therefore, more input from process designers is needed; and (3) in our practice of business process engineering, every solution generated by automatic algorithms must be examined and refined before it is put into real execution.

Thus, our solution approach can be extended to the scenario that allows choices and loops. However, in this chapter, we focus on a conflict-free approach to quickly identify the relevant part inside the service portfolio and generate solution backbones. These backbones can be combined and merged to form solutions that can contain choices and loops when required.

## 3.7 SUMMARY

It is necessary to have a method that enhances the reusability of a service portfolio by generating composition guidance when fulfilling a business requirement. This research can be seen as an important step towards the effort to bridge the gap between business and service domains in building enterprise SOA solutions. We utilize data relations in both domains and add data mediation constructs to make the data model in these domains complete and coherent. We devise three composition rules: sequential, parallel, and choice, based on the augmented data model. Based on the data relations and composition rules, we propose a formal method to derive all the possible composition candidates, given a service portfolio. First, we obtain a connected service net from the given service portfolio; then, we reduce the service net with respect to the given requirement (i.e., the input/output signature); and finally, we decompose the reduced service net into subnets, each of which represents a composition candidate. A prototype system is developed, and an example is given to validate our approach as well as the algorithm.

In summary, through our approach, we can quickly choose operations related to the business requirement and chain them together as a process. The contributions of this chapter are summarized as follows:

1. A lightweight approach making the best use of the existing service portfolio in enterprise SOA solutions. It does not need additional semantic information. What we need is data type and data relation definition in both business and service domains. Such information can be obtained by parsing

WSDL files, XML schemas, and the UML class definitions in a business domain. Minor effort is needed to set up the cross-domain data relations and add necessary data mediations.

2. As far as we know, no existing work tackles the problem of service composition by using Petri net decomposition. This idea can be seen as a combination of the bottom-up and top-down approaches in the service composition domain. That is, the generation of a service net is a bottom-up way to give a compact representation of the service portfolio. The decomposition of a service net is a top-down way to derive solution candidates with a desired structure. The introduction of service nets has two advantages: (1) a service net regarding a given service portfolios can be reused for multiple service composition requests and (2) when new services are added or services retire, a service net can be modified in an incremental way and does not need to be built from scratch.
3. Our approach does not preclude the integration with other ones, such as those that are semantic or rule based. The solution obtained by our approach provides hints to find a satisfactory solution. Even when no feasible solution is derived, in the decomposed nets, we can find fragments that may be relevant to and useful in finding a final solution.

Future work includes building a more comprehensive data model to derive better solutions and validating our approach via service libraries such as ITIL (Information Technology Infrastructure Library) and SCOR (Supply-Chain Operations Reference-model) or artificially generated large-scale service networks [91]. Our work does not address how the generated Petri nets are to be executed in a workflow engine. One feasible solution is to transform the resultant Petri nets into BPEL processes such that they can be executed in a BPEL-compliant engine. Well-established methods, such as those proposed in [57], can be used to serve this purpose.

## 3.8 BIBLIOGRAPHIC NOTES

Current research work on service composition methods can be divided into two categories: top-down and bottom-up approaches. The former focuses on building new solutions from scratch [92,93]. It addresses the issue of how to reflect the requirements and to refine them into finer grains of abstraction such that programmers can take over to implement them. It ignores the fact that enterprise solutions are built on top of an existing IT infrastructure. Designers need extra help in putting the solution design in the context of current IT infrastructure, including the current service portfolio.

Bottom-up approaches mainly focus on the automatic service composition methods. These methods can further be classified into three main categories: AI-planning [91,94–103,152], optimization [43,104,105], and automata-based approaches [40–42].

A AI-planning-based approach assumes that service providers have published semantic descriptions of their services, for example, input, output, precondition, and effect. The survey in [106] describes the problem of automatic service composition as a five tuple in which $S$ is the set of all possible system states and $S_0$ and $G$ are the initial and goal state regarding the service composition. $A$ is the set of all possible actions (i.e., all the service operations); $\Gamma = S \times A \times S$ defines the precondition and effect for each action. Then, if we start from the initial (or goal) state, with all the possible actions in $\Gamma$, various AI-planning methods can be used to derive a feasible plan to the goal (or initial) state. Researchers in this category usually use an ontology modeling language like OWL-S [25] to add semantic annotations on Web service description. Then, situation calculus [94,99], PDDL [95], rule-based approach such as SWORD [100], and HTN [96] are used to derive feasible solution(s). A Petri net-based planning framework is proposed in [99]. It is based on state space analysis, and some complexity results are given.

Optimization-based approaches are used to derive composite services that achieve the best QoS. Usually, the QoS constraints include local constraints imposed on a single service and global ones imposed on multiple services. Therefore, two selection approaches are used to solve these two kinds of constraints, respectively [107]. Optimization methods such as linear programming [43] and genetic algorithm [44] are used to solve the QoS constraints and yield feasible and optimal solution(s).

An automata-based approach uses automata to describe the behavior of a target composite service as well as participant services. The key of this approach is computing a *delegator* that coordinates the activities from those participant services such that the overall behavior corresponds to that of the composite service. If a delegator exists, the behavior of the target composite service can be achieved by synthesizing the participant services and delegating their individual behaviors [40–42].

However, current solutions have limitations when they are used in real business scenarios. First, most of them assume a coherent representation of requirement (target service) and participant services. Few of them consider the gap between business and service domains. As we already saw earlier in this chapter, these two domains usually have different domain models with different concerns. This gap hampers the effective use of the AI-planning-, optimization-, and automata-based approaches.

Second, many of the approaches use ontology to describe the behavior of services and related data. However, nowadays, in most enterprises, semantic information of their Web services is not always available to users. The planning-based approach needs much additional effort in adding semantic tags on top of the current Web service standard stack.

On one hand, current solutions need a more ideal usage scenario than those in reality. On the other hand, service portfolio contains abundant data to be investigated and used. We believe that from these data, considerable guidance can be derived to improve service composition. We also believe that our data-driven solution is a lightweight approach that can be used in conjunction with other approaches such as planning or optimization-based ones.

CHAPTER 4

# Analysis and Composition of Partially-Compatible Web Services

## 4.1 PROBLEM DEFINITION AND MOTIVATING SCENARIO

With the emergence of SOA (service-oriented architecture), service composition is gaining momentum as the potential *silver bullet* for the seamless integration of heterogeneous computing resources, rapid deployment of new business capabilities, and enhanced reuse possibilities to a variety of legacy systems [108]. Existing service composition specification languages such as BPEL (Business Process Execution Language) and WS-CDL (Web Services Choreography Description Language) provide the mechanisms to *directly compose* two (or more) services by specifying that a message sent by one interface is received by the other (and vice versa). This kind of interface link is achieved by using constructs such as *Partner Link* in BPEL and *Channel* in WS-CDL. In this chapter, we use BPEL to describe the internal logic of Web services.

Direct composition is made based on the following assumptions:

1. The incoming messages of one service are the exact ones provided by its partner(s); the outgoing messages of one service are the exact ones consumed by its partner(s).

*Business and Scientific Workflows: A Web Service-Oriented Approach*, First Edition.
Edited by Wei Tan and MengChu Zhou.

2. Two services in a composition consent to the message format and exchange sequence such that their composition process always executes in a logically correct way (e.g., terminates properly).

The existing specifications and approaches in service composition mostly concentrate on direct composition that requires the services to be fully compatible. In practice, it may not be the case. Hence, we introduce the concept of *partial compatibility*. It refers to the situation where two (or more) Web services provide complementary functionality and could, in principle, be linked together. However, in reality, their interfaces and interaction patterns do not fit each other exactly. Hence, they cannot be directly composed. The problem of partial compatibility arises mainly because the services have to interact with one another in the ways not necessarily foreseen when they are separately developed. Consequently, the assumptions made for direct composition may no longer hold.

As presented later in this chapter, if two services have mismatches in their interfaces and interaction patterns, they cannot be directly composed. Moreover, even if they can be directly composed, we do not have confidence whether their composition is correct. Note that the meaning of correctness depends on specific requirements, but it usually requires terminability, liveness, and boundedness by using the terms from Petri nets [81]. However, current research in Web service composition mainly focuses on automatic composition methods [86,109–111] and formal verification of service composition [112]. Less attention is paid to the issue of partial compatibility.

Recently, the mediation approach is attracting more attention [46,48–50,113] because it is considered as an economic and labor-saving method to address the challenge of partial compatibility in real world Web service composition. The basic idea of mediation-aided composition is similar to the concept of an *adapter* to make two pieces of hardware compatible. The mediator wraps the various services such that they can appear homogeneous and be therefore integrated and composed more easily.

Figure 4.1 illustrates direct and mediation-aided compositions. Messages *A* and *B* are exchanged between Services 1 and 2. In Figure 4.1a, Service 1 first sends *A* and then waits for *B*; Service 2 first waits for *A* and then sends *B*. Services 1 and 2 can be directly composed by adding links between "Send *A*" and "Receive *A*", "Receive *B*" and "Send *B*". This composition is direct because nothing

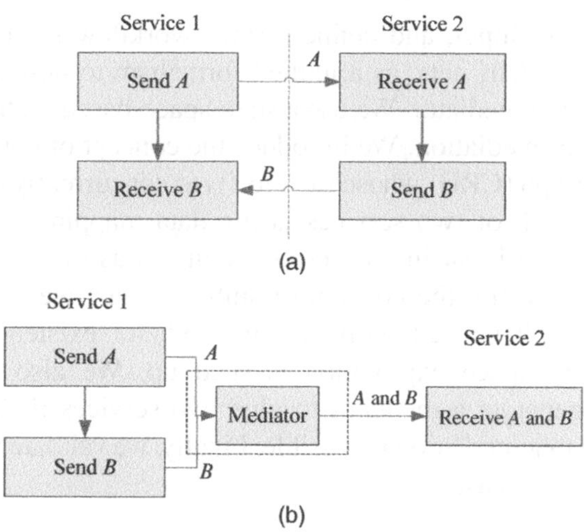


**Figure 4.1** (a) Direct composition and (b) mediation-aided composition.

is sitting in between their interaction. It is also correct because both services can terminate properly. In Figure 4.1b, Service 1 first sends *A* and then sends *B*; Service 2 waits for *A* and *B* to arrive simultaneously. Services 1 and 2 cannot be directly composed by simply adding links because Service 1 has two interfaces while Service 2 has only one. In this case we can add a module (i.e., *mediator*) between them. Its function is to combine messages *A* and *B* coming from Service 1 and forward it to Service 2. With the aid of this mediator, Services 1 and 2 can be composed and interact correctly.

Figure 4.1b presents a rather simple case of mediation-aided composition, and later, we present more powerful mediators that can intercept, store, transform, and forward messages between services.

In our work, we use colored Petri nets (CPNs) as an underlying formalism. This model provides not only a formalism to depict the internal logic and the message exchange behavior, but also rich analysis capability to support the solid verification of compatibility and mediation existence.

There is neither formal analysis on the existence of mediation nor methods to derive the mediator for two partially compatible BPEL Web services. In contrast, with the existing approaches assuming a Web service as a set of independent operations, our approach takes into account the conversational nature of Web services. We take the *de facto* standard, that is, BPEL, as our input, and define service workflow net (SWF-net), a kind of colored Petri nets, as a unified formalism to describe services, composition, and mediator. We use a state-space-based method to check the existence of mediation. We introduce the concept of communicating reachability graph (CRG) whose function is to concurrently construct the reachability graph of two services, using data mapping (that needs to be provided as an input in our current solution) as the communication mechanism. By using the concept of stubborn sets, we verify that the CRG contains all needed properties in mediator existence checking. Moreover, state-space exploration is sped up. We also propose the guidance to generate a mediator to glue two services if through CRG we can verify that mediation is possible. Finally, we validate the approach through a real-life case.

### 4.1.1 A Motivating Scenario

The motivating scenario comes from the composition of eBay and a third-party checkout (TPC) service [114]. It is an excerpt of a real business scenario—simple yet illustrative enough to explain the proposed concept, algorithm, and result.

As an online auction and shopping service provider, eBay allows a third party to handle a seller's checkout processes. When buyers on eBay finish shopping and want to check out, they are directed to a checkout system provided by a third-party checkout service provider. The eBay and third-party checkout services are to be composed to fulfill the requirement of the online shopping and checkout business. They provide complementary functionality, but because they are developed by different entities, they do not fit each other as exactly as one desires.

Figure 4.2 shows the BPEL of both eBay and TPC services. When a buyer wins an auction, the eBay service starts the checkout and then invokes a TPC service by passing *OrderID*, *UserID*, and *SecretID*. Next, eBay receives invocation from TPC (*Receive FetchToken*) with *UserID* and *SecretID*, and replies with *Token*, which is a required parameter in subsequent interactions. Finally, eBay receives invocation from TPC with *Token*, *OrderID*, and *UserID* (*Receive GetOrderData*) and replies with *OrderData*. On the TPC side, the TPC service initiates its own process upon receiving *Order* and *PartnerID*. Then it invokes *GetOrderTrans* with *OrderID* and *UserID* and waits for an asynchronous reply with *OrderData* from the online merchant (*Receive*

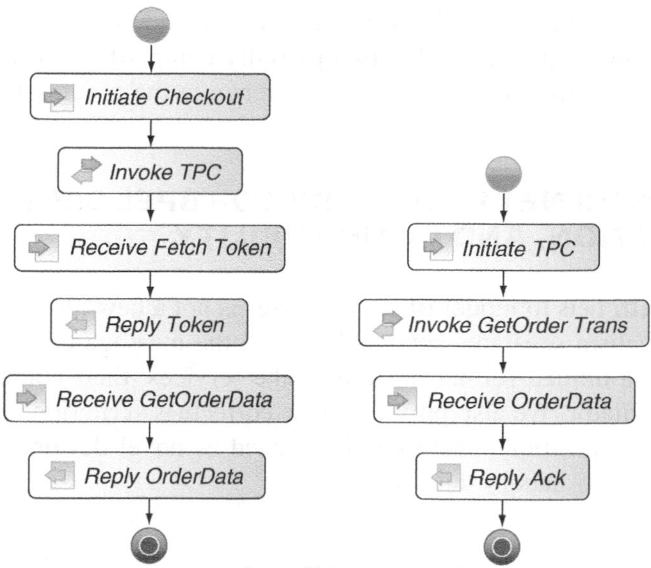


**Figure 4.2** BPEL of eBay and TPC services.

*OrderData*). TPC returns an *Ack* after it receives *OrderData* (*Reply Ack*). With the order data retrieved, TPC shows to the user the items purchased and shipping address, and the buyer follows the TPC flow to complete the checkout process. Note that this step is not relevant to the problem we are going to address, and thus it is not shown in Figure 4.2.

Obviously these two services cannot be directly composed because of the following reasons:

1. The messages exchanged between their operations do not match exactly; and
2. The numbers of their operations and input/output messages are not identical.

Besides, without formal analysis, the correctness of their composition cannot be guaranteed.

In the aforementioned scenario, there is no way to compose eBay and TPC services directly. In other words, the current direct composition approaches fail to do so. To solve this problem, Section 4.2 gives the formalism for *BPEL service*, *composition*, *mediation*, and *mediation-aided composition*. Section 4.3 introduces the method to check whether there is any mediator to glue two partially compatible services, and Section 4.4 introduces the method to generate the mediator.

## 4.2 PETRI NET FORMALISM FOR BPEL SERVICE, MEDIATION, AND COMPATIBILITY

Using Petri nets to model BPEL processes is not a new idea. However, our formalism separates control flow with the message exchange and provides a unified formalism to describe services, their composition, and a mediator. We also provide a new correctness criterion regarding service composition. These can be viewed as novel developments in applying Petri nets to this area.

### 4.2.1 CPN Formalism for BPEL Process

To formally analyze the compatibility and mediation issue in BPEL services composition, we first define a formal model. Then, we present how to transform a BPEL process to this model. Service workflow net is an extension of workflow nets defined in Chapter 2, with the capability of describing message exchanges among services, based on the concept of colored Petri nets.

**Definition 4.1. (Service Workflow Net, SWF-net)** A service workflow net is a colored Petri net $(P, T, F, \Sigma, C)$, where

1. $P$ is a finite set of places satisfying
   (a) $P = P_I \cup P_M$ and $P_I \cap P_M = \varnothing$;
   (b) $P_I$ is a set of internal places, and
   (c) $P_M$ is a set of message places satisfying the condition that $\forall p \in P_M$, $(\bullet p = \varnothing \wedge |p\bullet| = 1) \vee (p\bullet = \varnothing \wedge |\bullet p| = 1)$.
2. $T$ is a finite set of transitions;
3. $F \subseteq (P \times T) \cup (T \times P)$ is a flow relation and $(P_I, T, F)$ is a WF-net;
4. $\Sigma$ is a finite set of color sets. Color set $E = \{e\} \in \Sigma$ has a unique element, which is the color of the control tokens in $P_I$; and
5. $C$ is the color function from $P$ to $\Sigma$, and $\forall p \in P_I$, $C(p) = E$.

**Remarks:**

1. Internal places in $P_I$ represent the internal control logic, and message places in $P_M$ represent the messages exchanged among services.
2. $(P_I, T, F)$ forms an ordinary WF-net as defined in Chapter 2.
3. The internal places are tagged with color $e$ that stands for the control tokens in $(P_I, T, F)$, which is unique.
4. The message places are tagged with the color sets that represent message types.

To differentiate input/output message places, we define *message polarity* for message places, denoted $\Psi$.

$$\forall p \in P_M$$
$$\Psi(p) = \begin{cases} +1; {}^{\bullet}p = \varnothing \wedge |p^{\bullet}| = 1 & \text{(incoming message)} \\ -1; p^{\bullet} = \varnothing \wedge |{}^{\bullet}p| = 1 & \text{(outgoing message)} \\ 0; p^{\bullet} = {}^{\bullet}p = \varnothing & \text{(constant data)} \end{cases}$$

The idea of message polarity comes from Reference [113], and it is notated as shown in Table 4.1.

**EXAMPLE 4.1.**

Figure 4.3 shows the SWF-net of the eBay service illustrated in Figure 4.2.

In this net, $P_I = \{p_1, p_2, p_3, p_4\}$ and $P_M = \{p_5, p_6, p_7, p_8, p_9\}$.

$\Sigma = \{\{e\}, Order, UserID \times SecretID, Token, Token\times\ OrderID\times UserID, OrderData\}$, and the color mapping function $C$, that is, the color set definition of each place in $P$, is as follows:

$e$ denotes the color of all control tokens in all the places in $P_I$. *Order*, which denotes the set of all possible *order* messages, is the

**Table 4.1** The Polarity of Places

| Massage place | ○ | ○→ | →○ | Otherwise |
|---|---|---|---|---|
| Polarity ($\Psi$) | 0 | +1 | −1 | Undefined |

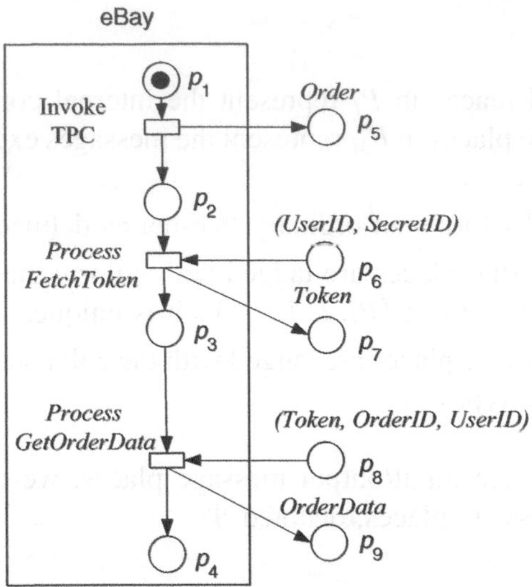


**Figure 4.3** The SWF-net of the eBay service illustrated in Figure 4.2.

color set of $p_5$. *UserID* × *SecretID*, which denotes the set of all valid combinations of *user id* and *secret id*, is the color set of $p_6$. *Token*, which denotes the set of all possible *token* messages (different from the control token in $P_I$), is the color set of $p_7$. *Token* × *OrderID* × *UserID*, which denotes the set of all valid combinations of *token*, *order id*, and *user id*, is the color set of $p_8$. *OrderData*, which denotes the set of all possible *order data* messages, is the color set of $p_9$.

$$\Psi(p_5) = \Psi(p_7) = \Psi(p_9) = -1 \quad \text{and} \quad \Psi(p_6) = \Psi(p_8) = +1$$

Let us explain the color set used in this example. Suppose that there are two users in this system, that is, $UserID = \{u_1, u_2\}$, and each user has his/her own *token* and *secret id*. Therefore, we have $Token = \{tk_1, tk_2\}$, $SecretID = \{s_1, s_2\}$, in which $tk_1$ and $tk_2$ are the tokens of $u_1$ and $u_2$, respectively; $s_1$ and $s_2$ are the *secret ids* of $u_1$ and $u_2$, respectively. Suppose that there are two items to buy or we have two types of orders, that is, $Order = \{o_1, o_2\}$, and correspondingly $OrderData = \{od_1, od_2\}$ in which $od_1$ and $od_2$ are the full content of $o_1$ and $o_2$, respectively. Then $UserID \times SecretID = \{(u_1, s_1), (u_2, s_2)\}$ and $Token \times OrderID \times UserID = \{(tk_1, o_1, u_1), (tk_2, o_1, u_2), (tk_1, o_2, u_1),$

$(tk_2, o_2, u_2)\}$. Note that the combination of *user id, secret id,* and *token* is valid only when it represents the same user. For example, none of $(u_1, s_2)$, $(u_2, s_1)$, $(tk_1, o_1, u_2)$, and $(tk_2, o_1, u_1)$ is valid using the aforementioned criterion. Here, for simplicity, we assume two users and two orders. However, in reality, there can be many users and many orders. We further note that in the compatibility analysis we only need to know the color set (i.e., type information) of each place rather than the number of colors a color set has.

The elements *<receive>*, *<reply>*, *<invoke>*, *<sequence>*, *<if>*, *<pick>*, *<flow>*, *<while>*, *<repeatUntil>*, and *<link>* are key ones to describe the control logic of BPEL. Because our work tackles the issue of service compatibility in the control logic aspect, it does not consider BPEL constructs such as *compensation, fault handler, assign, correlation set, link condition,* and *variables.*

Figure 4.4 illustrates how to transform some BPEL elements into SWF-net ones. BPEL activities and internal control logic are modeled with internal places and transitions; the messages exchanged are modeled with message places. In Figure 4.4, message places are explicitly denoted as $pm$, $pm_1$ and $pm_2$, and other places are all internal places. In Section 4.3 we illustrate how these two BPEL processes illustrated in Figure 4.2 are transformed into SWF-nets.

### 4.2.2 CPN Formalism for Service Composition

Before defining service composition, we define the fusion of two colored Petri nets.

**Definition 4.2. (Fusion of colored Petri nets)** Given two colored Petri nets $N_i = (P_i, T_i, F_i, \Sigma_i, C_i, M_{0i})$, $i = 1$ and 2, satisfying that $P_C = P_1 \cap P_2 \neq \varnothing, \forall p \in P_C, C_1(p) = C_2(p)$, and $M_{01}(p) = M_{02}(p)$, $N = (P, T, F, \Sigma, C, M_0)$ is the fusion of $N_1$ and $N_2$ via places if the following requirements are satisfied:

1. $P = P_1 \cup P_2$,
2. $T = T_1 \cup T_2$, $T_1 \cap T_2 = \varnothing$,
3. $F = F_1 \cup F_2$,
4. $\forall p \in P$, if $p \in P_1$, $C(p) = C_1(p)$; else $C(p) = C_2(p)$, and
5. $\forall p \in P$, if $p \in P_1$, $M_0(p) = M_{01}(p)$; else $M_0(p) = M_{02}(p)$.

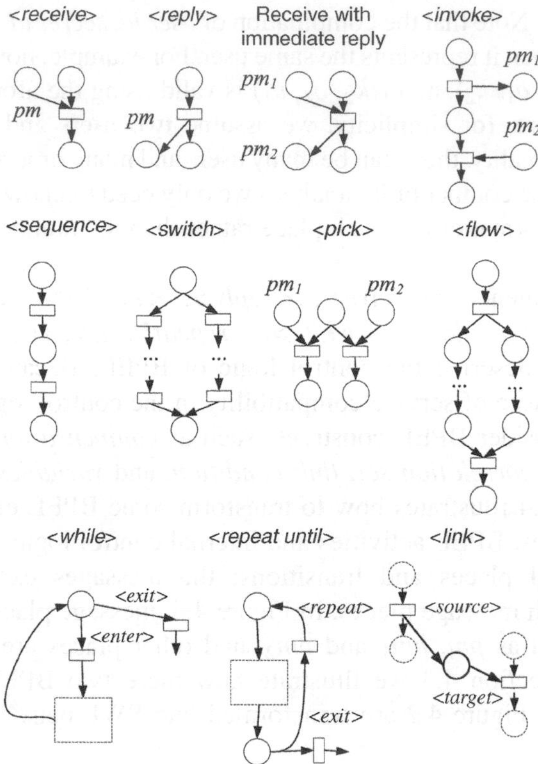


**Figure 4.4** Transforming BPEL into SWF-net.

We claim that two colored Petri nets $N_1$ and $N_2$ are *fusible* if they can be fused via a set of common places with identical color sets and marking, and in this case, the fusion of $N_1$ and $N_2$ via common places $P_C$ is denoted $N_1 \oplus_{P_C} N_2$.

**Remarks:** In order to do place fusion, we should first label the places that we want to merge in two nets with identical labels, and we should also guarantee that places that we do not want to merge are with different labels. $P_C$ is the set of common places in colored Petri nets, which have identical color set definitions and markings in two nets.

Definition 4.2 is based on the definition given in Reference [115]. However, when we consider the problem of service composition, there are some specific requirements:

1. Only message places can be merged, and thus we should pay special attention when we define $P_C$.
2. When we merge two message places from two services, we require that not only their color sets be identical, but also their polarity be contrary.

Given these requirements that are specific to service composition, we define the composition of two SWF-nets.

**Definition 4.3. (Composition of SWF-nets)** Given two SWF-nets $N_i = (P_{Ii} \cup P_{Mi}, T_i, F_i, \Sigma_i, C_i)$, $i=1$ and 2, $N = (P_I \cup P_M, T, F, \Sigma, C)$ is the composition of $N_1$ and $N_2$ if

1. $P_{I1} \cap P_{I2} = \varnothing$, $P_I = P_{I1} \cup P_{I2}$,
2. $P_M = P_{M1} \cup P_{M2}$, $P_C = P_{M1} \cap P_{M2} \neq \varnothing$,
3. $\forall p \in P_C$, $p$ in $N_1$ and $p$ in $N_2$ have contrary polarity, that is, $\Psi_1(p)\Psi_2(p) = -1$. $\Psi_1$ and $\Psi_2$ are the polarity functions of $N_1$ and $N_2$, respectively, and
4. $N = N_1 \oplus_{P_C} N_2$.

The composition of two SWF-nets $N_1$ and $N_2$ via common message places $P_C$ is denoted $N = N_1 \otimes_{P_C} N_2$. We claim that operator $\otimes_{P_C}$ can be extended to other colored Petri nets as long as their places are classified into two disjoint categories, that is, internal places ($P_I$) and message places ($P_M$). Later we use this operator when we define composition via mediation.

Figure 4.5 presents the method to transform BPEL composition to SWF-net composition. In Figure 4.5, the composition of *<invoke>* and *<receive>*/*<reply>* is modeled with SWF-net composition.

### 4.2.3 Mediator and Mediation-Aided Service Composition

When one service provides functionality that another service requires but two services were not programmed to collaborate in advance, one may often find that it is impossible to directly compose them. In our formalism, there does not exist a set $P_C$ such that $N = N_1 \otimes_{P_C} N_2$.

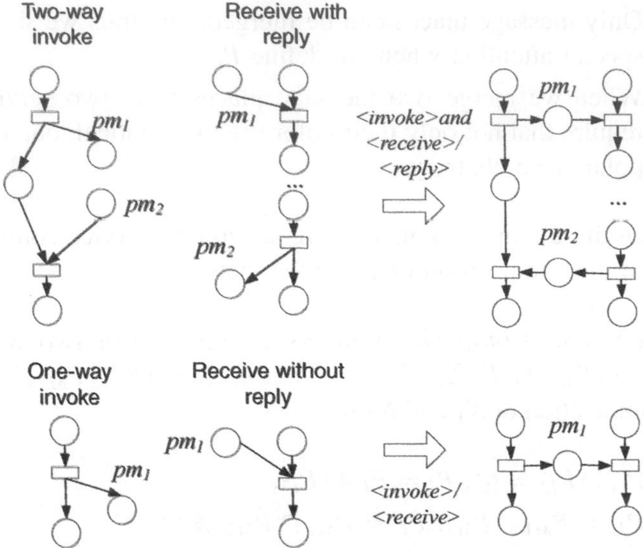


**Figure 4.5** Transform BPEL composition to SWF-net composition.

We introduce the concept of *mediation* to deal with this difficult issue. Informally, *mediation* (*or mediator*) is a piece of code that sits between two services and closes the differences between their interfaces. Formally, we model a mediator as a colored Petri net, which has interfaces to the two services that need to be composed to collaborate. All messages exchanged by the two services go through the mediator.

**Definition 4.4. (Mediation/Mediator)** A mediator $\mathbf{M} = (P_m, T_m, F_m, \Sigma_m, C_m)$ is a place-bordered colored Petri net. The polarity of the border places can be 0, $-1$, or $+1$.

**Remarks:** A place-bordered Petri net is a net in which (1) every transition has at least one input and one output places; and (2) some places have input or output transitions but not both, which are called border places.

**Definition 4.5. (Composition via Mediator)** Given two SWF-nets $N_1$, $N_2$ and a mediator **M**, $N_1 \otimes_{P_{C1}} \mathbf{M} \otimes_{P_{C2}} N_2$ is the composition of $N_1$ and $N_2$ via **M**.

**Remarks:**

1. Intuitively, service composition is used to synthesize two SWF-nets via message places with identical color set and contrary polarity.
2. If $P_{C1} \cap P_{C2} \neq \varnothing, \forall p \in P_{C1} \cap P_{C2}$, $p$ in $N_1$ and $p$ in $N_2$ have contrary polarity, that is, $\Psi_1(p)\Psi_2(p) = -1$, and in $\mathbf{M}$, $\Psi_{\mathbf{M}}(p) = 0$.
3. $N_1 \otimes_{P_C} N_2$ is a special case of $N_1 \otimes_{P_{C1}} \mathbf{M} \otimes_{P_{C2}} N_2$, where $P_C = P_{C1} = P_{C2}$, and $T_m = F_m = \varnothing$.

Now we can give the definition of service compatibility.

**Definition 4.6. (Compatibility of Two Services)** Given two SWF-nets $N_1$ and $N_2$, $N$ is their composition, that is, $N = N_1 \otimes_{P_C} N_2$. $M_0 = M_{10} \times M_{20}$, and $M_e = M_{1e} \times M_{2e}$. $M_{i0}$ and $M_{ie}$ are the initial and end markings of $N_i$, respectively. $N_1$ is compatible with $N_2$ with respect to $P_C$ if the reachability graph of $N$ is well formed, that is,

1. $\forall M \in \mathbf{R}(N, M_0)$, there is a firing sequence $\sigma$ and a marking $M_\sigma$ such that $M[\sigma\rangle M_o$ and $M_o \geq M_e$; and
2. Given $M \in \mathbf{R}(N, M_0)$ with $M \geq M_e$, if $\exists p \in P, M(p) > M_e(p)$, then $p \in P_{M1} \cup P_{M2}$.

In addition, two SWF-nets, $N_1$ and $N_2$, are compatible with mediator $\mathbf{M}$ if the reachability graph of $N_1 \otimes_{P_{C1}} \mathbf{M} \otimes_{P_{C2}} N_2$ is well formed.

The meaning of Definition 4.6 can be explained as follows:

1. Once the interaction begins, it will complete successfully.
2. When the interaction completes, both services reach their ending state, and possibly there are remaining messages that are sent out by one service but not consumed by the other.

*Weak soundness* [56] requires a stronger condition than the aforementioned compatibility does, and *soundness* [81] requires even more than *weak soundness* does. This relaxation roots from the observation that services are more autonomous and loosely coupled. Hence, Definition 4.6

is more reasonable in stating what condition should be satisfied when two services are believed to be compatible.

Definitions 4.5 and 4.6 only concern the composition of two services. Our method can easily be extended to a multiservice composition scenario by stepwise composition and analysis. Hence, we focus our discussion on two-service composition thereafter.

## 4.3 COMPATIBILITY ANALYSIS VIA PETRI NET MODELS

The solution approach is illustrated in Figure 4.6. First, transform two BPEL services to be composed into SWF-nets. Then verify whether they are directly composable. If not, request data mapping information. Next, use data mapping to build a communicating reachability graph

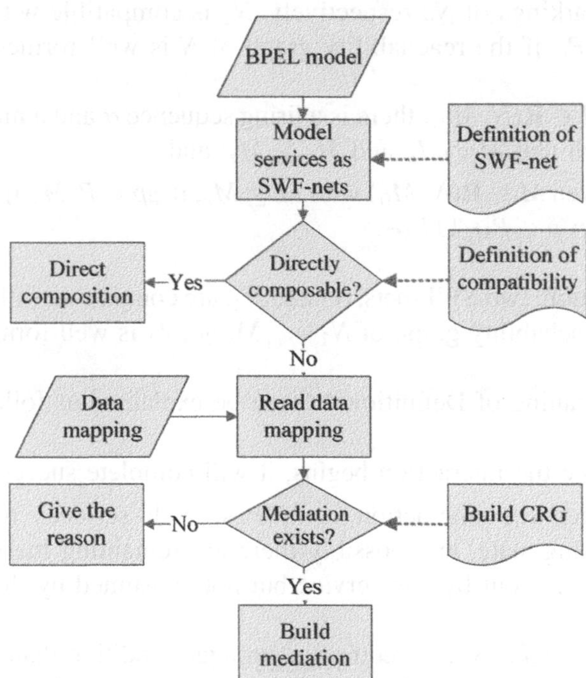


**Figure 4.6** The proposed solution approach.

(CRG) to verify whether there exists a mediator to glue them. If yes, generate it. In this section, we use the motivating scenario presented in Section 4.1 to explain our solution approach.

### 4.3.1 Transforming Abstract BPEL Process to SWF-net

The method to transform BPEL services to SWF-nets has been given in Section 4.2. Figure 4.7 depicts the result of transforming two BPEL services in Figure 4.2 into their corresponding SWF-nets. In Figure 4.7, message *Order* is defined as the composition of *OrderID, UserID* and *SecretID*; while message *COReq* is defined as the composition of *Order* and *PartnerID*. Transitions *ProcessFetchToken*, *ProcessGetOrderData*, and *ProcessOrderData* all represent *receive* plus (immediate) *reply* in the original BPEL process. We have made this simplification to obtain a more compact state space while preserving all the behavioral characteristics. In Figure 4.7 we group the message places of two SWF-nets into a dotted rectangle called *composition*.

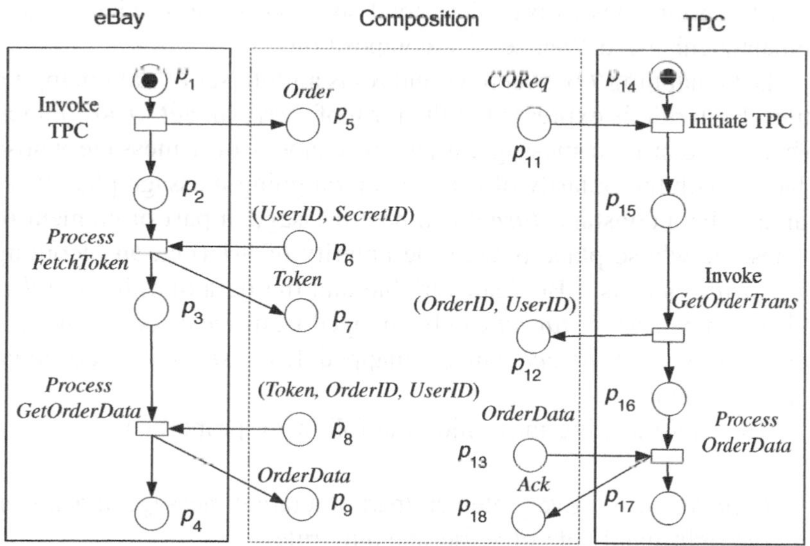


**Figure 4.7** Two SWF-nets: eBay and third-party checkout (TPC).

### 4.3.2 Specifying Data Mapping

The functionality of data mapping is to define rules to relate (syntactically/semantically equivalent) elements of two messages such that two interfaces belonging to different services can be linked, and ultimately, services can be composed. In the specification of BPEL, messages exchanged between two Web services are modeled as an aggregation of parts and/or elements. Therefore, data mapping can be performed at the message, part or element levels.

It is noted that data mapping is a very challenging problem in the area of data integration, semantic Web, and SOA. We assume that the data mapping relation between two services to be composed is specified by service composers who intend to compose them. We then focus on how to detect the behavior mismatches between two services and how to build a mediator to glue them (if possible). Semantic Web service technology allows the semiautomatic and automatic annotation of Web services, and therefore, can be very helpful in the generation of data mapping relations between two services. Some prior works [97,116] focused on the data semantics and transformation between Web service interfaces. Instead, we focus on the behavior analysis and mediation via data transformation. Note that the proposed approach can be combined with the prior ones to provide a total solution to more adaptive and semantic-enhanced Web service composition.

Data mapping *I* between $N_1$ and $N_2$ is a finite set of data mapping rules. Each rule is expressed in the form of <*src*, *target*, *trans_flag*>, where *src* can be a message, a part or element of a message whose place is with the polarity of $-1$ (i.e., an outgoing message place); *src* can also be a constant. *target* can be a message, a part or element of a message whose place is with the polarity of $+1$ (i.e., an incoming one). *trans_flag* is a Boolean variable and the default value is *false*. It is set to be *false* if *target* can be mapped from *src* directly, and it is set to be *true* if *target* can be mapped from *src* with additional transformation.

The data mapping may enjoy the following properties:

*Completeness*. Every element/part of a target message appears on the right-hand side of some mapping rule.

*Accuracy*. Every element/part of a target message appears in at most one right-hand side of a mapping rule.

**Table 4.2** Data Mapping Table

| Source | Target |
|---|---|
| *eBay.Order* | *TPC.COReq.Order* |
| "eBay" | *TPC.COReq.PartnerID* |
| *eBay.Order.(UserID, SecretID)* | *eBay.(UserID, SecretID)* |
| *TPC.(OrderID, UserID)* | *eBay.(Token, OrderID, UserID).(OrderID, UserID)* |
| *eBay.Token* | *eBay.(Token, OrderID, UserID).Token* |
| *eBay.OrderData* | *TPC.OrderData* |

In the eBay example, we have the data mapping shown in Table 4.2. *eBay* and *TPC* stand for eBay and TPC services, respectively. Notations such as *eBay.Order* stand for message *Order* of *eBay*. For complex messages made up of multiple parts/elements, we use parentheses to aggregate the multiple parts/elements into one single message; for example, message *eBay.(UserID, SercretID)* stands for a message of eBay, and this message is made up of two elements, that is, *UserID* and *SercretID*; *eBay.(Token, OrderID, UserID).Token* stands for the element *Token* in message *(Token, OrderID, UserID)* of *eBay*. In row 2 of Table 4.2, "eBay" stands for a constant string whose content is *eBay*.

Our approach assumes that the data mapping between two services is accurate. It is easy to verify that the data mapping in Table 4.2 is complete and accurate.

### 4.3.3 Mediator Existence Checking

In order to check whether there exists a mediator to glue two partially compatible services, we introduce the concept of communicating reachability graph (CRG). Its basic idea is to construct the reachability graph of two services concurrently, using data mapping as a communication mechanism. That is, when the source data are ready, their target should be informed.

Given two SWF-nets $N_1$ and $N_2$, and a data mapping $I$, their CRG is a directed graph $\mathbf{G}(N_1, N_2, I) = (V, E)$, where $V \subseteq M_1 \times M_2$. There are two kinds of edges in CRG. One is an operation edge, that is,

$$E_O = \{\langle m, t, m' \rangle | m, m' \in V \quad \text{and} \quad m \xrightarrow{t} m',$$
$$\text{if } t \in T_1, m' = m'_1 \times m_2; \text{ else if } t \in T_2, \ m' = m_1 \times m'_2\}$$

The other is a mediation edge, that is,

$$E_M = \left\{ \langle m, t_M(m), m' \rangle | m, m' \in V \text{ and } m \xrightarrow{t_M(m)} m' \right\}$$

A mediation edge is constructed to act as a communication mechanism between two services. The meaning of $t_M(m)$ is given in Algorithm 4.1.

**Algorithm 4.1. (Method to Construct CRG)**

**Input:** SWF-nets $N_i = (P_{Ii} \cup P_{Mi}, T_i, F_i, \Sigma_i, C_i)$, $i = 1, 2$ and data mapping $I$.

The data mapping table used here is similar to Table 4.2, except that a new column named flag is added.

| Flag | Source | Target |
|---|---|---|
| | SrcMsg_1.Element_1 | TargetMsg_1.Element_1 |
| | ... | ... |
| | SrcMsg.Element_*n* | TargetMsg.Element_*n* |

**Output:** $\mathbf{G}(N_1, N_2, I) = (V, E)$

1. Initialize $(V, E) = (\{m_0 = m_{10} \times m_{20}\}, \varnothing)$; $m_0$ is untagged
2. While there are untagged nodes in $V$, do
   2.1 Select an untagged node $m \in V$ and tag it; Denote $m = m_1 \times m_2$.
   2.2 For each enabled transition, $t_i \in T_i$, at $m = m_1 \times m_2$, do
      2.2.1 Compute $m'$ such that $m \xrightarrow{t_i} m'$; if $i = 1$, $m' = m'_1 \times m_2$; else if $i = 2$, $m' = m_1 \times m'_2$
      2.2.2 If there exists $m''$ such that $m'' \xrightarrow{\sigma} m'$, $m'' \leq m' \wedge m'' \neq m'$, and $\exists p \in P \wedge p \notin P_{M1} \cup P_{M2}$ such that $m''(p) < m(p)$, then the algorithm fails and exits (Note that the unboundedness condition of CRG has been detected.)

2.2.3 If there is no $m'' \in V$ such that $m'' = m'$, then $V = V \cup \{m'\}$; (and $m'$ is untagged)

2.2.4 $E = E \cup \{(m, t_i, m')\}$

2.2.5 If $t_i^{\bullet} \cap P_{Mi} = p_m$ (i.e., new tokens are fed into message place $p_m$ with the firing of $t_i$)

(a) Flag all the rows whose source message is $C(p_m)$ in the data mapping table

(b) Compute $m''$ such that $m' \xrightarrow{t_M(m')} m''$. $m''$ is derived from $m'$ through virtual transition $t_M(m')$ by (i) unmarking $p_m$ if in all data mapping rules whose source message is $C(p_m)$, the target messages are satisfied, (ii) marking the place attached with the message, for each newly satisfied target message in step (a). (Note that a target message is *satisfied* if in the data mapping table all the rows it resides in are flagged.)

(c) If $m'' \neq m'$: tag $m'$; $V = V \cup \{m''\}$; $E = E \cup \{(m', t_M(m'), m'')\}$. (and $m''$is untagged.)

3. The algorithm succeeds with $\mathbf{G}(N_1, N_2, I)$ obtained.

Given eBay service $N_1$, TPC service $N_2$ in Figure 4.7, and the data mapping $I$ in Table 4.2, we can derive $\mathbf{G}(N_1, N_2, I)$ according to Algorithm 4.1 as Figure 4.8 shows. The operation edges are denoted with solid directed arcs and the names of operation transitions are labeled on them. The mediation edges are denoted with dashed directed arcs, and the data obtained by mediation are labeled on them. The first several steps to obtain the CRG in Figure 4.8 are as follows. At the beginning, eBay and TPC services are both at the initial state, with a token in $p_1$ and $p_{14}$, respectively. Other places are with no token except $p_{10}$ that represents *TPC.COReq.PartnerID* with a token representing a constant value "eBay". Starting from this initial state denoted by the initial bold ellipse in Figure 4.8, the eBay service can fire its "Invoke TPC" transition and deposit a token to $p_2$ and $p_5$, respectively as seen in the second ellipse. At this state, by checking Table 4.2 we can find that both parts of *TPC.COReq*, that is, *Order* and *PartnerID* are available, and *eBay.(UserID, SecretID)* is also available. Hence, a mediation transition can fire to deposit a token to $p_6$ and $p_{11}$,

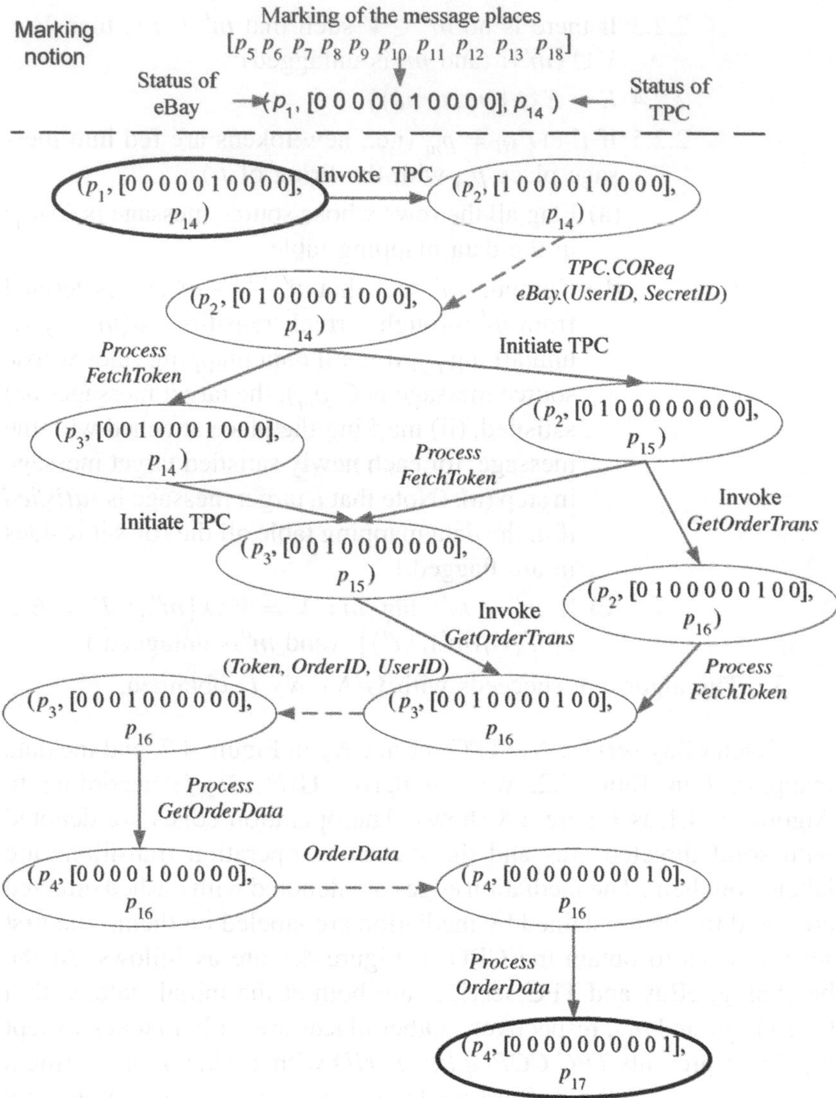


**Figure 4.8** The communicating reachability graph of eBay and TPC service.

respectively. This mediation transition is illustrated by a dashed directed arc from the second ellipse to the third one. From this state, we can further populate CRG by firing transitions in each service as well as mediation ones.

We prove that if $\mathbf{G}(N_1, N_2, I)$ satisfies a certain property, there exists a mediator to glue $N_1$ and $N_2$, and in Section 4.4 we give the method to generate it. We have the following theorem:

**Theorem 4.1.** Given an accurate data mapping $I$, and two SWF-nets $N_1$ and $N_2$, there exists a mediator $\mathbf{M}$ with respect to $I$, such that $N_1$ and $N_2$ can be composed via $\mathbf{M}$ if $\mathbf{G}(N_1, N_2, I)$ is well formed, that is,

1. $\forall M \in \mathbf{R}(M_0)$, there are an edge sequence $\sigma$ and a marking $M_\sigma$ such that $M[\sigma\rangle M_\sigma$ and $M_\sigma \geq M_e$; and
2. Given $M \in \mathbf{R}(M_0)$ with $M \geq M_e$, if $\exists p \in P$, $M(p) > M_e(p)$, then $p \in P_{M1} \cup P_{M2}$.

Its proof is given later. The proof shows that the CRG contains all needed properties in mediator existence checking. Moreover, in our method to build CRG, state-space exploration is sped up because CRG is generated as a reduced state space of the composed services, eliminating some intermediate states that are not relevant to the compatibility verification.

We can easily verify that $\mathbf{G}(N_1, N_2, I)$ in Figure 4.8 is well formed. Therefore, we claim that a mediator exists to glue $N_1$ and $N_2$.

Figure 4.9a shows two services with no mediator to glue them. Service *X* expects to receive message *B* and then sends message *A* in the next step. Service *Y* expects to receive message *A* and then sends message *B* in the next step. With data mapping <*X.A*, *Y.A*>, <*X.B*, *Y.B*>, the CRG (Figure 4.9c) is not well formed. Therefore, *X* and *Y* cannot be composed via mediation. Figure 4.9b shows the composition of services *X* and *Y* with the given data mapping, and the resulting net contains a deadlock in fact.

### 4.3.4 Proof of Theorem 4.1

The proof of Theorem 4.1 needs the concept of a stubborn set [117]. Intuitively, a set of transitions is called a stubborn set in a given marking, if each transition in it remains to be *stubborn* (i.e., enabled) when a transition outside it fires. This property infers that, in marking $M$, if $t \in T_S$, $t_1, t_2, \ldots, t_n \notin T_S$ and $M[t_1 t_2 \ldots t_n\rangle M_n[t\rangle M_n'$, then there is a marking $M'$ such that $M[t\rangle M'[t_1 t_2 \ldots t_n\rangle M_n'$.

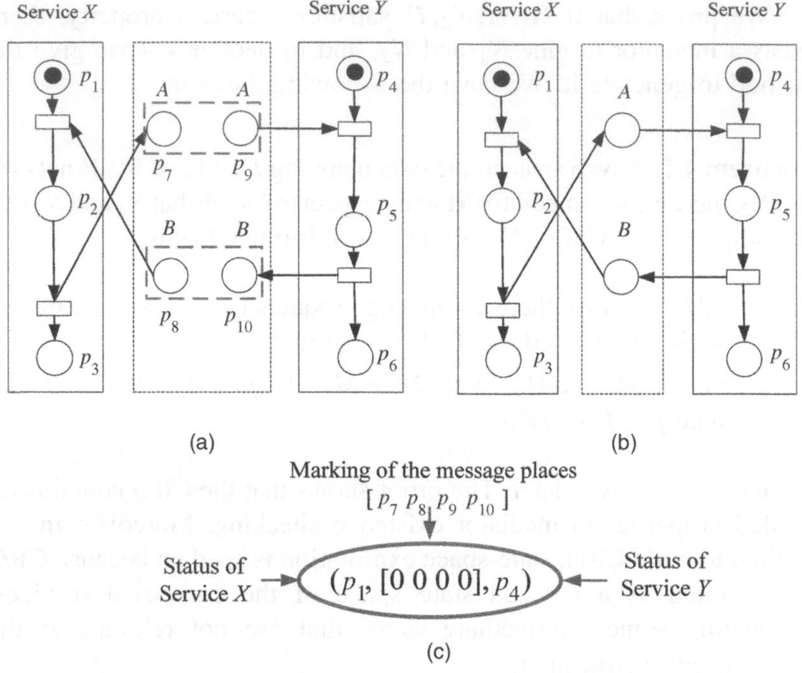


**Figure 4.9** (a) An example in which no mediator exists. (b) The composed service. (c) The CRG.

The following two lemmas are due to Reference [117].

**Lemma 4.1.** The ordinary state space is a labeled directed graph $(W, E)$, while the reduced state space generated by stubborn sets is a labeled directed graph $(\underline{W}, \underline{E})$.

If $s \in W$ and $s$ is a terminal state, then $s \in \underline{W}$ and $s$ is a terminal state of $\underline{W}$.

If $s$ is a terminal state of $\underline{W}$, then $s \in W$ and $s$ is a terminal state of $W$.

**Lemma 4.2.** There is an infinite occurrence sequence in the reduced state space if and only if there is an infinite occurrence sequence in the ordinary state space.

Theorem 4.1 claims that CRG is equivalent to the reduced state space generated using the set of mediation transitions as stubborn sets. Because we are only interested in terminal states in the state space, the reduced state space preserves all relevant properties. In other words, CRG is well formed if the two services can be composed with the help of a mediator.

*Proof of Theorem 4.1.* $\Rightarrow$ We are to prove that if $\mathbf{G}(N_1,N_2,I)$ is well formed, a mediator $\mathbf{M}$ that conforms to $I$ exists. Note that in Section 4.4, we will give the method to derive a mediator based on the information from a well-formed CRG, and denote the mediator as $\mathbf{M}=(P_m,T_m,F_m)$.

When we build the reachability graph of $N_1 \otimes_{P_{C1}} \mathbf{M} \otimes_{P_{C2}} N_2$ (denoted $\Gamma(N_1 \otimes_{P_{C1}} \mathbf{M} \otimes_{P_{C2}} N_2)$), if we use the stubborn set defined in the following equation,

$$\mathbf{S}(m)=\begin{cases}\{t_m\}, \text{ when } \exists t_m \in T_m, t_m \text{ is enabled at } m\\ T_1 \cup T_2 \cup T_m, \text{ otherwise}\end{cases} \tag{4.1}$$

we obtain a reduced reachability graph of $\Gamma(N_1 \otimes_{P_{C1}} \mathbf{M} \otimes_{P_{C2}} N_2)$, denoted $\Gamma_R(N_1 \otimes_{P_{C1}} \mathbf{M} \otimes_{P_{C2}} N_2)$.

The meaning of function $\mathbf{S}$ is explained as follows. When there is a mediation transition enabled, choose it as the single enabled transition in the stubborn set at marking $m$. If there are multiple mediation transitions enabled, choose any one of them as the single enabled transition in the stubborn set. When there is no mediation transition enabled, the stubborn set equals to the set of all transitions in $N_1 \otimes_{P_{C1}} \mathbf{M} \otimes_{P_{C2}} N_2$. By this means, we obtain a subgraph of $\Gamma(N_1 \otimes_{P_{C1}} \mathbf{M} \otimes_{P_{C2}} N_2)$.

According to Lemmas 4.1 and 4.2, $\Gamma_R(N_1 \otimes_{P_{C1}} \mathbf{M} \otimes_{P_{C2}} N_2)$ contains all terminal markings and one infinite path if there is one in $\Gamma(N_1 \otimes_{P_{C1}} \mathbf{M} \otimes_{P_{C2}} N_2)$. Because the verification of well-formedness only involves the terminal markings, $\Gamma_R(N_1 \otimes_{P_{C1}} \mathbf{M} \otimes_{P_{C2}} N_2)$ preserves all the information we require. On the other hand, it is easy to see $\mathbf{G}(N_1,N_2,I)$ is *equivalent* to $\Gamma_R(N_1 \otimes_{P_{C1}} \mathbf{M} \otimes_{P_{C2}} N_2)$ with respect to marking $M'$ ($M'=M_1 \times M_2$). Hence, if $\mathbf{G}(N_1,N_2,I)$ is well formed, $\Gamma_R(N_1 \otimes_{P_{C1}} \mathbf{M} \otimes_{P_{C2}} N_2)$ is also well-formed, and ultimately, $\Gamma(N_1 \otimes_{P_{C1}} \mathbf{M} \otimes_{P_{C2}} N_2)$ is well-formed. Therefore, we conclude that $\mathbf{M}$ serves as a mediator to make $N_1$ compatible with $N_2$.

$\Leftarrow$ We are to prove that if a mediator $\mathbf{M}$ that conforms to $I$ exists, $\mathbf{G}(N_1,N_2,I)$ is well-formed. As mentioned, if a mediator $\mathbf{M}$ that conforms to $I$ exists, $\Gamma(N_1 \otimes_{P_{C1}} \mathbf{M} \otimes_{P_{C2}} N_2)$ is well-formed, and since $\Gamma_R(N_1 \otimes_{P_{C1}} \mathbf{M} \otimes_{P_{C2}} N_2)$ is a subgraph of $\Gamma(N_1 \otimes_{P_{C1}} \mathbf{M} \otimes_{P_{C2}} N_2)$, it is also well-formed; and ultimately, $\mathbf{G}(N_1,N_2,I)$ is well-formed. □

**Remarks:** $\Gamma_R = (V,E), V \subseteq M_1 \times M_2 \times M_{\mathbf{M}}$; and $\mathbf{G} = (V',E'), V' \subseteq M_1 \times M_2$. $M_1$, $M_2$, and $M_{\mathbf{M}}$ are markings of $N_1$, $N_2$, and mediator $\mathbf{M}$, respectively. $\mathbf{G}$ and $\Gamma_R$ are *equivalent*, that is, there is a surjective mapping $\varphi$ between them such that $\forall v \in V$ and $\forall v' \in V'$, $\varphi(v) = v'$ if $\prod_{M_1 \times M_2}(v) = v'$. $(v_1,v_2) \in E \Rightarrow (\varphi(v_1),\varphi(v_2)) \in E' \vee \varphi(v_1) = \varphi(v_2)$. If in $\Gamma_R$ there is $v_1[t_1\rangle v_2[t_2\rangle v_3 \ldots [t_k\rangle v_{k+1}$, then $\varphi(v_1) = v'_1$, $\varphi(v_2) = \varphi(v_3) = \cdots = \varphi(v_{k+1}) = v'_{k+1}$. $t_1$, $t_2$, ..., $t_k$ are mediation transitions in $\Gamma_R$. $\prod_{M_1 \times M_2}$ is the projection function that projects the marking at $M_1 \times M_2 \times M_{\mathbf{M}}$ to $M_1 \times M_2$.

## 4.4 MEDIATOR GENERATION APPROACH

### 4.4.1 Types of Mediation

Here we first introduce the classification of mediators.

1. *Store/Forward Mediator*. A store/forward mediator is the simplest one. It stores the incoming message and forwards it to the receiver when needed.
2. *Transformation Mediator*. A transformation mediator transforms the incoming message and forwards it to the receiver when needed.
3. *Split Mediator*. A split mediator replicates the source message (or part/element of it) into multiple copies.
4. *Merge Mediator*. Corresponding to a split one, a merge mediator collects the multiple source messages/parts/elements and then combines them into one single target message.

The CPN models for these types of mediators are given in Figure 4.10.

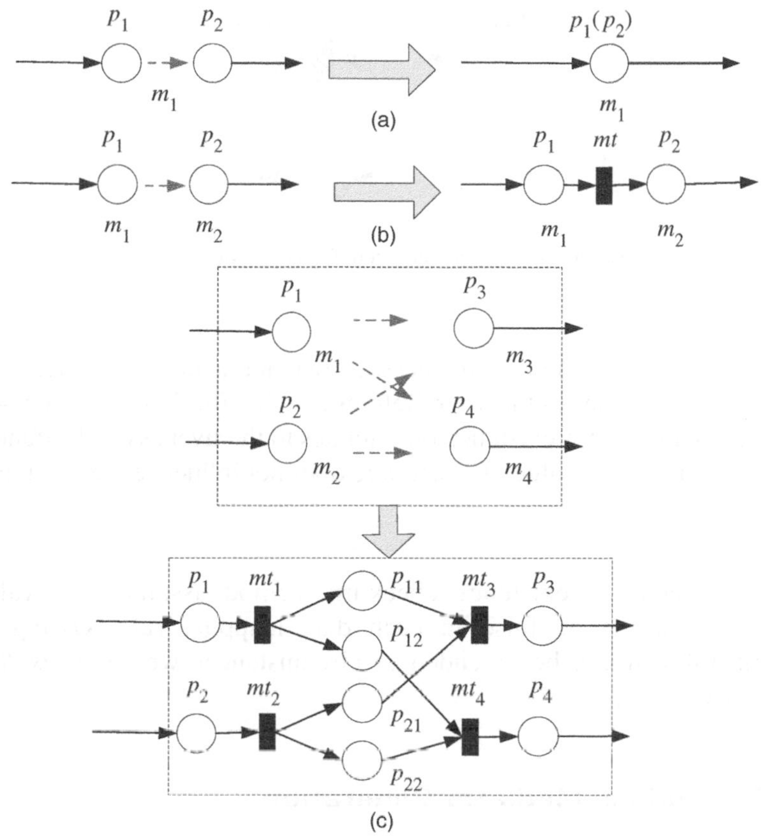


**Figure 4.10** (a) Store/forward mediator. (b) Transformation mediator. (c) Split/ merge mediator.

Given the different types of mediation, in Lemma 4.3 we prove that the value of *trans_flag* does not influence the existence of mediators. Hence it is ignored in the mediator existence checking algorithm.

**Lemma 4.3.** The value of *trans_flag* does not influence the existence of mediator.

*Proof*: For a data mapping rule <*src*, *target*, *trans_flag*>, the mediator generated is shown in Figure 4.11. The mediator with transformation can be reduced to the mediator without transformation, preserving

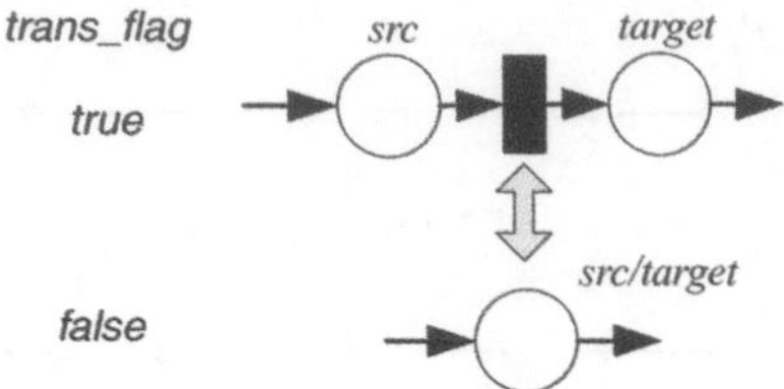


**Figure 4.11** Transformation mediator and store/forward mediator.

liveness, safeness, and boundedness. Note that this kind of reduction is called Fusion of Series Places in References [78,80]. From Theorem 4.1 we see that mediator existence only relates to the liveness and safeness property. Thus, the value of *trans_flag* does not influence the existence of mediators.

□

The mediator existence checking method assumes the value of *trans_flag* to be false in each data mapping rule. Owing to Lemma 4.3, it can be extended to circumstances where *trans_flag* is *true* or *false*.

### 4.4.2 Guided Mediator Generation

In Section 4.3 we use CRG to check the existence of a mediator between two services. If it is well formed, this section gives the method to build the mediator between message places of $N_1$ and $N_2$.

Recall the concept of data mapping, and its example in Table 4.2; we define *reference count* for each message $m_s$ in data mapping $I$. Message $m_1$ is referred by message $m_2$, if $m_1$ and $m_2$ appear in one row in the data mapping table. For example, in Table 4.2, the first row represents data mapping rule <*eBay.Order*, *TPC.COReq.Order*>, we say that message *Order* of eBay is referred by message *COReq* of TPC, and vice versa. The reference count for message $m$ is the number of data mapping rules whose source message is $m$.

For instance, in Table 4.2, the reference count of message *eBay.Token* is 1 since it is only referred by *eBay.*(*Token*, *OrderID*, *UserID*) while that of message *eBay.Order* is 2, since it is referred by both *TPC.COReq* and *eBay.*(*UserID*, *SecretID*).

Clearly, the reference count of a message can be easily derived from a data mapping table. Next, we define *active reference count* ($\Delta$) for each source message $m$ in data mapping $I$. $\Delta(m)$ is the number of data mapping rules whose source message is $m$, and the target of this data mapping is consumed in CRG. For example, the reference count of *eBay.OrderData* is 1; if in Figure 4.8 there is always a token left in $p_{13}$ in terminal marking $M_e$, the active reference count of *eBay.OrderData* is 0 because it means that although message *eBay.OrderData* is referred by one data mapping rule, the target message of this mapping is never consumed. A data mapping rule is *active* if the target message is consumed in at least one terminal marking $M_e$.

On the basis of the concept of data mapping and active reference count, we can build a mediator between two services. Algorithm 4.2 gives the method to do so. Its basic idea is illustrated in Figure 4.10, and its procedure is explained as follows.

For a message mapping where $\Delta(src) = \Delta(target) = 1$, use a *store/forward mediator*. In Figure 4.10a, if message $m_1$ is sent by $p_1$ and needed by $p_2$, we simply merge $p_1$ and $p_2$ to form a *store/forward mediator*.

For message mapping with transformation, use a *transformation mediator*. In Figure 4.10b, if $m_1$ is sent by $p_1$ and $m_2$ is needed by $p_2$, and $m_2$ can be transformed from $m_1$, we add a mediation transition $mt$ between $p_1$ and $p_2$ to form a *transformation mediator*.

For message *src* with $\Delta(src) > 1$, use a *split mediator*. For message *target* with $\Delta(target) > 1$, use a *merge mediator*.

In Figure 4.10c, if $m_1$ is sent by $p_1$ and referred by $m_3$ and $m_4$, $m_2$ is sent by $p_2$ and also referred by $m_3$ and $m_4$. We add split transitions $mt_1$ and $mt_2$ after $p_1$ and $p_2$, merge transitions $mt_3$ and $mt_4$ before $p_3$ and $p_4$, and we add $p_{11}$, $p_{12}$, $p_{21}$, and $p_{22}$ to connect these mediation transitions.

**Algorithm 4.2. (Generation of a Mediator)**

**Input:** SWF-nets $N_1$and $N_2$, and data mapping $I$

**Output:** $\mathbf{M} = (P_m, T_m, F_m, \Sigma_m, C_m)$

1. $P_m = P_{M1} \cup P_{M2}$, $T_m = F_m = \varnothing$

2. For each outgoing message place $p_i \in P_{M1} \cup P_{M2}$ with $\Psi(p_i) = -1$
   2.1 If $k_i = \Delta(C(p_i)) > 1$
      2.1.1 Add a mediation transition $t_i$ in **M**:
      $T_m = T_m \cup \{t_i\}$, add places $\{p_{i1}, p_{i2}, \cdots, p_{ik_i}\}$ in **M**:
      $P_m = P_m \cup \{p_{i1}, p_{i2}, \cdots, p_{ik_i}\}$
      2.1.2 $F_m = F_m \cup \{(p_i, t_i), (t_i, p_{i1}), (t_i, p_{i2}), \ldots, (t_i, p_{ik_i})\}$
3. For each incoming message place $p_j \in P_{M1} \cup P_{M2}$ with $\Psi(p_j) = +1$
   3.1 If $k_j = \Delta(C(p_j)) > 1$
      3.1.1 Add a mediation transition $t_j$ in **M**:
      $T_m = T_m \cup \{t_j\}$, and add place $\{p_{j1}, p_{j2}, \cdots, p_{jk_j}\}$ in **M**:
      $P_m = P_m \cup \{p_{j1}, p_{j2}, \cdots, p_{jk_j}\}$
      3.1.2 $F_m = F_m \cup \{(t_j, p_j), (p_{j1}, t_j), (p_{j2}, t_j), \ldots, (p_{jk_j}, t_j)\}$
4. For each active data mapping rule without transformation, and the source and target message places are $p_i$ and $p_j$, respectively, Merge$(p_i^\bullet, {}^\bullet p_j)$
5. For each active data mapping rule with transformation, and the source and target message places $p_i$ and $p_j$, respectively, AddTransformation$(p_i^\bullet, {}^\bullet p_j)$
6. Return $\mathbf{M} = (P_m, T_m, F_m, \Sigma_m, C_m)$

In Algorithm 4.2, two functions, that is, Merge$(p_i^\bullet, {}^\bullet p_j)$ and AddTransformation$(p_i^\bullet, {}^\bullet p_j)$ are used. Merge$(p_i^\bullet, {}^\bullet p_j)$ is to merge a place $p_{ik} \in (p_i^\bullet)^\bullet$ with a place $p_{jk} \in {}^\bullet({}^\bullet p_j)$. If $p_i^\bullet$ and/or ${}^\bullet p_j$ is null, use $p_i$ and/or $p_j$ instead of $p_{jk}$ and $p_{jk}$. AddTransformation$(p_i^\bullet, {}^\bullet p_j)$ is to add a transition $t_{ikj}$ between a place $p_{ik} \in (p_i^\bullet)^\bullet$ and a place $p_{jk} \in {}^\bullet({}^\bullet p_j)$, that is, $T_m = T_m \cup \{t_{ikj}\}$, and $F_m = F_m \cup \{(p_{ik}, t_{ikj}), (t_{ikj}, p_{jk})\}$. If $p_i^\bullet$ and/or ${}^\bullet p_j$ is null, use $p_i$ and/or $p_j$ instead of $p_{ik}$ and $p_{jk}$. Note that if $(p_i^\bullet)^\bullet > 1$ or ${}^\bullet({}^\bullet p_j) > 1$, choose a different $k$ each time these two functions are invoked such that each place in $(p_i^\bullet)^\bullet$ will merge with a different place in ${}^\bullet({}^\bullet p_j)$, and each newly added transition will have different source and target places in $(p_i^\bullet)^\bullet$ and ${}^\bullet({}^\bullet p_j)$.

With the proposed method, a mediator between eBay and TPC is generated as shown in Figure 4.12. The mediation transitions are denoted with black rectangles to differentiate them from operation transitions belonging to eBay and TPC services. With the generated mediator **M**, the

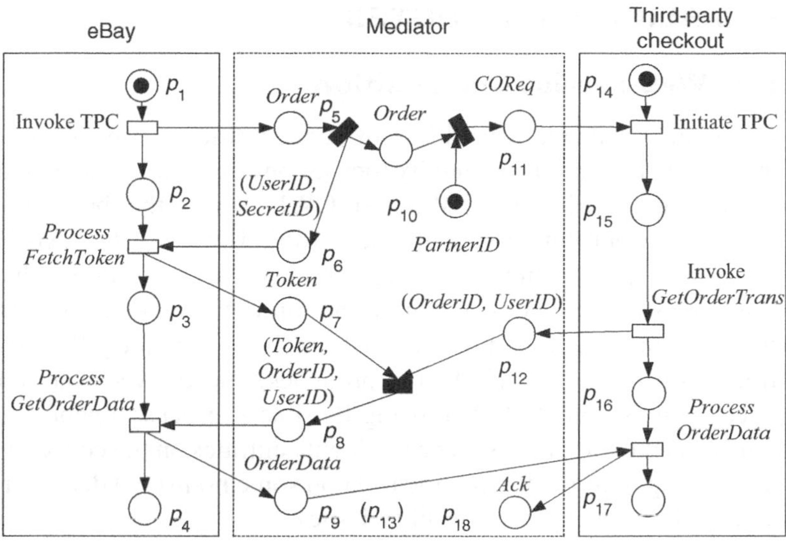


**Figure 4.12** Mediation-aided service composition.

reachability graph of $N_1 \otimes_{P_{C1}} \mathbf{M} \otimes_{P_{C2}} N_2$ is well-formed, that is, eBay and TPC services are compatible with the aid of mediator **M**.

For mediator development/deployment, we use IBM Business Process Manager [33]. A program takes the BPEL services defined as input, transforms the BPEL services into SWF-nets, and analyzes their compatibility. If two BPEL services are partially compatible, a mediator Petri net is generated and transformed back into a mediator BPEL service. The mediator BPEL service consists of such activities as *receive*, *assign*, and *invoke* and the links among them. Once all source messages are ready, the target message is generated and the corresponding interface is invoked. In our BPEL run-time, that is, IBM Business Process Manager, each *porttype* is equipped with a message queue. Thus, the mediator can simply forward the target message whenever all the source messages are ready, being unaware of when the target messages will be consumed. The mediator BPEL assembles the two original BPEL services and makes them run smoothly with each other. Otherwise, if two services are not compatible, our program can point out where the incompatibility is and give instructions to correct the incompatibility, for example, by adding data mapping or changing a message sequence.

## 4.5 BIBLIOGRAPHIC NOTES

### 4.5.1 Web Service Composition

Industry and academia have different concentrations in Web service composition. Industrial community focuses on composition languages, for example, BPEL, WS-CDL, and OWL-S and the build-time/ run-time environment to support them [86]. However, the existing composition specifications only support direct composition, which seems to be straightforward and often too rigid. Academic community focuses on automatic composition (through AI planning [95,109], optimization [43,111], and other approaches) and the verification of service composition [112,118] (using Petri nets, process algebra, and automata as the formalisms). The work concentrates on the conceptual level, making reasonable simplification on some nontrivial details (for example, the partially compatibility issue).

### 4.5.2 Business Process Integration

Compatibility problems also exist when two or more business processes are to be integrated [119]. Compared to traditional business processes, Web services are autonomous, loosely coupled, and defined in a standard format. Consequently, mediation can be used as a preferable approach than a method to modify internal structures when gluing partially compatible services.

### 4.5.3 Web Service Configuration

Briefly, there are two methods to make partially compatible services work smoothly with each other, that is, mediation [47] and configuration [46]. Configuration is a heavyweight approach that changes the original service within some predefined variable points to make it work smoothly with other services. Casati and Shan [46] propose a configuration-based approach that enables the dynamic and adaptive composition of services.

### 4.5.4 Petri Net Model of BPEL Processes

There are some studies about the modeling and analysis of a *single* BPEL process using Petri nets [55,57,120]. Hinz et al. [57] present a Petri net model for a BPEL process, and this model covers the exceptional behavior, for example, faults, events, and compensation. Lohmann et al. [120] use Petri nets to decide the controllability of a service, that is, the existence of a partner process, and compute its operating guideline. Ouyang et al. [55] present a comprehensive and rigorously defined mapping of BPEL constructs into Petri net structures. Other works focus on the analysis of the *direct* composition of two or more BPEL services [56,121,122]. Compared with the work in [56,121,122], we clearly move one step forward to tackle the issue of *indirect* composition.

### 4.5.5 Component/Web Service Mediation

Compared with configuration, mediation is a relatively lightweight approach. The idea of mediation-aided service composition is stimulated by the related work in the software engineering area. For example, *generative programming* [123] is a style of computer programming that uses automated source code creation through generic classes, prototypes, templates, aspects, and code generators to improve the productivity of programmers.

Yellin and Strom [113] propose a method to augment object-oriented component interfaces with *protocols* that include sequencing constraints. They define *adaptors* that can be used to bridge the differences between components and present the method to automatically generate adaptors. Our work is stimulated by [113], but significantly different from it in the following aspects. First, the automata-based approach has limitations in modeling the concurrent behavior of Web services, for example, the *flow* construct in BPEL, while Petri nets are good at modeling such behavior. Second, the automata-based approach focuses on a message exchange sequence but ignores the different exchange styles; for example, more subtle behaviors such as one-way *invoke*, two-way *invoke* and *receive* with/without *reply*, cannot be modeled by automata, while Petri nets can describe them well as illustrated in this chapter. Third, in the automata model in [113], all the state transitions are triggered by external messages. Thus, the internal nondeterminism cannot be modeled, for example, the *if* construct in BPEL; while our SWF-net can model internal as well as external nondeterminism. Last, the automata-based approach can only model the synchronous semantics of composition, while Petri net-based one can model both synchronous and asynchronous semantics. This

**Table 4.3** A Comparison of Related Work on Service Composition/Analysis

| | MO | AC | CM | MC | AM | CP |
|---|---|---|---|---|---|---|
| Ouyang et al. [55] | PN | Y | N | N | N | N |
| Hamadi and Benatallah [122] | PN | N | Y | N | N | N |
| Kongdenfha [50] | N/A | N | Y | Y | N | N |
| Brogi and Popescu [51] | YAWL | Y | Y | Y | N | N |
| Nezhad [52] | FSM | N | Y | Y | Y | N |
| Our approach | CPN | N | Y | Y | N | Y |

work uses asynchronous semantics that is realistic in industrial service composition.

The work in [47,49] provides various scenarios of mismatch patterns in Web service composition. However, a comprehensive classification is missing. Some scenarios are presented with the corresponding solutions. These solutions seem elementary (presented with natural language) and are based on proprietary models. Hence, they can hardly be used in practice.

Based on their previous work [49], Kongdenfha et al. [50] propose the use of an aspect-oriented programming (AOP) approach to weave adaptation solutions into the partially compatible services. The work in [51] proposes a method to automatically generate a mediator between two services. Nezhad et al. [52] also propose an automata-based method to model the protocol of service interactions and to identify mismatches automatically. They use a schema matchmaking technique to handle the issue of message mapping, and propose some heuristic methods for deadlock resolution between two services.

A comparative summary of previous efforts in this area is given in Table 4.3. The columns of the table correspond to the following criteria where Y means yes and N means no:

**MO** indicates the formal model used, FSM for finite state machines, PN for Petri nets, CPN for colored Petri nets, and YAWL for Yet Another Workflow Language.

**AC** indicates whether the formalism provides a representation of advanced BPEL constructs, for example, event handler, fault handler, and scope.

**CM** indicates whether the formalism considers the composition of multiple services.

**MC** indicates whether a mediation code generation method is given.

**AM** indicates whether a method for automatic message mapping between services is given.

**CP** indicates whether correctness proof for a given method is given.

CHAPTER 5

# Web Service Configuration with Multiple Quality-of-Service Attributes

## 5.1 INTRODUCTION

Web services and their related design and composition methodologies are increasingly used to integrate disparate software components to accomplish many challenging tasks. A Web service is defined as a Web-accessible function that is well defined, self-contained, and does not depend on the context of other Web services. When any single Web service fails to accomplish a service requestor's multiple function requirements, multiple Web services need to be dynamically configured together to form a Web service composition to satisfy both functional and nonfunctional requirements. The latter are characterized by quality of service (QoS). The QoS study is important and covers the following areas:

1. QoS specification and description, that is, QoS modeling. QoS serves as a key index for discriminating candidate Web services and Web service compositions with identical functionality. Quantifiable QoS parameters and measurements include reliability, capacity, availability, and cost. The QoS information can be collected from service providers, for example, cost; or from service requesters' feedback, for example, execution time;

*Business and Scientific Workflows: A Web Service-Oriented Approach*, First Edition.
Edited by Wei Tan and MengChu Zhou.

or from a third party, for example, service reputation. Such information should be collected in a fair manner.

2. Composition of Web services according to QoS requirements. Web service composition has to deal with behavioral interface, choreography, and orchestration. Behavioral interface denotes the behavioral aspects of the interactions for a given individual service during the composition. Orchestration considers one particular service that directs the logical order of all other services, whereas choreography considers the case where individual services work together in a loosely coupled network. They are often accomplished via Business Process Execution Language (BPEL). The QoS of the composed service is determined by the QoS of its underlying component services. The aggregation functions for the computation of the QoS through component services need to be identified. It is not hard to imagine that there may be many feasible Web service compositions that can meet the functional requirement but carry different QoS values. Therefore, the QoS of the resulting composite service is a determinant factor in satisfying the different requirements and preferences of different users. For example, a user may demand for reliability to be maximized while another user may demand for total cost to be minimized. Different users may weigh QoS attributes differently. Thus, it is necessary to consider the preferences of users and optimize the Web service composition in terms of the QoS requirements. Various methods can be utilized.
3. Dynamic environment where composite services are invoked. It can be explained from two aspects. First, a service composition operates under a dynamic and heterogeneous environment, and its run-time performance fluctuates with the varying quality of the services. Second, when a Web service becomes unusable or unreliable, the other Web services in the composition that interact with it may need to be altered in order to adapt to the new environment. Various QoS-aware Web service selection strategies are required.
4. Web service configuration. Service configuration and service composition complement each other in nature. The former is function-oriented and offers the lower-level business

functions required by the orchestration. It is often done under Service Component Architecture (SCA). On the other hand, service composition is mainly process-oriented and provides the higher-level orchestration. Compared with process-oriented service composition, function-oriented service configuration enjoys more agility and flexibility. For example, if a Web service is configured by two services, these two services may be executed in sequence or parallel depending on their implementation. Moreover, service configuration under SCA can protect business logic and improve testability, for example, configuration information can be used by service fault management to track defects. SCA builds on service encapsulation through the assembly of heterogeneous services. After the components that provide services and consume other services are implemented, they are assembled to build the business application through the wiring of service references to services [124]. An SCA module is assembled by configuring and wiring together components, entry points, and external services. Entry points are the representation of interfaces that are offered for use by components outside a module. If a component in a module references the services provided outside of it, they are represented as external services. SCA assembly operates at two levels, that is, the assembly of loosely connected components within a system and within a module. A dynamic configuration can be modeled as a functional assembly of the overall requested function. For example, in Figure 5.1, system A can be wired by subsystems B, C, and D, or wired by X and Y. Subsystem C can be wired by module components E and F, whereas E has two candidate modules G and H for its implementation. The SCA configuration also becomes a service, which can be accessed and reused in a uniform manner. Multiple service components can be configured and assembled into groups called composites, to provide specific business capabilities that can be a part of other services. For example, C in Figure 5.1 can be a composite and can be referenced by other services. Since the assembly of an SCA system mirrors the assembly of a module, we do not distinguish among subsystems, modules, and services in the book.

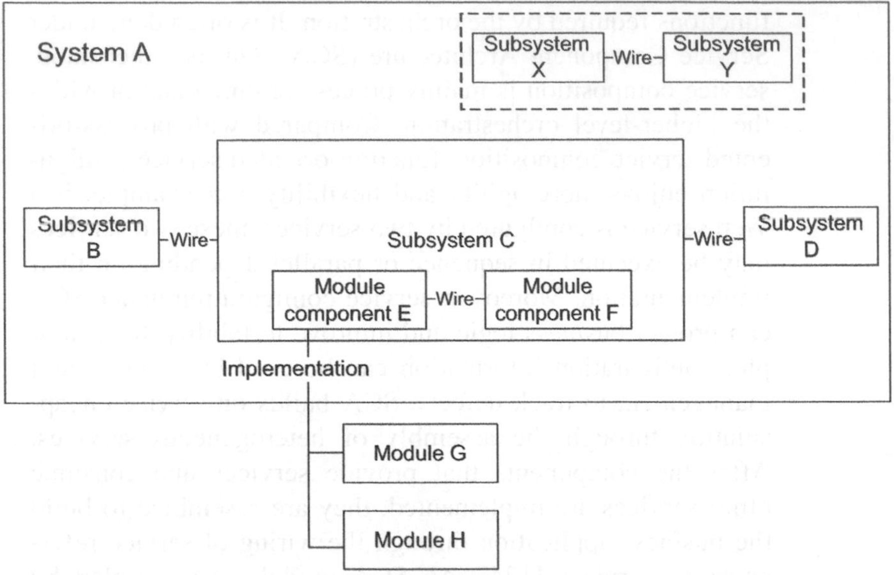


**Figure 5.1** An example of system assembly and disassembly.

The main difficulty of deploying services under SCA is that there are multiple service assembly methods and many configuration choices interweaved to satisfy both functional and nonfunctional requirements. We model the configuration problem as service functional configuration (SFC). A Web service may have multiple SFCs, for example, in Figure 5.1, system A can be configured by wiring subsystems B, C, and D, or subsystems X and Y. However, only one configuration can be selected at one time. The optimal choice should meet both a user's functional and QoS requirements.

As a dynamically formed digraph to present all of the references, service dependency graph (SDG) is popularly used to depict the functional dependency relationship among Web services [125]. However, although SDG provides a means for Web service configuration descriptions in order to ensure functional interoperability among collaborating Web services, it deals with only the functional aspect. It can hardly support the dynamic configuration of Web services to deal with nonfunctional requirements. Moreover, the SCA specification set being developed under the open SOA collaboration [32] and most of the current research on SCA does not incorporate QoS [126].

Thus, service requestors face a large number of choices of service configurations that can provide a similar function. An environment with changeable QoS of the component services makes the selection problem even more challenging. Therefore, selecting an optimal configuration remains difficult.

In this chapter, we address the optimal configuration issues by concentrating on

(a) the formal modeling and definition of Web service configuration by using a formal methodology, i.e, Petri nets; and

(b) an optimal QoS search algorithm under varying configuration constraints.

For the first issue, we introduce a formally defined configuration net named service configuration net (SC-net) based on Petri nets in order to help select candidate configurations. The main advantages of adopting Petri nets as a modeling language are twofold. First, as a graphical and mathematical tool, Petri nets can provide a uniform environment for dealing with large and complex Web service configurations. Second, by firing the transitions in the SC-net, we can generate a set of candidate configurations automatically and thus minimize the human efforts in searching for a configuration. For the second issue, before we present our optimal QoS search algorithm, we carry out structural analysis to discover the essential properties of the SC-net we build. The analysis results clarify that the set of basis solutions of a state-shift equation of an SC-net net is identical to the set of the solutions that correspond to realizable configuration processes. Based on this, we formulate Web service configuration under single and multiple QoS attributes as a linear programming problem. This greatly alleviates the solution complexity.

The rest of the chapter is organized as follows: Section 5.2 discusses Web service quality attributes, their measurement, and aggregation function to be used in optimal configuration. Section 5.3 introduces assembly Petri nets and their properties. It also discusses how to model the configuration problem formally. Section 5.4 specifies the optimal Web service configuration problem and presents a real example to certify the validity of the analysis results and solution methodology. Section 5.5 introduces the implementation of the methodology. Finally, Section 5.6 concludes the chapter.

## 5.2 QUALITY-OF-SERVICE MEASUREMENTS

### 5.2.1 QoS Attributes

Each functionality of a service can be evaluated by several QoS properties and parameters. The QoS parameters are sorted into run time, transaction support, configuration management and cost, and security-related ones. Each parameter comprises several metrics and submetrics. In this chapter, we focus on configuration-related QoS attributes. Generally, there are two kinds of QoS attributes, that is, cost and benefit. For cost attributes, the higher the value, the less optimal the solution, and for benefit attributes, the higher the value, the better the solution. These include availability and reliability. Some of the QoS attributes can be measured quantitatively as shown in Table 5.1.

### 5.2.2 Aggregation

In the following discussion, a dummy web service is the one to be decided during the service composition/configuration process and a nondummy one is the one whose QoS values are available, to be formally defined via a disassembly Petri net in the next section. A place in the net corresponds to an atomic service (called a leaf place), a service to be instantiated by an atomic one, or a composite one. The latter two cases lead to non-leaf places. Suppose that we have $q$ QoS

**Table 5.1** QoS Attributes and Measures Used for Evaluating Candidate Configurations

| QoS attributes | Measures |
|---|---|
| Cost | The fee to be paid by a service requestor for invoking a Web service each time |
| Availability | The attribute for evaluating an immediate availability of a Web service. It can be computed as the ratio of the service accessible time to the total time of observation |
| Reliability | The probability of receiving the result within the expected duration time after a Web service is successfully invoked |
| Successful execution rate | The probability that a request is correctly responded within the anticipated time indicated in a Web service invocation context, for example, an operation is successfully completed |

attributes to evaluate, that is, $\psi_{1-q}$. The SFC QoS attributes are the cumulative effect of the QoS attributes of the nondummy Web service places that instantiate the modules of the SFC. The dummy Web service places included in the SFC do not have QoS values. To compute them, we assume that a QoS attribute for a candidate SFC is a function of the QoS attribute of all the component services. We explain each attribute's aggregation function as follows:

1. *Cost*. The cost of an SFC is the sum of the costs of all the Web services involved. Suppose that the reusability frequency for Web service denoted by $p$ is $p_f$, that is, $p_f = 1$ if the Web service is used once, and $p_f > 1$ if the Web service is reused.

   Let $C(p', \zeta)$ be the set of all Web services in an SFC, and $\psi_1(C(p', \zeta))$ and $\psi_1(p, \zeta)$ denote the cost of the SFC and the Web service $p$ at time $\zeta$, respectively. Then we have $\psi_1(C(p', \zeta)) = \sum_{p \in C(p',\zeta)} \psi_1(p, \zeta) * p_f$.
2. *Availability*. The availability of an SFC is given by the product of the availability of all the Web services involved.

   Let $\psi_2(C(p', \zeta))$ and $\psi_2(p, \zeta)$ denote the results after applying the logarithm function to the availability of an SFC and the availability of the Web service $p$ at time $\zeta$, respectively. Then the original product relations among availability values of all the Web services are converted into addition relations, that is, $\psi_2(C(p', \zeta)) = \sum_{p \in C(p',\zeta)} \psi_2(p, \zeta) * p_f$. Then we transform the nonlinear aggregation function into a linear one.

### 5.2.3 Computation of QoS

Suppose that we have $N_c$ SFC candidates. The *j*th QoS attribute for the *i*th SFC is denoted as $\psi_{i,j}$, $1 \le i \le N_c$, $1 \le j \le q$ where $q$ denotes the number of QoS parameters under consideration. Different SFC candidate corresponds to different solution vector $\alpha_i$, $1 \le i \le N_c$.

To compute $\psi_{i,j}$ by the linear formulation of $\alpha_i$, according to the definition of SFC and the linear aggregation function, for the *j*th QoS attribute we associate a $1 \times (m + n)$ QoS attribute vector $V_j$. Suppose that $V_j = (V_m \, V_n)$, where $V_m$ and $V_n$ are $1 \times m$ and $1 \times n$ vectors, respectively. Elements in $V_m$ are associated to $m$ places, whereas elements in $V_n$ are associated to $n$ transitions accordingly. Note that these places and transitions are in a disassembly Petri net to be defined in the next section. The values of the elements in $V_j$ are determined in the following algorithm:

**Algorithm 5.1. (Association)**

**Step 1**. If the *j*th QoS attribute is cost, we associate a positive large enough number $L^+$ to nonleaf Web service places (to be updated during a configuration process). If the *j*th QoS attribute is benefit, we associate a negative large enough number $L^-$.

**Step 2**. Every leaf Web service place $p$ is associated with QoS attribute $\psi_j(p, \zeta)$. Note that a leaf Web service place corresponds to a known service whose QoS values are given already.

**Step 3**. For every nonleaf and nondummy Web service place $p$, we associate $\psi_j(p, \zeta)$ to all of its output transitions $t \in p^{\bullet}$.

**Step 4**. For every nonleaf and dummy Web service place $p$, we associate a number 0 to all of its output transitions $t \in p^{\bullet}$.

In the following theorem, we need the knowledge of disassembly Petri nets to be discussed next. Note that $\alpha_i$ is $(M_i\ x_i)^{\mathrm{T}}$ where $M_i$ is the marking of the net corresponding to the *i*-th candidate SFC and $x_i$ is the firing vector that leads initial marking $M_0$ to $M_i$.

**Theorem 5.1.** *The jth QoS attribute for the i-th candidate SFC, that is,* $\psi_{i,j}$ *, can be computed as* $V_j * \alpha_i$.

*Proof:* Since $\alpha = (M_i\ x_i)^{\mathrm{T}}$, $V_j * \alpha$ is equal to $V_m * M_i + V_n * x_i$. For the Web service $s$ denoted by the nonleaf Web service place, the reusability frequency of the Web service in the configuration is equal to the firing number of the transitions $t \in p^{\bullet}$ where $p \in P_s$. Then the QoS attribute of a nonleaf Web service place can be aggregated through $V_n * x_i$.

For the Web service denoted by the leaf Web service place $p$, the reusability frequency of the Web service in the configuration is equal to the number of tokens in marking $M_i(p)$. Then the QoS attribute of leaf Web service places can be aggregated through $V_m * M_i$. Dummy Web services chosen in a configuration do not affect the final result. Since the aggregation functions can be treated linearly, the conclusion holds. □

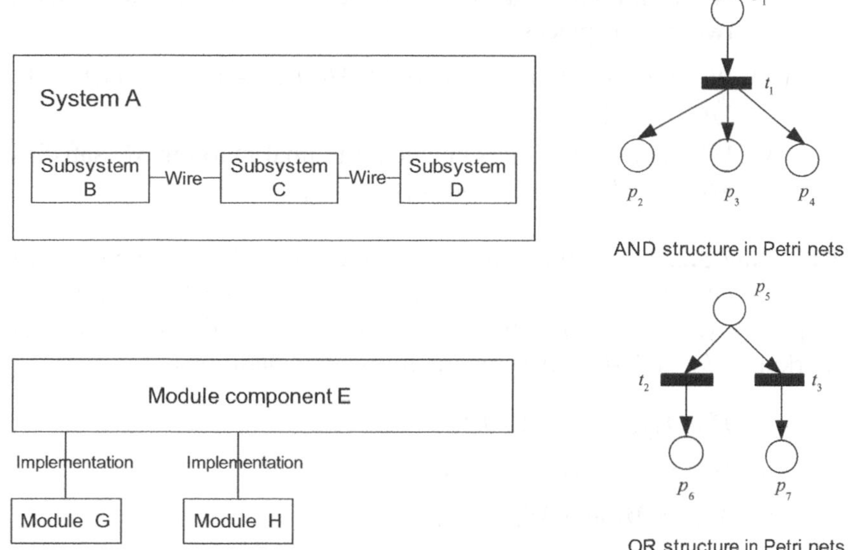


**Figure 5.2** Modeling SCA function assembly through Petri nets.

## 5.3 ASSEMBLY PETRI NETS AND THEIR PROPERTIES

### 5.3.1 Assembly and Disassembly Petri Nets

Assembly in SCA is the process of composing business applications by configuring components that provide service functions. We transform the assembly relationship in SCA into Petri nets, that is, transform function combination and function selection to AND and OR structures in Petri nets in Figure 5.2. The following definitions are used.

**Definition 5.1.** A disassembly Petri net is an ordinary Petri net ($P$, $T$, $F$, $W$) with $M_0$ and $M_f$ as their initial and final markings, respectively, satisfying the following conditions:

(i) A place $p_0 \in P$ is called a root such that it has no input transition but has at least one output transition.

(ii) A subset of places $P' \subset P$ are called a set of leafs such that they have no output transitions, that is, $P'^{\bullet} = \phi$.

(iii) A transition in $T$ has one and only one input place and at least two output places.

(iv) Its initial marking $M_0$ satisfies $M_0(p_0) = 1$ and $M_0(p) = 0$, $\forall p \in P - \{p_0\}$.

(v) When no transition is enabled, the final marking $M_f$ satisfies $M_f(p) = 1$, $\forall p \in P'$ and $M_f(p) = 0$, $\forall p \in P - P'$.

**Definition 5.2.** Given that a disassembly Petri net is an ordinary Petri net $(P, T, F, W)$ with $M_0$ and $M_f$ as their initial and final markings, respectively, an assembly Petri net is $(P, T, F', W')$ with initial and final markings $M'_0$ and $M'_f$ satisfying the following conditions:

(i) $F' = \{(y, x)|(x, y) \in F\}$,

(ii) $W'(x, y) = W(y, x)$, and

(iii) $M'_0 = M_f$ and $M'_f = M_0$.

Postset of $t$ is the set of output places of $t$, denoted $t^\bullet$. Preset of $t$ is the set of input places of $t$, denoted $^\bullet t$. Post (Pre) set of $p$ is the set of output (input) transitions of $p$, denoted $p^\bullet$ and $^\bullet p$, respectively. In Figure 5.2, $t_1{}^\bullet = \{p_{2-4}\}$, $^\bullet t_1 = \{p_1\}$, $p_5{}^\bullet = \{t_{2-3}\}$, and $(p_5{}^\bullet)^\bullet = t_2{}^\bullet \cup t_3{}^\bullet = \{p_{6-7}\}$. A place is called a leaf place if $p^\bullet = \varnothing$. In Figure 5.2, $p_{2-4}$ and $p_{6-7}$ are leaf places. The net's execution rules, as discussed in Chapter 2, are applicable to assembly and disassembly Petri nets.

A circuit in a Petri net is a sequence of nodes $x_1, x_2, \ldots,$ and $x_n$ if $x_i = \{x_{i+1}\}$, $i = 1, 2, \ldots,$ and $n - 1$, and $x_n = \{x_1\}$. An acyclic Petri net is a net such that it contains no circuit in it.

**Definition 5.3.** Service set $S = WS \cup \{s_{\text{dummy}}\}$ where $WS = \{s_{1-z}\}$ is a finite set of real Web services, and $s_{\text{dummy}}$ is dummy service that denotes a composition or selection of real Web services. We call a Web service an atomic Web service if it does not reference other services.

**Definition 5.4.** Service configuration net (SC-net): An acyclic Petri net is an SC-net if

(i) there is a place denoted $p'$ with no input arc, which corresponds to the service requested by a user. $M_0(p') = 1$ and $M_0(p) = 0$, $\forall p \neq p'$;

(ii) every atomic Web service in $S$ is denoted by a leaf place;

(iii) every other Web service $s \in S$ excluding those mentioned in items 1 and 2 is mapped to a place set $P_s \subset P$. Every Web service place $p \in P_s$ has the same function and nonfunctional attributes and can be treated as the duplication of $s$. The number of duplications is equal to the reusability frequency of $s$ in the configuration;

(iv) each nonleaf place has only one input arc and at least one output arc;

(v) each transition has only one input arc and at least one output arc; and

(vi) $\forall t \in T$, if $|t^{\bullet}| > 1$ there is an AND relationship among places in $t^{\bullet}$. $\forall t \in T$, and if $|t^{\bullet}| = 1$, ${}^{\bullet}t = p$ and $|p^{\bullet}| > 1$, there is an OR relationship among transitions in $(p^{\bullet})^{\bullet}$.

Note that the proposed SC-net falls into the class of disassembly Petri nets [80]. Based on the definition of the SC-net, we state SFC and a realizable configuration process.

**Definition 5.5.** An SFC at time $\zeta$ is denoted $C(p', \zeta)$ such that (a) $p' \in C(p', \zeta)$, and (b) $\forall p \in C(p', \zeta)$, if $p^{\bullet} \neq \emptyset$, $\exists t \in p^{\bullet}$ and $\forall p'' \in t^{\bullet}$, $p'' \in C(p', \zeta)$.

**Definition 5.6.** A realizable configuration process is a sequence of transition firings from the initial marking $M_0$ to a current marking $M$. $M$ is called a realizable configuration state.

If we denote system A, subsystems X, Y, B, C, and D, module components E and F by $p'$ and $p_{3-9}$, respectively, we can obtain an SC-net in Figure 5.3 for the configuration of system A in Figure 5.1. There are three candidate configurations, that is, $C_1(p', \zeta) = \{p', p_1, p_{3-4}\}$, $C_2(p', \zeta) = \{p', p_2, p_{5-8}\}$, and $C_3(p', \zeta) = \{p', p_2, p_{5-7}, p_9\}$. The firing transitions determine the configuration processes, for example, $M_0[t_1 > M_1[t_3 > M_2$ corresponds to $C_1(p', \zeta)$ whereas $M_0[t_2 > M_3[t_4 > M_5[t_5 > M_6$ corresponds to $C_2(p', \zeta)$. Note that since the subgraph in the dotted trapezoid denotes the configuration information for subsystem C, if C can be referenced by other services, the subgraph can also be reused for configuration description according to the property 3 of Definition 5.3.

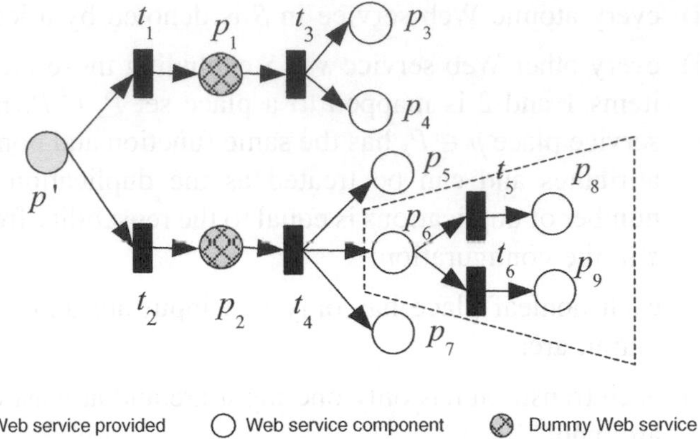


**Figure 5.3** SC-net representation of the configuration of system A.

In order to derive the candidate Web service configurations automatically and obtain a more efficient QoS search algorithm, in this section, we analyze the graph and the algebraic structural properties of the SC-net.

## 5.3.2 Definition of Incidence Matrix and State-Shift Equation

**Definition 5.7.** For an SC-net with $m$ places and $n$ transitions, following [80], the incidence matrix $A = [a_{ij}] = W(t_j, p_i)$-$W(p_i, t_j)$ is an $m \times n$ matrix of integers.

For example, for the SC-net in Figure 5.3, the incidence matrix

$$A = \begin{bmatrix} -1,1,0,0,0,0,0,0,0,0 \\ -1,0,1,0,0,0,0,0,0,0 \\ 0,-1,0,1,1,0,0,0,0,0 \\ 0,0,-1,0,0,1,1,1,0,0 \\ 0,0,0,0,0,0,-1,0,1,0 \\ 0,0,0,0,0,0,-1,0,0,1 \end{bmatrix}^T.$$

**Definition 5.8.** The state-shift equation is $[E\ \text{-}A]\alpha = M_0$, where $A$ is the incidence matrix, $\alpha = \binom{M}{x}$ is an $(m+n) \times 1$ column vector, and

$E$ is an $m \times m$ unit matrix. $x$ is an $n \times 1$ column vector of nonnegative integers. $M$ and $M_0$ denote the current and initial markings, respectively.

$x$ is called the firing count vector and the $j$th element of $x$ denotes the number of times that $t_j$ must fire to transform $M_0$ to $M$. The state-shift equation can be easily transformed to another type denoted by $Ax = M - M_0$. If we use $({}^{\bullet}p)$ and $(p^{\bullet})$ to denote the $k$th fired input transition and the $l$th fired output transition of $p$, we can rewrite the state-shift equation as $M_0(p) = M(p) - \sum({}^{\bullet}p)^k + \sum(p^{\bullet})^l$.

### 5.3.3 Definition of Subgraphs and Solutions

In this section, we define subgraphs in an SC-net and solutions for the state-shift equation and clarify the relationship between the structural properties of subgraphs and the algebraic characteristics of solutions.

**Definition 5.9.** In an SC-net, a subgraph that corresponds to a realizable configuration process (CP) consists of the fired transitions, their input places, and the nonzero element of current marking $M$.

For example, for the SC-net in Figure 5.3, a realizable CP can be $CP_1 = \{(P,T)|P = \{p'\}, T = \varnothing\}$, $CP_2 = \{(P,T)|P = \{p', p_1\}, T = \{t_1\}\}$ or $CP_3 = \{(P,T)|P = \{p', p_1, p_3, p_4\}, T = \{t_1, t_3\}\}$. In CP, $p'$ has single output arc and the other nonleaf place has single input arc and single output arc.

**Theorem 5.2.** *The set of places of a CP in which no transition can be enabled under M is a candidate SFC.*

*Proof:*

1. Since $p'$ does not have any input arc and $M_0(p') = 1$, we have $M(p') + \sum(p'^{\bullet})^l = 1$. Then $M(p') = 1$ or $\sum(p'^{\bullet})^l = 1$, which means the set of places of CP contains $p'$. This satisfies property (a) of SFC in Definition 5.5.
2. Without loss of generality, suppose that $M_0[t_1 > M_1[t_2 > M_2 \ldots [t_n > M$. Since each transition has only one input arc, suppose that the input places of the fired transitions are $p'$, $p_1$, $p_2$, . . . , denoted as a place set $P_F$. Since no transition under $M$ can be enabled, $\forall p_i \in P_F$ in CP, $\exists t_{i+1} \in p_i^{\bullet}$, $\forall p \in t_{i+1}^{\bullet}$, $p$ is in $P_F$ or $M(p) > 0$. This satisfies property (b) of SFC. □

For example, given $CP_1$ to $CP_3$ defined in the previous page. Since $t_1$ and $t_2$ are enabled in $CP_1$, $t_3$ is enabled in $CP_2$, and no transition can be enabled in $CP_3$, only the set of places of $CP_3$ is a candidate SFC.

**Definition 5.10.** In an SC-net, a subgraph that corresponds to a Solution of the State-shift Equation (SSE) consists of the transitions corresponding to nonzero elements of $x$, their input and output places, and places corresponding to nonzero elements of $M$.

For example, for the SC-net in Figure 5.3, a solution of the state-shift equation can be $\alpha_1 = (0, 0.2, 0.8, 0, 0, 0, 0, 0, 0, 0.2, 0.8, 0, 0, 0, 0)^T$ or $\alpha_2 = (0, 0.1, 0, 0.9, 0.9, 0, 0, 0, 0, 0, 1, 0, 0.9, 0, 0, 0)^T$, then two SSEs are $\text{SSE}_1 = \{(P,T)|P = \{p', p_1, p_2\}, T = \{t_1, t_2\}\}$ and $\text{SSE}_2 = \{(P,T)|\ P = \{p', p_1, p_3, p_4\}, T = \{t_1, t_3\}\}$, respectively.

If an SSE corresponds to a CP, and the final marking corresponds to a realizable configuration state, then the solution of the state-shift equation is a *realizable solution.*

**Definition 5.11.** If the column vectors of $[E\ \text{-}A]$ corresponding to nonzero elements of the solution are linearly independent of one another, the solution is a basis solution.

**Definition 5.12.** If all elements of a solution are nonnegative integer, this solution is called nonnegative integer solution.

**Theorem 5.3. [127]** *Column vectors corresponding to the nonzero elements of the realizable solution in* $[E\ \text{-}A]$ *are linearly independent.*

**Theorem 5.4.** *A solution is a nonnegative integer solution if and only if it is a realizable solution.*

*Proof:* From Definition 5.9, it is obvious that if a solution is a realizable one, it is a nonnegative integer one.

Necessity: Consider the Web service place $p'$. Following the equation $M_0(p') = M(p') + \sum(p'^{\bullet})^l = 1$, we have $M(p') = 1$ and $\sum(p'^{\bullet})^l = 0$ or $M(p') = 0$ and $\sum(p'^{\bullet})^l = 1$. When $M(p') = 1$ and $\sum(p'^{\bullet})^l = 0$, the other elements of the solution have to be 0. This means that the corresponding SSE consists only of place $p'$. In this case, the configuration process is in the initial state and this solution is obviously a realizable solution. When $M(p') = 0$ and $\sum (p'^{\bullet})^l = 1$, by the nonnegative integer property of the solution, $p'$ has a single output arc.

Consider a nonleaf place $p$. We have $M_0(p) = M(p) - M_0(p) = M(p) - \sum ({}^{\bullet}p)^k + \sum (p^{\bullet})^l = 0$. From item (iv) in Definition 5.4, we have $M(p) + \sum (p^{\bullet})^l = 1$. Since $p$ is a nonleaf place, we have $M(p) = 0$, then $\sum (p^{\bullet}) = 1$ and $p$ has only one output transition. □

**Theorem 5.5.** *A solution is a basis solution if and only if it is a nonnegative integer solution.*

*Proof:* From Theorems 5.3–5.4, it is obvious that if a solution is a nonnegative integer solution, it is a basis solution. We prove the necessity by contradiction that we show that the solution whose element is not a nonnegative integer is not a basis solution.

Consider the solution whose element is not nonnegative integer. Its SSE can be regarded as the composition of some CPs. There are two cases:

1. Besides the leaf place of SSE, there does not exist a place with $M(p) > 0$; and
2. Besides the leaf place of SSE, there exists a place with $M(p) > 0$.

In case (1), from the leaf places to the output transition of the root place $p'$, we add the column vectors successively. We can generate two or more nonzero column vectors of which only the element corresponding to the Web service place $p'$ is not 0, and the other elements are all 0. This means that the column vectors are not linearly independent and the solution is not a basis solution.

In case (2), we can extract the subgraph whose root place satisfies $M(p) > 0$ and its successive places and transitions from SSE. From the leaf places to the output transition of the root place $p$, we add the column vectors successively. We can then generate two or more nonzero column vectors of which only the element corresponding to the Web service place $p$ is not 0, and the other elements are all 0. This means that the column vectors are not linearly independent, and the solution is not a basis solution. □

For example, $SSE_1$ in Figure 5.3 as given before satisfied the condition of case (1). We can generate two nonzero column vectors of which only the element corresponding to the Web service place $p'$ is 1,

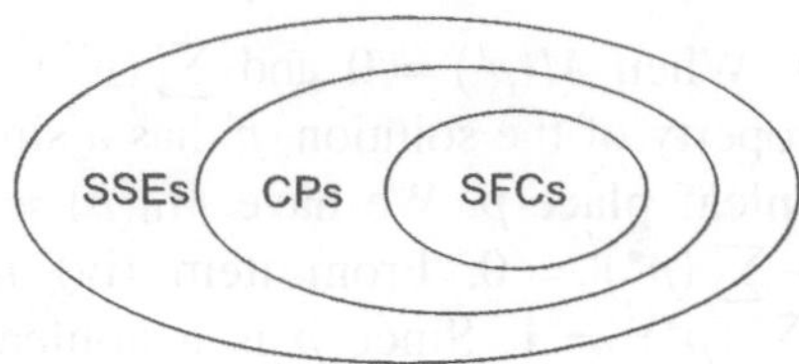


**Figure 5.4** Relationship among the set of solutions correspondent to SSEs, CPs, and SFCs. SSE, a subgraph in SC-net that corresponds to a solution of the state-shift equation; CP, a subgraph in SC-net that corresponds to a realizable configuration process; SFC, service dependency configuration.

and the other elements are all 0. $SSE_2$ satisfies the condition of case (2), we can extract the subgraph $\{(P,T)|P=\{p_1,p_{3-4}\},T=\{t_3\}\}$, and we can then generate two column vectors of which only the element corresponding to the Web service place $p_1$ is 1, and the other elements are all 0. In both cases, the solution is not a basis solution.

**Theorem 5.6.** *A solution corresponds to a CP if and only if it is a basis solution.*

*Proof:* From Theorems 5.4–5.5, it is obvious. □

From Theorem 5.2, the set of places of a CP in which no transition can be enabled under $M$ is a candidate SFC, whereas Theorem 5.6 represents that the set of the CPs is correspondent to the set of the basis solutions of $[E\ \text{-}A]\alpha = M_0$. Relationship among the set of solutions correspondent to SSEs, CPs, and SFCs is shown in Figure 5.4. We can conclude that the set of basis solutions of a state-shift equation of the SC-net is identical to the set of solutions that correspond to realizable configuration processes. If we formulate nonfunctional objectives in a way that can restrict the search space of the set of solutions correspondent to CPs with optimal QoS to the set of solutions correspondent to the SFCs, we can then search the optimal QoS configuration by a linear programming technique.

## 5.4 OPTIMAL WEB SERVICE CONFIGURATION

A linear programming problem is a kind of problem that has three inputs, that is, a set of variables, an objective function, and a set of constraints [128]. Linear programming attempts to optimize the objective function by adjusting the values of the variables under constraints. The results are the optimal value of the objective function and the values of variables at this optimum. The objective function and the constraints are both linear.

The $(m+n) \times 1$ column vector $\alpha = \binom{M}{x}$ can be treated as the variable vector for the linear programming problem. The state-shift equation, that is, $[E\ \text{-}A]\alpha = M_0$, can be taken as the constraints.

A Web service user may have single or multiple QoS objectives. For example, a user may want the total cost minimized with the configuration availability maximized. From Theorem 5.1, for the *j*th QoS attribute, we have

$$\psi_j = V_j * \alpha \tag{5.1}$$

### 5.4.1 Web Service Configuration under Single QoS Objective

If the *j*th QoS attribute is cost, the search problem of optimal configuration is formulated as follows:

$$\text{Minimize } \psi_j = V_j * \alpha \tag{5.2}$$

If the *j*-th QoS attribute is benefit, it is formulated as follows:

$$\text{Maximize } \psi_j = V_j * \alpha \tag{5.3}$$

Both are subject to the same constraints: $[E\ \text{-}A]\alpha = M_0$ and $\alpha \geq 0$, where $\alpha = \binom{M}{x}$ and $M_0 = (1, 0, 0, 0, 0, \ldots, 0)^T$

**Lemma 5.1.** The SSE with the optimal QoS is a CP.

*Proof:* From Theorem 5.6, the set of basis solutions of a state-shift equation of the SC-net is identical to the set of solutions that correspond to realizable configuration processes. Since the optimal value of the objective function of the linear programming occurs with a basis solution, the SSE with the optimal QoS is a CP.

□

**Theorem 5.7.** *The association algorithm can limit the SSE with the optimal QoS to be achieved only when an SSE corresponds to an SFC.*

*Proof:* From Lemma 5.1, the SSE with the optimal QoS is a CP. Then we finish our proof by contradiction. We suppose that there exists a CP with the optimal QoS that does not correspond to an SFC.

By Theorem 5.2, there exists a transition that can be enabled under $M$. According to the structural characteristics of the SC-net, no transition in CP under $M$ can be enabled if every nonleaf place $p \in P$ satisfies $M(p) = 0$. Then there exists at least one nonleaf place $p \in P$ satisfying $M(p) > 0$. According to Step 1 in the association algorithm, there are two cases.

1. If the *j*th QoS attribute is cost, after aggregation through $V_m * M$, $V_j * \alpha$ will be too large; and
2. If the *j*th QoS attribute is benefit, after aggregation through $V_m * M$, $V_j * \alpha$ will be too small.

Considering the objective function stated in (2) and (3), $V_j * \alpha$ can achieve the optimal value neither in case (a) nor in case (b). Therefore, the conclusion holds. □

Note that the approach we apply in Step 1 in the association algorithm is analogous to the "big M method," which is widely used in linear programming to force an artificial variable to be zero [128].

### 5.4.2 Web Service Configuration under Multiple QoS Objectives

If a Web service user has multiple QoS objectives, the optimal configuration problem can be treated as multi-attribute decision-making (MADM) [129], in which alternatives are the candidate SFCs to be evaluated and attributes are the QoS measures of SFCs under consideration. Simple additive weighting (SAW) [130] is an important method for MADM. We adopt SAW as follows. We first normalize every QoS attribute $\psi_j$ to $\Gamma_j$ to allow a comparable scale for all cost and benefit QoS attributes. Then we apply a weight $w_j$ for the *j*th QoS attribute to represent relative importance or value trade-offs of different attributes. Finally, we calculate $f = \sum_{j=1}^{q} \Gamma_j * w_j$ for each candidate configuration. The greater the $f$ value, the more preferred the SFC. Through comparing $f$ values for all candidate SFCs, the optimal configuration with the maximal one is chosen. Then, we formulate the search problem of optimal configuration as follows:

$$\text{Maximize } f = \sum_{j=1}^{q} \Gamma_j * w_j$$

Subject to $[E\ \text{-}A]\alpha = M_0$ and $\alpha \geq 0$, where $\alpha = \begin{pmatrix} M \\ x \end{pmatrix}$ and $M_0 = (1, 0, 0, 0, 0, \ldots, 0)^T$

## 5.4.3 Experiments and Performance Analysis

Now consider the example of sales management service configuration as shown in Figure 5.5. The services in dotted rectangles are dummy

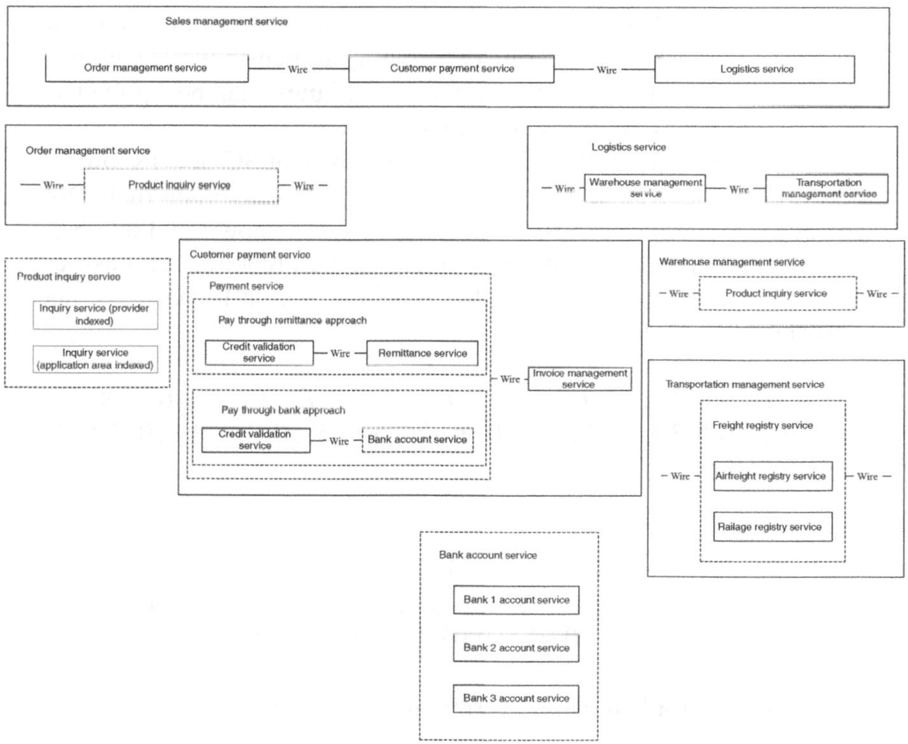


**Figure 5.5** Sales management service configuration.

services while others are real services. The *sales management service* references a series of other services to perform the sales processing service. These services are *order management service*—for recording details of the order; *customer payment service*—for checking the credit of the customers and taking the payment associated with the order; and *logistics service*—for checking availability of the ordered goods (*warehouse management service*) and for getting the goods dispatched to the customer (*transportation management service*).

The *customer payment service* can be assembled through two approaches, the *remittance service* and the *bank account service*. The available *Bank* 1–3 *account services* that are external services can be referenced by the *customer payment service*. There are also two kinds of product inquiry services, that is, provider indexed and application area indexed. The product inquiry services are referenced by both *order management service* and *warehouse management service*.

The simplest MADM problem focuses on two attributes. This subclass of problems is known as dual attribute optimization. To illustrate the approach, we use two quality dimensions, that is, cost $\psi_1$ and availability $\psi_2$. Other quality attributes can be applied or included without any substantial changes.

According to Definition 5.3, the correspondent SC-net is shown in Figure 5.6. The Web services that $p'$ and $p_{1-22}$ denote and their QoS attributes, for example, cost and availability, are shown in Table 5.2.

Using the previously introduced aggregation functions and association algorithm, we have the QoS attribute vector for cost $V_1$ and availability $V_2$ as follows:

$$V_1 = (L^+, L^+, L^+, L^+, L^+, L^+, 40, L^+, L^+, L^+, L^+, L^+, L^+, 10, 100, 25, 20, L^+, 60, 30, 28, 22, 25, 10, 50, 20, 50, 35, 60, 0, 0, 0, 0, 0, 0, 0, 0, 0, 0, 0, 0, 0)$$

$$V_2 = (L^-, L^-, L^-, L^-, L^-, L^-, -0.11, L^-, L^-, L^-, L^-, L^-, L^-, -0.36, -0.04, -0.11, -0.08, L^-, -0.05, -0.02, -0.06, -0.19, -0.13, -0.01, -0.17, -0.08, -0.11, -0.03, -0.05, 0, 0, 0, 0, 0, 0, 0, 0, 0, 0, 0, 0, 0)$$

Then the problem can be formulated as follows:

$$\text{Maximize } f = \sum_{j=1}^{2} \Gamma_j * w_j$$

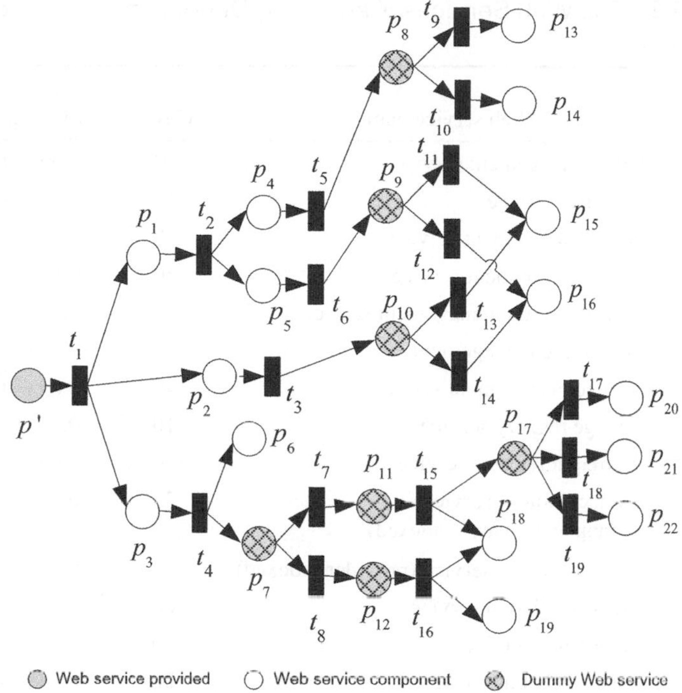


**Figure 5.6** Correspondent SC-net.

Subject to $[E \text{ -}A]\alpha = M_0$

$\alpha = \binom{M}{x}$ and $\alpha \geq 0$, $M_0 = (1, 0, 0, 0, 0, \ldots, 0)^T$and $A$ is the incidence matrix of the net.

Suppose that $L^+ = 1000$, $L^- = -8$ and the weight for cost and availability are 0.2 and 0.8, respectively. The problem can be solved by a simplex algorithm or interior-point algorithm. The result is

$$\alpha = (0,0,0,0,0,0,1,0,0,0,0,0,0,0,1,0,2,0,1,1,0,0,0,1,1,1,1,\\ 1,1,0,1,0,1,0,1,0,1,0,1,0,0,0)^T$$

The corresponding SFC contains $p'$, $p_{1-6}$, $p_{14}$, $p_{16}$ (reuse once), $p_{18}$, and $p_{19}$.

**Table 5.2** The Web Services $p'$ and $p_{1-22}$ Denote and Their QoS Attributes

| Places | Web service name | Cost | Availability (after taking logarithm) |
|---|---|---|---|
| $p'$ | Sales management service | 10 | 0.99 (−0.01) |
| $p_1$ | Logistics service | 50 | 0.84 (−0.17) |
| $p_2$ | Order management service | 20 | 0.92 (−0.08) |
| $p_3$ | Customer payment service | 50 | 0.89 (−0.11) |
| $p_4$ | Transportation management service | 35 | 0.97 (−0.03) |
| $p_5$ | Warehouse management service | 60 | 0.95 (−0.05) |
| $p_6$ | Invoice management service | 40 | 0.89 (−0.11) |
| $p_{13}$ | Railage registry service | 10 | 0.70 (−0.36) |
| $p_{14}$ | Airfreight registry service | 100 | 0.96 (−0.04) |
| $p_{15}$ | Product inquiry service (application area indexed) | 25 | 0.89 (−0.11) |
| $p_{16}$ | Product inquiry service (provider indexed) | 20 | 0.92 (−0.08) |
| $p_{18}$ | Credit validation service | 60 | 0.95 (−0.05) |
| $p_{19}$ | Remittance service | 30 | 0.98 (−0.02) |
| $p_{20}$ | Bank 3 account service | 28 | 0.94 (−0.06) |
| $p_{21}$ | Bank 2 account service | 22 | 0.83 (−0.19) |
| $p_{22}$ | Bank 1 account service | 25 | 0.88 (−0.13) |
| $p_{7-12,17}$ | Dummy service | $L^+$ | $L^-$ |

In order to make our configuration adapted to the dynamic environment, we can perform sensitivity analysis [131] after the optimal configuration is found. Generally, in the standard linear programming problem, if there is any change in the values of coefficient matrix (i.e., $[E\ -A]$), the right-hand side vector (i.e., $M_0$), or objective function coefficients (i.e., $V_i$ and $w_i$), the optimal solution is likely to change. However, when the perturbations are within a certain range, the current optimal solution may remain unchanged. This invariance of the optimal solution is a desirable property that helps significantly reduce the computational complexity when perturbations occur and/or we are uncertain about the exact values of coefficients. In the SFC problem, the coefficient matrix and the right-hand side vector often stay unchanged, while the objective function coefficients $V_i$ often fluctuate according to the variable environment by supposing that Web service user's preference on $w_i$ stays unaffected. Since we treat the SFC problem as two-attribute MADM in the above-mentioned case, when more than one attribute and/or more than one Web service change, the problem becomes more complicated. We take an example that the attributes of remittance service ($p_{19}$) can change while the attributes of other Web services in the optimal configuration remain unchanged. Through sensitivity computation, we deduce that the maximum range of cost perturbation is 18.14 and the maximum range of reliability perturbation is 3.45% for *remittance service* when the optimal configuration stays unchanged.

## 5.5 IMPLEMENTATION

We present our implementation framework in Figure 5.7. There are mainly four roles in the framework: Web service user, service configuration manager, Universal Description, Discovery, and Integration (UDDI) registry, and Web services. The service configuration manager contains two major components, that is, service configuration planner and service configuration optimizer.

We describe the interaction between roles in our framework according to the life cycle of a Web service [132].

*Registration Stage.* Web service providers publish their Web service and invocation interfaces they intend to offer in Web Service Definition Language (WSDL) and register the Web services to a common registration table located at UDDI. Schema Application Programming Interface (API) in UDDI defines four

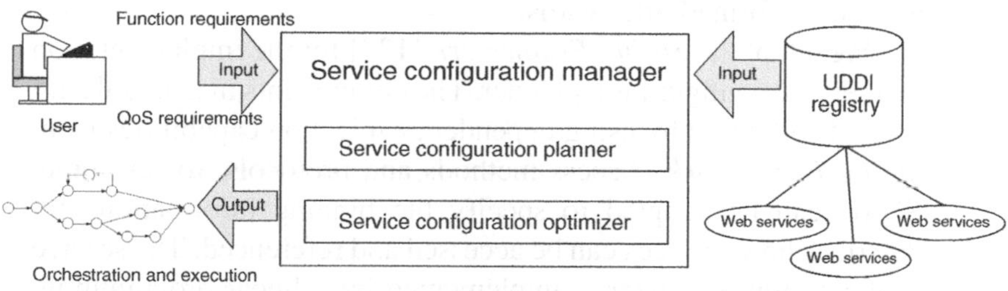


**Figure 5.7** Implementation framework for SC-net.

data types mainly in functional aspects, that is, businessEntity, businessService, bindingTemplate, and tModel. We extend the UDDI data model with Web service quality information and encapsulate QoS information following a uniform template formalized by the Extensible Markup Language (XML) Schema definition in [133]. Since QoS metadata in XML format can be sent to UDDI through Simple Object Access Protocol (SOAP), the new UDDI registry can provide a service configuration manager with both the function and the QoS attributes of the Web services.

*Configuration Stage.* The Web service user inputs the function and QoS requirement to the service configuration manager. In the case study of sales management service configuration, the salesman may require the function of recording details of the order, checking the credit of the customers, delivering the goods, and so on. The relative importance of different QoS attributes reflecting user subjective preference or perception is also provided, for example, the weight for cost and availability are 0.2 and 0.8, respectively. First, according to the functional requirement, the service configuration planner automatically selects services based on whether they meet the configuration's structural constraints and match interfaces. An SC-net corresponding to the configuration is built. The service configuration planner may check the potential problems due to missing services and unsatisfied interfaces. Second, the service configuration optimizer obtains the QoS requirement from the user and accesses to QoS metadata about services from the extended UDDI data model. The QoS aggregation function is computed. Through the association algorithm defined earlier, a linear programming problem is specified. Finally, the service configuration optimizer finds the optimal configuration. Sensitivity analysis can also be performed afterwards.

We adopt the *Spring Framework* [134] for the implementation of a service configuration planner. The components in a module are created and wired by using dependency injection capabilities from *Spring Framework*. Access methods and protocols, for example, SOAP, can be adopted to specify the binding information that describes how services can be accessed and referenced. The service configuration optimizer is implemented by a linear programming solver based on the simplex algorithm.

*Orchestration Stage.* The optimal configuration is deployed in the execution environment. The Web service orchestration and deployment are done with the CIMFlow-System [135], which is a formerly developed central workflow management system. In CIMFlow-System, we use a process modeler module to establish a workflow model and task allocator module to receive the task allocation request and assign tasks to specific Web service interfaces.

*Execution Stage.* After deployment, the business process can be executed and supported by the workflow engine in CIMFlow-System. When a transaction instance is generated, the service configuration manager determines which services should be used in the configuration by interacting with the CIMFlow-System. The optimal configuration information is sent back to CIMFlow-System for dynamic binding. Run-time performance analysis and optimization are also conducted with the CIMFlow-System, for example, the turnaround time calculation and optimal execution path selection [136].

## 5.6 SUMMARY

The Web service framework ushers in a new revolution in traditional computing. By assembling service components, the service component architecture provides a programming model for the creation and assembly of business systems using a service-oriented architecture. However, many Web service-related problems still remain open, including Web service modeling, service discovery, service selection, service configuration, service deployment, and execution. This work deals with functional and nonfunctional constraint modeling and configuration of services under constraints. This work can be treated as a complement to the SCA policy framework to support the specification of functional requirement and QoS expectations.

This chapter presents a service functional configuration net based on Petri nets for the Web service presentation and automatic assembly. The configuration specifications for the module and component services are described through the structure of disassembly Petri nets. The candidate configurations are generated automatically through firing the transitions in such Petri nets. Next, by carefully analyzing the structure of the configuration net and the algebraic property of the state-shift equation of Petri nets, we discover that the set of all candidate configuration processes is identical to the set of all basis solutions of the state-shift equation, which leads to the useful conclusion that the functional constraint of a configuration can be replaced by the state-shift equation. Then, after compiling the QoS attributes and aggregation function to compute the QoS for the whole configuration, we formalize the optimal Web service configuration problem as a linear programming problem. Hence, more efficient algorithms can be applied and large-size configuration problems can be solved. Finally, we implement the proposed functions and algorithms as the service configuration manager and incorporate the Web service registration, orchestration, and invocation functions into the framework. The implementation framework is a platform from component design to concrete deployment.

The proposed approach in this chapter lacks such features as concurrency and synchronization. Actually, a service configuration net models a set of components that are used to make a particular business function. It models the way in which they are configured. It does not model the time sequences involved in executing particular service operations. The techniques proposed in this chapter need to be extended to deal with business process sequencing and run-time-related QoS. The approaches based on Petri nets and elementary siphons will be explored [137].

## 5.7 BIBLIOGRAPHIC NOTES

*QoS Specification and Description.* Menasce [138] presents an overview of the current QoS-related research in Web services area. Ran [139] summarizes a set of quantifiable QoS parameters and measurements, for example, reliability, capacity, availability, and cost, into multiple QoS categories. tModel in UDDI registries is used to formalize representation models for each QoS parameter. Perryea and Chung [140] group Web services into several communities according to nonfunctional requirements. Xiong and Fan [133] propose a uniform QoS attribute definition framework in order to coordinate QoS properties from both Web service provider's and user's perspectives. Liu et al. [141] extend the QoS model by including both generic and domain specific criteria. The QoS information is usually collected from service providers, service requesters' feedback, and a third party. Its accuracy is critically important and yet difficult to guarantee.

*Web Service Composition under QoS Constraints.* Local and global optimizations are used. Ardagna and Pernici [142] discriminate global and local QoS constraints. The local optimization is done at a task level, that is, choosing for each task the Web service with the best QoS. Casati and Shan [46] propose eFlow to suit adaptive and dynamic features of Web services required by different individual users and to cope with a highly dynamic business environment. To prevent service providers from deviating from the advertised QoS as such deviation causes losses to the users, Jurca et al. [143] propose a novel QoS monitoring mechanism to collect the ratings and compute the actual quality delivered to the users. Huang et al. [144] present a moderated fuzzy Web service discovery approach to model users' subjective and fuzzy opinions and to assist service users and providers in reaching a consensus.

Compared with the local optimization approach, the global optimization is done at the process level where services are selected for each task to obtain the optimal global quality. Lamparter et al. [145] use utility function policies to model the multiple preferences of users. But the utility function is hard to quantify for a multi-attribute decision. Gao et al. [146] combine different service paths as a weighted multistage graph and transform the selection of the optimal execution plan into the selection of the longest path. Since the service path is defined as a sequential chain of service operations, there is limitation when the search methods are used in complex service execution. To overcome the disadvantages, Zeng et al. [107] use a state chart to describe a workflow execution sequence in detail, that is, the control-flow, and then arrange a set of candidate Web services that can equally accomplish the function for each activity in the state chart. Their work is further improved by Gao et al. [147] by adding more quality dimensions, that is, capacity and load, to their QoS model. However, it suffers from several drawbacks. First, they use 0-1 integer programming [148] to obtain the solution, which is NP-hard. This chapter proposes the use of a linear programming method that is solvable in polynomial time (complexity class P). Second, they assume that every candidate

Web service is associated with only one workflow task. However, a Web service probably contains many invocation interfaces and operations that can support many workflow tasks in fact. Moreover, these Web services can be reused as many times as possible. Third, the Web service execution sequence is relatively rigid according to the state chart that defines the control-flow. Canfora et al. [44] propose to use genetic algorithms instead of integer programming to deal with a large set of candidate Web services.

*Dynamic Environment*. A number of studies, for example, METEOR-S [111], SwinDeW [149], and GlueQoS [150], deal with QoS -aware Web service selection under a dynamic environment.

*Web Service Configuration*. Liang and Su [125] propose a service dependency graph (SDG) based on an AND/OR graph to discover Web services. Guo et al. [151] propose an optimized peer-to-peer overlay network for service discovery.

CHAPTER 6

# A Web Service-Based Public-Oriented Personalized Health Care Platform

## 6.1 BACKGROUND AND MOTIVATION

In the last 50 years, developing countries have witnessed the dramatic population growth. Moreover, many countries, especially those that are developed, are facing the clear trend of population aging due to longer life expectancies. These occurrences make the shortage of health care and medical resources more and more obvious and severe. Furthermore, the inconsistency between the per-capita level of medical resources and the growing demand from people for health care is becoming more serious. The growth of total population and the trend of aging have a significant impact on the structure and pattern of health care services. Thus the construction of new service systems that help provide more efficient health care services for people with limited medical resources has emerged as a serious and urgent challenge.

The problems faced in the field of health care such as the aging of population, the increase in the number of chronic patients, the rise in medical expenses, and the need to improve the quality of medical services are common around the world today. To solve them,

*Business and Scientific Workflows: A Web Service-Oriented Approach*, First Edition.
Edited by Wei Tan and MengChu Zhou.

information technology (IT) must be more readily deployed to this field. In recent years, medical information systems have played an increasingly important role in supporting doctors and nurses, enhancing the quality of medical services, reducing medical expenses, and improving the care of chronic patients. Therefore, medical informatization has drawn much attention in various countries, for example, the research and development of hospital information systems (HIS), electronic medical record (EMR) systems, picture archiving and communication systems (PACS), and National Health Information Network in the United States, the EMR systems and PACS in the United Kingdom, the electronic health record (EHR) system in Canada, the National E-Health Technology Architecture in Australia, the Red System in Denmark, the Grenoble Integrated HIS of No.8 health center in France, and the "Jin Wei" Project in China.

The majority of previous studies have focused on (1) informatization for hospitals and medical institutions within organizations, regional medical informatization, or the construction of health information infrastructure, and (2) standardization, such as HL7 (Health Level Seven), Digital Imaging and Communications in Medicine (DICOM), and IHE (Integrating the Healthcare Enterprise). Little effort was made toward the development of health care service systems for general individual users.

The health care community has recognized the need to transform from the current hospital-centralized and treatment-based mode, to a prevention-oriented and comprehensive one in which hospitals, communities, families, and individuals are closely involved. The new mode will have to provide individuals with intelligent health information management and health care services. In addition, it will allow them to enjoy medical prevention and health care services in their daily lives just as today's Internet shopping and teleconferences.

The advancement of information technologies brings more opportunities for innovations in health care. Technologies such as service-oriented architecture, cloud computing, and autonomic computing can facilitate the construction of service systems with higher reusability, flexibility, extensibility, and robustness. Currently, the computing model is transitioning toward one that is user-centered. A new computing model is bound to change the original business model of the entire medical and health care industry. However, most of the existing medical information software is based on mediocre application architectures where various functions are not packaged in the form of services. The existing systems fail to adequately meet users' diverse, uncertain, and personalized needs, and to adapt to the dynamically changing application environments. Consequently, these systems fail to provide more personalized customizations that can proactively recommend the most suitable medical and health care services to different individuals.

The new prevention-oriented comprehensive health care mode calls for individual-oriented personalized health care service platforms. Fortunately, service-oriented technologies are mature enough to help one implement such platforms. Section 6.2 describes a general public-oriented service platform that can provide customizable and personalized health care services for individuals. Its architecture, main services, service composition needs, and user preferences are given. Section 6.3 discusses key service composition techniques to build the platform. Section 6.4 highlights its implementation status. Section 6.5 concludes the chapter.

## 6.2 SYSTEM ARCHITECTURE

This section gives an overview of the system architecture of the Public-oriented Health care Information Service Platform (PHISP). It explains some basic concepts and definitions including:

1. PHISP system architecture involving body sensor networks, a cloud platform, and a health care service system;
2. Services encapsulated in PHISP;
3. Specifications of composite services; and
4. User/domain preferences.

### 6.2.1 The System Architecture of PHISP

First, we present the health care service platform, that is, PHISP. It intends to provide personalized health care services for the general public. Its architecture is given in Figure 6.1. It consists of three main

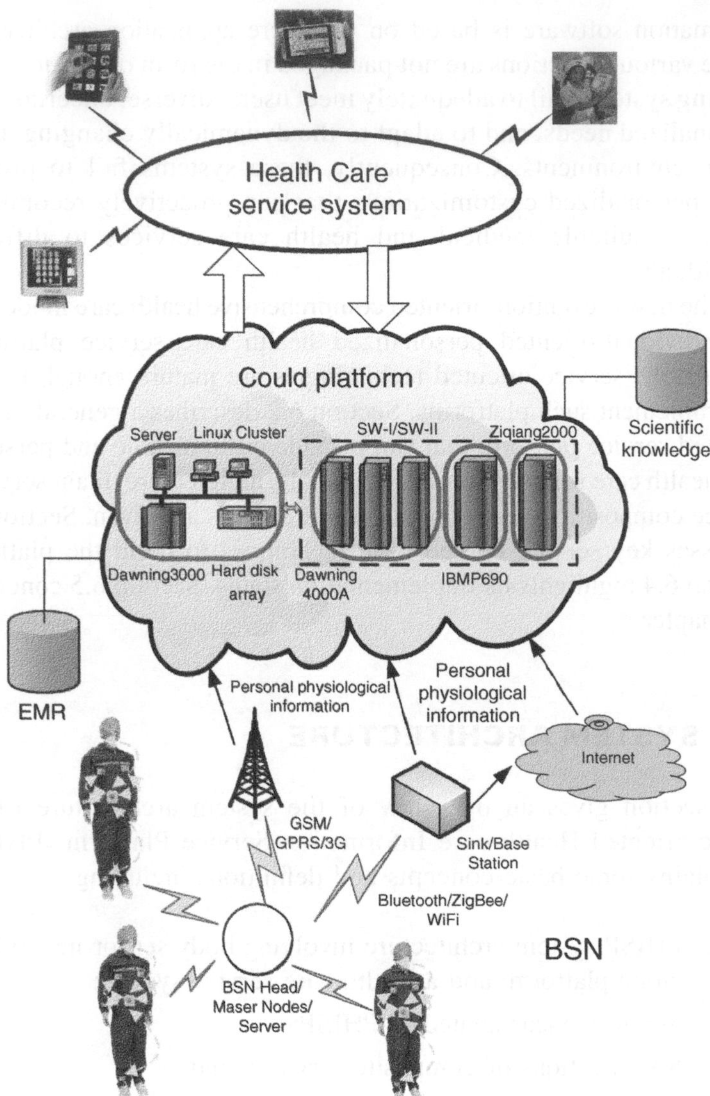


**Figure 6.1** PHISP architecture.

components, that is, *body sensor networks* (BSN), a *cloud platform*, and a *health care service system*, as described as follows:

1. Body sensor networks (BSN). According to individual's different treatments and personalized needs, appropriate health

information collection terminals (i.e., sensors) must be configured for each individual. A BSN is used to realize the multimode acquisition, integration, encryption, and real-time transmission of personal health information in living, working, or hospital environment. As shown in Figure 6.1, various communication and computer networking technologies can be used. They include Bluetooth, WiFi, and GSM/GPRS/3G/4G digital cellular networks. GSM stands for Global System for Mobile Communications, which is a technology for the second-generation (2G) digital cellular networks. GPRS represents General Packet Radio Services, which is expanded from GSM and is often referred to as the 2.5G technology.

2. *Cloud platform.* Based on the cloud computing technology, one can achieve the rapid storage, management, retrieval, and analysis of massive health data mainly including electronic medical record (EMR) repository, scientific knowledge base of health care, and personal health data acquired from BSN.
3. *Health care service system.* It includes a personal health information management system, a dynamic personal health monitoring system, a real-time early-warning system, a personal health risk assessment and guidance system, a seasonal disease early-warning system, a decision-making library for various diseases, and many typical disease care services. Some of the services will be in detail described in Section 6.2.2.

Next, we discuss the following design and implementation technologies used to realize PHISP:

1. SOA and Web service technology;
2. Activity diagrams for specifying composite services; and
3. Service composition methods with choice and parallel structures.

### 6.2.2 Services Encapsulated in PHISP

PHISP utilizes the design idea of SOA and Web service technology for its design and implementation. The majority of its functional modules are developed and packaged in the form of services as discussed as follows:

- *Physiological Information Acquisition Service* (*Physi_Info_Acquir*). This service can acquire general physiological signals such as body temperature, blood pressure, saturation of blood oxygen, electrocardiogram, and some special signals according to different deployed sensors.
- *Environmental Information Acquisition Service* (*Envir_Info_Acquir*). This service can acquire temperature, humidity, air pressure, and other environmental information for a given user.
- *Subjective Feeling Acquisition Service* (*Subj_Feel_Acquir*). This service can acquire a user's subjective feelings, food intake, and so on. The information is often provided by users or their caretakers via a terminal that could be a computer or cell phone.
- *Coronary Heart Disease-Oriented Data Analysis and Diagnosis Service* (*Coronary_Analy_Diagno*). This service can analyze physiological information, environmental information, and subjective feelings via a series of analysis models and then produce preliminary diagnostic results. The models are specifically designed and built for coronary heart disease.
- Cerebral apoplexy-oriented data analysis and diagnosis service (*Cere_Apop_Analy_Diagno*) and diabetes-oriented data analysis and diagnosis service (*Diabetes_Analy_Diagno*), which are similar to *Coronary_Analy_Diagno* but for cerebral apoplexy and diabetes, respectively.
- *Personal Health Risk Assessment Service* (*Health_Risk_Assess*). Based on the preliminary diagnostic results and EMR information of a patient, this service can assess the status of a patient's health risk. We can divide the risk into three levels:
  - RL = 0 represents that the patient is in the normal condition.
  - RL = 1 represents that the patient has some signs of disease.
  - RL = 2 represents that the patient is ill and requires a doctoral appointment.
- *Personal Health Guidance Service* (*Health_Guid*). According to the preliminary diagnostic results and EMR information of a

patient, this service can provide the patient with preventive measures, indicate the items needing his/her attention, and offer other health guidance.

- *Personal Health Real-Time Warning Service* (*Real_Time_Warn*). This service can warn a user about the signs of a certain disease.
- *All-Round Intervention Service* (*All_Round_Interven*). When a user has any signs of illness, this service enforces all-round intervention and instructs the patient to deal with the case.
- *Active Seasonal Disease Warning Service* (*Season_Disea_Warn*). This service can warn users about any seasonal disease information, and provide them with some preventive measures and guidance.
- *Emergency Alarm Service* (*Emerg_Alarm*). This service can alert a user and his/her family doctor and/or associated hospital when he/she is ill.
- *Electronic Medical Record Service* (E_M_R). With a user's ID number and other authentication mechanisms, this service can output the user's medical history information.
- *Geographic Information Service* (*Geograph_Info*). With a user's ID number and other authentication mechanisms, this service can acquire the user's geophysical location.
- *Activating Emergency Service* (Activ_Emerg). After the emergency alarm is confirmed, this service can activate some related emergency services.
- *Medical Teaching Resources Video-on-Demand Service* (Video_on_Demand). According to a user's needs and requests, this service plays the corresponding videos on demand.

### 6.2.3 Composite Service Specifications

A composite service is specified as a combination of other composite or atomic services described in terms of service ontology and according to a set of control and data flow dependencies among them. To describe conditional branch structures more vividly, we use activity diagrams in UML to represent these dependencies [152].

An activity diagram shows a business process or software process as a flow of work through a series of actions. It includes action, control flow, initial node, activity final node, decision node, guard, and merge node. Moreover, it can express concurrency. It uses a fork node to divide a single flow into concurrent ones, and uses a join node to combine concurrent flows into a single one. In UML activity diagrams, an action is denoted by a rounded rectangle, and labeled with an action name of a given service class as defined in a service ontology. The flow of control is denoted by connectors (transitions) between actions. A decision node represents a conditional branch in a flow, and it has one input and two or more outputs. A merge node is required to merge flows that are split with a decision node, and it has two or more inputs and one output. Both decision and merge nodes are denoted by diamonds. The initial node of an activity diagram is denoted by a filled circle, while the final one is denoted by two concentric circles.

A simplified UML activity diagram specifying a "treating a stroke patient" composite service is shown in Figure 6.2. In the example, various information acquisition services and electronic medical records service can be executed in parallel in order to acquire physiological signals, environmental information, subjective feelings, and medical history information of the patient. Then they are analyzed by the cerebral apoplexy-oriented data analysis and diagnosis service, and the risk level is determined by the personal health risk assessment service. According to different risk levels, different solutions are generated. The decision node in the middle part of Figure 6.2 starts a branch structure. Three transitions (connectors) stem from the node, and are labeled with disjoint guards—conditions that specify whether a particular route can be taken or not.

### 6.2.4 User/Domain Preferences

User preferences are a key component of Web service composition. They are critical for the following reasons.

First, according to users' requirements, a family of solutions can be induced by a composition method. User preferences enable a user to specify the properties of solutions that make them more or less desirable. The composition method can use them to generate preferred solutions.

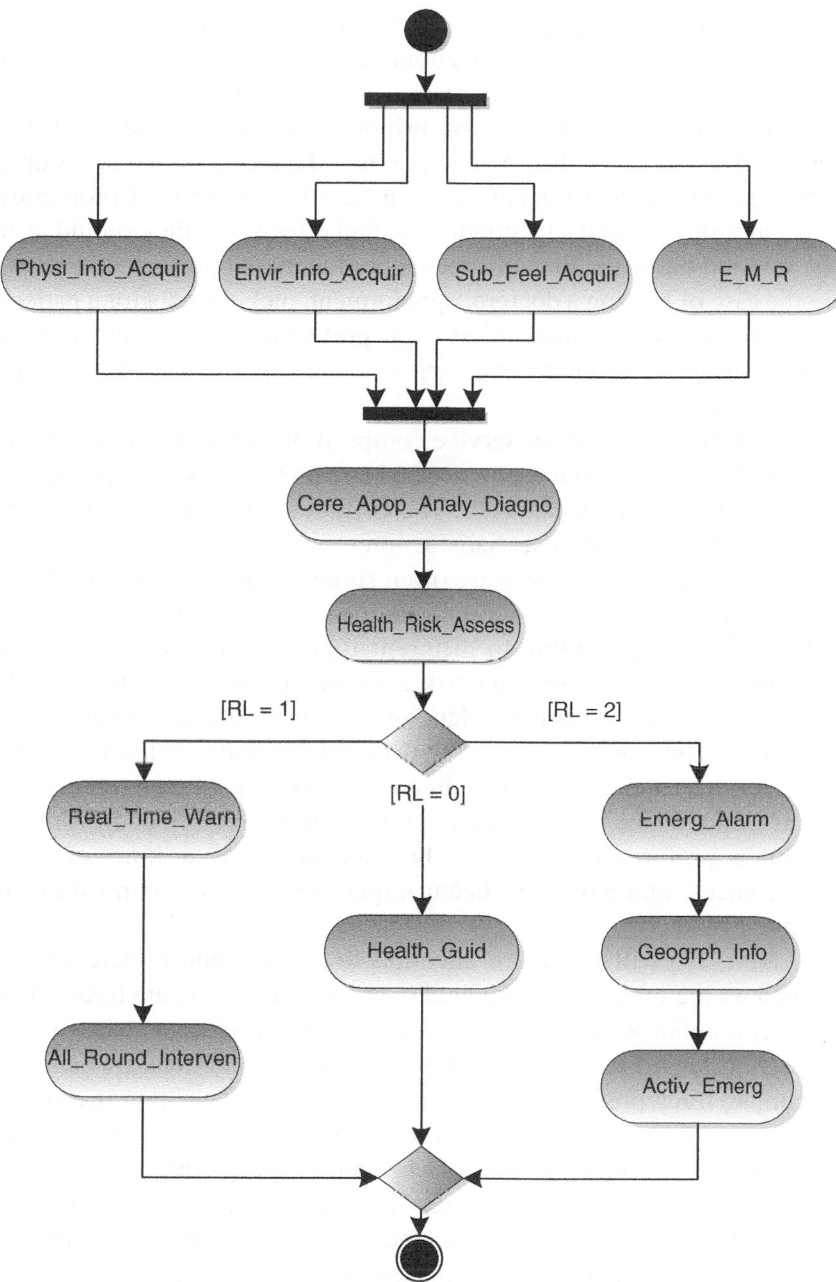


**Figure 6.2** Activity diagram of a composite service: treating a stroke patient.

Second, user preferences can affect how the composition is performed. A key component of Web service composition is the selection of specific services used to realize the composition. In a typical planning or reasoning process, primitive actions are selected for composition based on their preconditions and effects. Similar to actions, services are selected for composition based on functional properties such as inputs, outputs, preconditions, and effects, but they should also be selected based on domain-specific nonfunctional properties such as, in the case of making a doctoral appointment, picking a doctor a patient likes or trusts. By integrating user preferences into Web service composition, preferences over services can be specified to lead to the most desired solution.

Last but not the least, service composition is user-oriented, and it should be centered on a user's needs. User preferences and constraints are clearly parts of his/her needs. Therefore, we should not neglect them so as to maximize the user satisfaction.

In a specific field, there are often some common requirements or preferences, named as domain preferences. For example, in the field of health care, according to different illness degree of a patient as obtained via a diagnosis and risk assessment service, a doctor will propose different treatment plans or prescribe different health care services. The corresponding relationship between different health care services and the results of diagnosis service is often fixed in such a case, and, hence, this is domain preference for service composition. Domain preferences can also be considered as a kind of user preferences, and have significant impact on service composition in a given field.

Next, we will pay more attention to user/domain preferences in which we are interested in the field of health care. There are three types of user/domain preferences of interest. The first type occurs when a user prefers a class of services over another if certain conditions are met. For example, Lucy prefers to go to a doctor's office by walking instead of taking bus if the walking time is less than 20 min and the weather is pleasant. The second type occurs when a user prefers different services when they have different conditions. For example, Lucy goes to see her eye doctor if her eyes bother her; and her dentist if she has toothache. The last type occurs when a user assigns priorities over services with similar functionalities. For example, Lucy prefers to go to Lab A instead of Lab B for test services if both are available.

The following forms are proposed to express the user/domain preferences discussed earlier.

- *Type I. condition?*$\mathrm{WS}_1$ : $\mathrm{WS}_2$;
- *Type II. switch(condition){case* $C_1 : WS_1$; *case* $C_2 : WS_2; \ldots;$ *case* $C_n : WS_n$; *}*; and
- *Type III.* $WS_1 \gg WS_2 \gg \cdots \gg WS_n$.

The above-mentioned expressions are similar to some general expressions in software engineering and programming languages. Especially, the first two expressions are the conditional ones commonly used in C, C++, and Java. The first one evaluates the expression "*condition*" first. If it is TRUE, then executes service $WS_1$, and otherwise executes service $WS_2$. The second one also evaluates the truth value of expression "*condition*" first, and then executes the corresponding service accordingly. The third expression means that $WS_1$ has higher priority than $WS_2$, and $WS_2$ has higher priority than $WS_3$, and so on. In other words, $WS_2$ will be executed only if $WS_1$ fails, and $WS_3$ will be executed only if $WS_1$ and $WS_2$ both fail, and so forth.

## 6.3 WEB SERVICE COMPOSITION WITH BRANCH STRUCTURES

### 6.3.1 Basic Ideas and Concepts

In PHISP, we combine several key technologies and methodologies for service composition, so as to provide customizable and personalized medical and health care services for individuals. However, achieving automatic Web service composition (WSC) to support more control constructs for better performance is a challenging issue. In the domain of health care, workflows like Figure 6.2 can be generated by domain experts using domain knowledge. However, when the system is general public-oriented, the needs of users are often uncertain, diverse, and personalized. Consequently, defining all the possible workflow templates in advance becomes very difficult if not impossible. Thus, generating composite services with sophisticated control constructs automatically is very meaningful and important, even in this specific domain. This section focuses on the service composition techniques that can well support branch or choice structures.

The prior WSC methods based on sequential process models face some difficulties when applied to the field of health care. In this field, user needs are often uncertain, diverse, and personalized where some domain preferences exist. Composite services with only sequential process models can neither meet the diverse needs of users nor reflect their domain preferences. For example, classical artificial intelligence-based planning techniques can derive only linear sequences of actions. They require that the outcome of each action is known in advance. However, many services cannot meet such a requirement since their outcomes can be determined only after their execution, for example, diagnosis services or risk assessment services. Different outcomes usually require different services/processes to follow in the composite service.

In our platform, we introduce branch structures when needed into the process model of a composite service during service composition. Thus, the composite service can reflect user and domain preferences and meet the diverse and personalized needs of users, thereby overcoming the deficiencies of the existing methods that rely on sequential structures.

Activity diagrams are used to represent the feasible composite solutions. Each action node $n_k$ in the generated activity diagram represents an available service from the service community. Moreover, a state $S_k$ is associated with $n_k$ to denote the current status. It contains the currently available input and output parameters and evaluation results of some involved conditions. They are the basis for the next step reasoning.

We present one main algorithm and three subprocedures, which are used to process the three aforementioned user preferences, respectively. In the main algorithm, we start the service reasoning from the initial state. For such reasoning, many existing methods to compute state $S_k$ and the set of invocable services $\Omega(S_k)$ can be adopted. After every step of reasoning, a set of executable services is obtained. A subprocedure is called when such needs arise in order to deal with the user preference.

In a subprocedure, we first need to examine whether the truth value of condition formula in the preference can be acquired. After its truth value is found, we introduce a branch structure into the diagram. Specifically, a decision node is introduced into the diagram first, and guards are set for the corresponding control flows. Then, a merge node is introduced into the diagram to merge flows that are split by the decision node. At the end of the algorithm, a set of activity diagrams representing all the feasible composite services is obtained.

### 6.3.2 Service Composition Planner Supporting Branch Structures

Service composition planner (SCP) is the main algorithm that can introduce branch and choice structures into the composite service. It has three subprocedures, that is, processing preference with conditional expression (PPCE), processing preference with multiple cases (PPMC), and processing preference with priority (PPP). These subprocedures deal with the following user/domain preferences, respectively:

1. Service preference with *condition*?$\mathrm{WS}_1$ : $\mathrm{WS}_2$;
2. Service preference with *switch(condition){case* $C_1$ : $WS_1$; *case* $C_2$ : $WS_2$; . . . ; *case* $C_n$ : $WS_n$; *}*; and
3. Priority: $WS_1 \gg WS_2 \gg \cdots \gg WS_n$.

In the following algorithm, $C$ is a set of available services. $Req = (I_A, O_E; Pref, QoS)$ represents the user's request where $I_A$ and $O_E$ are the input and output parameters. *Pref* represents a set of personalized preferences defined by the service requester or common preferences in a specific domain; while QoS represents a set of standards of the service's quality parameters defined by the service requester.

It outputs a set of activity diagrams, each of which represents a feasible composite service. $n_j, j = 0, 1, 2, \ldots$ represents an action node. $S_j$ represents its state information. In the following algorithms, set NS is used to record all the action nodes to be processed later. Note that the subprocedures maintain the connection with the main algorithm SCP through this set.

**Algorithm SCP. (*C; Req*): Service Composition Planner**

**Input:**

$C = (WS_1; WS_2; \ldots ;WS_n)$, service community, a set of available services; and
$Req = (I_A, O_E; Pref, QoS)$, the user's request.

**Output:**

$ADG = (adg_1; adg_2; \ldots; adg_m)$, a set of activity diagrams representing all the feasible composite services.

1. Establish the initial node, and denote it by $n_0$;
2. The corresponding state of $n_0$ is $S_0$;
3. $NS = \{n_0\}$; $RS = \phi$;
4. **while** $NS \neq \phi$ **do**
5. $\forall n' \in NS$, suppose that its corresponding state is $S'$;
6. **if** $S' \supseteq O_E$ **then**
7. $RS = RS \cup \{n'\}$; $NS = NS - \{n'\}$;
8. **else**
9. According to $S'$, do one step reasoning to obtain all the executable services, noted as $\Omega(S')$;
10. $NS_{temp} = \phi$;
11. **for** each service $w \in \Omega(S')$ **do**
12. Introduce an action node into the graph, labeled with the name of service $w$, and draw a connector from $n'$ to it;
13. Denote the new action node by $n_i$, and compute its corresponding state $S_i$;
14. $NS = NS \cup \{n_i\}$, $NS_{temp} = NS_{temp} \cup \{n_i\}$;
15. **end for**
16. **if** there exists Type I user preference **then**
17. Call subprocedure **PPCE**;
18. **end if**
19. **if** there exists Type II user preference **then**
20. Call subprocedure **PPMC**;
21. **end if**
22. **if** there exists Type III user preference **then**
23. Call subprocedure **PPP**;
24. **end if**
25. $NS = NS - \{n'\}$;
26. **end if**
27. **end while**
28. **if** $RS = \phi$ **then**
29. **print** "There is no solution!"
30. **Exit.**
31. **else**
32. Introduce an activity final node into the diagram, denoted as $n_f$;

33. **for** each action node $n_j \in RS$ **do**
34. Draw a connector from $n_j$ to $n_f$;
35. **end for**
36. **end if**
37. Remove all the action nodes that cannot be connected to the finial node $n_f$ from the diagram, and also their associated connectors;
38. Since each path from the initial node to final node in the generated diagram is a feasible solution to the service composition problem, partition the diagram into several activity diagrams while keeping each conditional branch structure in every composite service since a branch structure cannot be divided.

In the algorithm, each action node $n_j$ in the generated activity diagram represents an available service from community $C$. Moreover, an information state $S_j$ is associated with $n_j$ to denote the current status after executing the service that the node represents. It contains the currently available input and output parameters, as well as information indicating the conditions that are presently true. These paramaters are used in the next step reasoning. In service composition based on input and output parameters only, state $S_j$ can be just a collection of parameters obtained by executing a sequence of services—starting from the initial node, and ending at the current node along a path of the diagram. The associated state of the initial node $n_O$ is $S_O = I_A$, which is the set of available inputs that the service requester provides. At $S_j$, we have a set of services $\Omega(S_j)$, each of which can be invoked.

After every step of reasoning, we check the set of newly obtained executable services to see whether any concerned service mentioned in *Pref* appears or not. If yes, we have to introduce a branch structure into the activity diagram under certain conditions as given in *Pref*.

At the end of the algorithm, the set *RS* records all the action nodes whose corresponding states can satisfy the user requirement. According to these nodes, we can find all the feasible solutions from the constructed diagram. $RS = \varnothing$ indicates that there are no solutions to this WSC problem.

It is worth noting that we can use any existing reasoning method to compute state $S_j$ and the set of invocable services $\Omega(S_j)$ under $S_j$ in the algorithm. Many such methods can do this job. Some simple ones are based only on inputs and outputs of services [153], while others are based on inputs, outputs, preconditions, and effects [154]. At the end of the algorithm, we may obtain several solutions to a specific WSC problem. For each feasible one, according to the QoS parameters of each component service, we can compute the value of QoS parameters of the whole composite service as shown in Chapter 5. Then we can select the best solution that can satisfy user requirements for QoS parameters and have the optimal performance.

For a Type I user preference, that is, *conditions*? $WS_1$: $WS_2$, we use the PPCE algorithm as follows.

**Algorithm PPCE. Processing Preference with Conditional Expression**

1. **if** A = $\{w', w''\} \subseteq \Omega(S')$ **then**
2.    Suppose that $n'_A$, $n''_A \in NS_{\text{temp}}$ representing the action nodes corresponding to services $w'$ and $w''$ respectively;
3.    *flag* = **false**;
4.    According to state $S'$, examine whether the truth value of *Cond* in user preference can be found;
5.    **if** found to be true **then**
6.       Introduce a decision node into the diagram, and draw a connector from $n'$ to it;
7.       *flag* = **true**;
8.    **else if** there is some node $n_k \in NS_{\text{temp}} - \{n'_A, n''_A\}$, such that the truth value of *Cond* can be found to be true under its corresponding state $S_k$ **then**
9.       Introduce a decision node into the diagram, and draw a connector from $n_k$ to it;
10.       *flag* = **true**;
11.    **else**
12.       Suppose $NS' = NS_{\text{temp}} - \{n'_A, n''_A\}$;
13.       **while** $NS' \neq \phi$ **do**
14.          $\forall n_t \in NS'$ with state $S_t$;
15.          **if** $S_t \supseteq O_E$ **then**
16.             $RS = RS \cup \{n_t\}$; $NS' = NS' - \{n_t\}$; $NS = NS - \{n_t\}$;
17.          **else**
18.             According to $S_t$, do one step reasoning to obtain all the executable services, denoted $\Omega(S_t)$;
19.             $NS'_t = \phi$;
20.             **for** each service $w \in \Omega(S_t)$ **do**

Introduce an action node $n_i'$ into the diagram, labeled with the name of service $w$, draw a connector from $n_t$ to it, and compute $S_i'$ of $n_i'$;
$NS_t' = NS_t' \cup \{n_i'\}$;
**end for**
$NS' = NS' \cup NS_t' - \{n_t\}$; $NS = NS \cup NS_t' - \{n_t\}$;
**if** there is some node $n_l' \in NS_t'$, such that the truth value of *Cond* can be found to be true under its corresponding state $S_l'$ **then**
Introduce a decision node into the diagram, and draw a connector from $n_l'$ to it;
*flag* = **true**;
**Exit** the **while** loop;
**end if**
**end if**
**end while**
**end if**
**if** *flag* = **true then**
Draw a connector from the decision node to $n_A'$, set a guard along this new connector with the condition *Cond*, then delete the original connector pointed to it;
Draw a connector from the decision node to $n_A''$, set a guard along this new connector with the condition $\neg Cond$, then delete the original connector pointed to it. Note that $\neg Cond$ means *Cond*'s complement.
Introduce a merge node $n_M$ into the diagram, draw a connector from action node $n_A'$ and $n_A''$ to it respectively; and compute the corresponding state $S_M$ of $n_M$;
$NS = NS - \{n_A', n_A''\} \cup \{n_M\}$;
**else**
The conditional branch is failed. Delete the related nodes;
**Exit**.
**end if**
**end if**

In the reasoning process, once the services mentioned in a user's preference (i.e., $w'$ and $w''$ in PPCE) appear, we will examine whether the truth value of condition formula *Cond* can be acquired and prepare to introduce a conditional branch structure into the diagram. We need to check three cases as follows.

In the first case, *Cond* can be evaluated under the current state $S'$. In this case, we can introduce a decision node into the diagram directly, whose input comes from action $n'$ (which is being processed in SCP).

In the second case, *Cond* cannot be evaluated under $S'$. However, in the set of services $\Omega(S')$ which can be executed currently, there is a service such that the state obtained after executing it can result in the truth value of *Cond*. Under this circumstance, we introduce a decision node after the action corresponding to the service.

If both above-mentioned cases are not satisfied, we continue the reasoning process based on the action set $NS_{\text{temp}}$ which corresponds to the invocable service set $\Omega(S')$, until there exists an action whose state can result in the truth value of *Cond*. Here, the reasoning process is similar to the one utilized in SCP.

After the decision node is introduced no matter which case is satisfied, we draw connectors from it to $n'_A$ and $n''_A$ (corresponding to the two services designated), respectively. Meanwhile, set the corresponding guard (*Cond* or $\neg$*Cond*) for these two control flows. Then we introduce a merge node into the diagram, whose two inputs originate from $n'_A$ and $n''_A$, respectively. After that, we compute the corresponding state $S_M$ of merge node $n_M$, and add $n_M$ into $NS$ to complete the connection with SCP. The merge node is also with a state for reasoning here for the simplicity of our algorithm. An important point needs to be noted here. We believe that the services in different branches of the same conditional structure have some similarities. For instance, they may have the same outputs and effects. Therefore, we think that the states obtained and the state of the merge node by executing services $w'$ and $w''$ under some state are equivalent, and can be used as the state of the merge node. Here, we deal with this in such a way for simplicity. Moreover, the services appearing in the same conditional branch structure always have similar functionalities. If it is not the case, minor modification to our algorithm is needed. The merge node will not be introduced, and states $S'_A$ and $S''_A$ should be recalculated.

For Type II preferences, that is,

$$switch(condition)\{case\, C_1 : WS_1;\ case\, C_2 : WS_2; \ldots ; case\, C_n : WS_n;\},$$

algorithm **PPMC** is used to introduce multiple branch structures into the activity diagram when some conditions are satisfied.

**Algorithm PPMC. Processing Preference with Multiple Cases**

1. **if** $A = \{w_1, w_2, \ldots, w_n\} \subseteq \Omega(S')$ **then**
2. Suppose that $n_{p1}, n_{p2}, \ldots, n_{pn} \in NS_{\text{temp}}$ representing the action nodes correspond to services $w_1, w_2, \ldots$, and $w_n$, respectively;
3. *flag* = **false**;
4. According to state $S'$, examine whether the truth value of formula *Cond* in user preference can be found;
5. **if** it is found **then**
6. Introduce a decision node into the diagram, and draw a connector from $n'$ to it;
7. *flag* = **true**;
8. **else if** there is a node $n_l \in NS_{\text{temp}}$—$\{n_{p1}, n_{p2}, \ldots, n_{pn}\}$ such that the truth value of *Cond* can be found under its corresponding state $S_l$ **then**
9. Introduce a decision node into the diagram, and draw a connector from $n_l$ to it;
10. *flag* = **true**;
11. **else**
12. Suppose $NS' = NS_{\text{temp}}$—$\{n_{p1}, n_{p2}, \ldots, n_{pn}\}$;
13. **while** $NS' \neq \emptyset$ **do**
14. $\forall n_t \in NS'$ with state $S_t$;
15. **if** $S_t \supseteq O_E$ **then**
16. $RS = RS \cup \{n_t\}$; $NS' = NS' - \{n_t\}$; $NS = NS - \{n_t\}$;
17. **else**
18. According to $S_t$, do one step reasoning to obtain all the executable services, denoted $\Omega(S_t)$;
19. $NS'_t = \phi$;
20. **for** each service $w \in \Omega(S_t)$ **do**
21. Introduce an action node $n'_i$ into the diagram, labeled with the name of service $w$, draw a connector from $n_t$ to it, and compute $S'_i$ of $n'_i$;
22. $NS'_t = NS'_t \cup \{n'_i\}$;
23. **end for**
24. $NS' = NS' \cup NS'_t - \{n_t\}$; $NS = NS \cup NS'_t - \{n_t\}$;
25. **if** there is a node $n'_l \in NS'_t$, such that the truth value of *Cond* can be found under its corresponding state $S'_l$ **then**
26. Introduce a decision node into the diagram, and draw a connector from $n'_l$ to it;

```
          flag = true;
          Exit the while loop;
        end if
      end if
    end while
  end if
  if flag = true then
    for i = 1 to n do
      Draw a connector from the decision node to n_pi, set a guard
          along this new connector with the condition C_i and then
          delete the original connector pointed to it;
    end for
    Introduce a merge node n_M into the diagram, draw a connector
        from action nodes n_p1, n_p2, . . . , and n_pn to it respectively;
        and compute the corresponding state S_M of n_M;
    NS = NS − {n_p1, n_p2, . . . , n_pn} ∪ {n_M};
  else
    The conditional branch is failed. Delete the related nodes;
    Exit.
  end if
end if
```

In the reasoning process, once the services mentioned in the user preference (i.e., $w_1, w_2, \ldots, w_n$ in PPMC) appear, we will examine whether the truth value of condition formula *Cond* can be acquired and prepare to introduce a branch structure into the diagram. We need to check three cases as follows, which are processed similarly to those in PPCE.

In the first case, *Cond* can be evaluated under the current state $S'$. In this case, we can introduce a decision node into the diagram directly, whose input comes from the action $n'$ (which is being processed in SCP).

In the second case, *Cond* cannot be evaluated under $S'$. However, in the set of services $\Omega(S')$ that can be executed currently, there is a service such that the state obtained after executing it can result in the truth value of *Cond*. Under this circumstance, we introduce a decision node after the action corresponding to the service.

Third, if none of the aforementioned cases is satisfied, we continue the reasoning process based on the action set $NS_{\text{temp}}$ which corresponds to the invocable service set $\Omega(S')$, till there exists an action whose state can result in the truth value of *Cond*. Here, the reasoning process is similar to the one in SCP.

After the decision node is introduced, no matter which case is satisfied, we draw connectors from it to $n_{p1}$, $n_{p2}$, . . . , and $n_{pn}$ (corresponding to the services designated), respectively. Meanwhile, set the corresponding guard $(C_1, C_2, \ldots, C_n)$ for these control flows. Then we introduce a merge node into the diagram, whose inputs originate from $n_{p1}$, $n_{p2}$, . . . , and $n_{pn}$, respectively. After that we compute the corresponding state $S_M$ of merge node $n_M$, and add $n_M$ into *NS* to complete the connection with **SCP**. The merge node is also with a state for reasoning here for the simplicity of our algorithm.

If none of these three cases is met, the multiple branch structure cannot be introduced into the diagram at present.

For Type III preference: $WS_1 \gg WS_2 \gg \cdots \gg WS_n$. First, for types of $WS_1 \gg WS_2$, algorithm PPP is proposed as follows.

**Algorithm PPP. Processing Preference with Priority**

1. **if** $\{w', w''\} \subseteq \Omega(S')$ **then**
2. Suppose $n'_A$, $n''_A \in NS_{temp}$ representing two action nodes corresponding to service $w'$ and $w''$ with states $S'_A$ and $S''_A$, respectively;
3. Introduce a decision node into the diagram, and draw a connector from $n'_A$ to it;
4. Draw a connector from the decision node to $n''_A$, set a guard along this new connector with the condition "Fail", and delete the original connector pointed to it;
5. Introduce a merge node $n_M$ into the diagram, draw a connector from action node $n''_A$ to it; then draw a connector from the decision node to it, meanwhile, set a guard along this new connector with the condition "Succeed"; compute the corresponding state $S_M$ of $n_M$;
6. $NS = NS - \{n'_A, n''_A\} \cup \{n_M\}$;
7. **end if**

Similar to procedure PPCE, once the services included in user preferences appear, we begin to introduce a conditional branch structure into the activity diagram that is being constructed. However, the situation is much simpler here. After detecting that two services ($w'$ and $w''$) can be executed, a decision node is introduced into the diagram directly. Its input comes from the action $n'_A$, the corresponding action of service $w'$ that has higher priority in user preferences. One output of the decision node points to action $n''_A$, the corresponding action of service $w''$ with lower priority, and a guard is set for this control flow with the condition "Fail". Thus, service $w''$ can execute only after $w'$ fails. Then, we introduce a merge node into the diagram in order to merge these two branches. Finally, we add $n_M$ into $NS$ to complete the connection with SCP.

Second, for types of $WS_1 \gg WS_2 \gg \cdots \gg WS_n$, PPP can be called repeatedly to deal with it. For example, if a user's preference is of the form $WS_1 \gg WS_2 \gg WS_3$, it can be represented as $WS_1 \gg (WS_2 \gg WS_3)$, in which $WS'_2 = (WS_2 \gg WS_3)$ can be viewed as a whole. Thus, a conditional branch structure can be introduced by executing the subprocedure once, and a fictional service $WS'_2$ is used in the Else branch. The subprocedure is then executed to refine $WS'_2$; a nested If-Then-Else structure can result.

### 6.3.3 Illustrating Examples

Consider an online drug purchase example. It involves a series of core tasks: searching drugs, submitting an order, paying for the order, and finally shipping the drugs. Note that we abstract and simplify several existing scenarios to form this example to illustrate the proposed algorithms.

Available services and user request are listed in Table 6.1. For the sake of simplicity, only the inputs and outputs of every service are given. The QoS information is omitted, and this will not affect the illustration of our method.

There are six available services, each of which accepts certain inputs and produces certain outputs. They are as follows:

1. Given the drug name information (DrugName), service *SearchDrugs* returns the code, price, and description information (DrugCode, DrugPrice, DrugDescription) of the drug.
2. Given the information of drug code (DrugCode) and purchase amount (DrugQuantity), service *SubmitOrder* returns order information (OrderInformation) and the amount required to pay (Payment).
3. Given the information of account number (AccountNumber) and password (AccountPassword), service *AccountQuery* returns the account balance (AccountBalance).

**Table 6.1** An Illustrative Example

| Service name | Input parameters | Output parameters |
|---|---|---|
| SearchDrugs | DrugName (DN) | DrugCode (DC)<br>DrugPrice (DP)<br>DrugDescription (DD) |
| SubmitOrder | DrugCode (DC)<br>DrugQuantity (DQ) | OrderInformation (OI)<br>Payment (Pa) |
| AccountQuery | AccountNumber (AN)<br>AccountPassword (AP) | AccountBalance (AB) |
| PayInFull | AccountNumber (AN)<br>AccountPassword (AP)<br>Payment (Pa) | PaidNotification (PaN) |
| PayByInstallments | AccountNumber (AN)<br>AccountPassword (AP)<br>Payment (Pa) | PaidNotification (PaN) |
| Shipping | OrderInformation (OI)<br>PaidNotification (PaN) | ShippedNotification (SN) |
| User Request | DrugName (DN)<br>DrugQuantity (DQ)<br>AccountNumber (AN)<br>AccountPassword (AP) | OrderInformation (OI)<br>ShippedNotification (SN) |

4. Given the information of account number (AccountNumber), account password (AccountPassword), and the amount required to pay (Payment), service *PayInFull* returns the notification of payment completion (PaidNotification).
5. Given the information of account number (AccountNumber), account password (AccountPassword), and the amount required to pay (Payment), the service *PayByInstallments* also returns the notification of payment completion (PaidNotification).
6. Given the order information and notification of payment completion (PaidNotification), service *Shipping* returns the notification of delivery (ShippedNotification).

The available inputs provided by a service requester and the outputs that he/she expects are included in the user request. Furthermore, the user preference is: *AccountBalance* > *Payment?PayInFull*: *PayByInstallments* in which "*AccountBalance* > *Payment?*" is denoted by *Cond*.

The inference method in our algorithm can be simply based on input and output parameters of a service. In other words, each state $S$ that is associated with an action can be just viewed as a set of input and output parameters. Under $S$, a service *WS* can be executed if and only if its input set $I$ can be covered by $S$ (i.e., $I \subseteq S$).

By executing SCP, we first establish the initial node $n_0$, where its related state is $S_0 = I_A = \{DN, DQ, AN, AP\}$. Under this state, we know that the set of invocable services is $\Omega(S_0) = \{SearchDrugs, AccountQuery\}$, since the input requirements of these two services can be satisfied by the available parameters at $S_0$. Two action nodes $n_1$ and $n_2$, labeled with *SearchDrugs* and *AccountQuery*, respectively, are introduced into the diagram. $S_1 = S_0 \cup \{DC, DP, DD\}$ and $S_2 = S_0 \cup \{AB\}$ are their corresponding states. Since the user preference is of Type I, we call subprocedure PPCE. However, the services in user preference (i.e., *PayInFull* and *PayByInstallments*) have not appeared yet. Then we continue the while-repeat procedure in SCP. We obtain node $n_1$ from set *NS*, and the set of invocable services is $\Omega(S_1) = \{SubmitOrder, AccountQuery\}$. Two action nodes $n_3$ and $n_4$ are introduced into the diagram for them, and $S_3 = S_1 \cup \{OI, Pa\}$ and $S_4 = S_1 \cup \{AB\}$ are their corresponding states. The services in which we are interested have not appeared yet. Thus, we continue the while-repeat procedure. Similarly, for node $n_2 \in NS$, the set of invocable services is $\Omega(S_2) = \{SearchDrugs\}$. An action node $n_5$ is introduced for it and its corresponding state is $S_5 = S_2 \cup \{DC, DP, DD\}$. Continuing the while-repeat procedure, node $n_3$ is taken from set *NS*. The set of invocable services is $\Omega(S_3) = \{AccountQuery, PayInFull, PayByInstallments\}$, and three action nodes $n_6$, $n_7$, and $n_8$ are introduced into the diagram for them. $S_6 = S_3 \cup \{AB\}$ and $S_7 = S_8 = S_3 \cup \{PaN\}$ are their corresponding states. The services in the user preference appear now. Then we execute subprocedure PPCE.

The formula *Cond* in the user preference cannot be evaluated under state $S_3$, but it can be evaluated under $S_6$ (i.e., the second case in PPCE). Then, according to the algorithm, a conditional branch structure is introduced into the diagram after action node $n_6$, and the corresponding state of the merge node $n_{M1}$ is $S_{M1} = S_6 \cup \{PaN\}$. We now return to the main algorithm SCP and continue the while-repeat procedure. At present $NS = \{n_4, n_5, n_{M1}\}$. For $n_4$ and $n_5$, two action nodes $n_9$ and

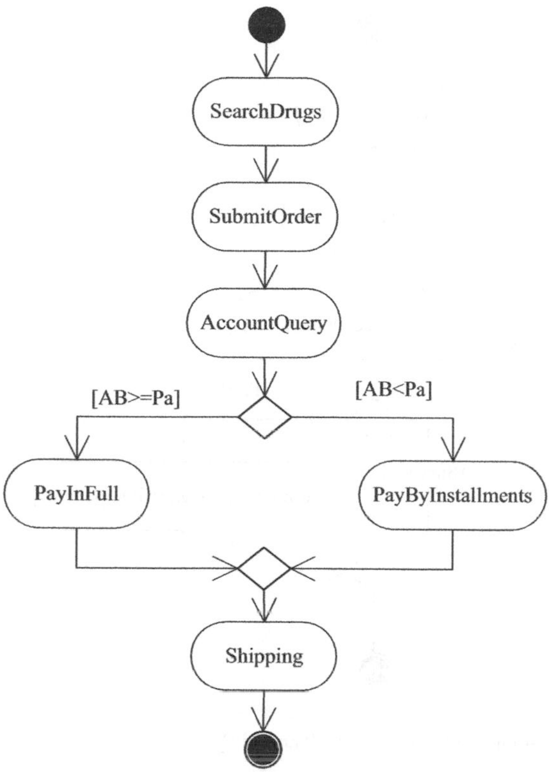


**Figure 6.3** A solution obtained via SCP and PPCE.

$n_{10}$ are introduced into the diagram for the same invocable service *SubmitOrder*. Then, for $n_9$ and $n_{10}$, we execute PPCE, and two conditional branch structures are introduced into the diagram after them respectively, in the way to deal with the first case in PPCE. After that, we continue the while-repeat procedure in SCP. Three action nodes, labeled with the same service *Shipping*, are introduced into the diagram after the three merge nodes, respectively. Next, these three nodes are included into the set *RS*, and the while-loop ends. Successively, an activity final node $n_f$ is introduced into the diagram. In the generated diagram, there are three paths from the initial node to the activity final node. Therefore, we can partition it into three diagrams.

A feasible solution to this WSC problem is shown in Figure 6.3. The guard "$AB >= Pa$" in the figure represents "$AccountBalance > Payment$", while "$AB < Pa$" represents "$AccountBalance < Payment$".

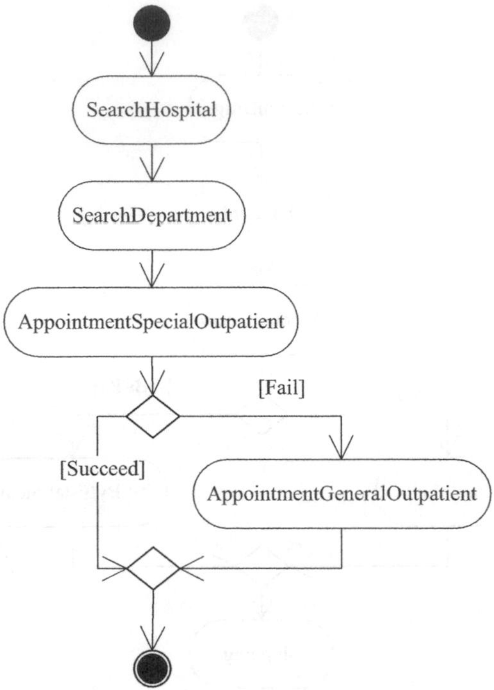


**Figure 6.4** A solution obtained via SCP and PPP.

Consider another example of online appointment registration. There are four available services: *SearchHospital, SearchDepartment, AppointmentSpecialOutpatient*, and *AppointmentGeneralOutpatient*. A requester has the user preference as *AppointmentSpecialOutpatient* $\gg$ *AppointmentGeneralOutpatient*. In other words, the appointment service of *Special* outpatients has a higher priority over general outpatients.

According to SCP and its subprocedure PPP, the resulting solution is shown in Figure 6.4. The execution process of SCP for this example is simple and therefore left for readers as an exercise.

The proposed algorithm SCP is polynomial in the size of action nodes in the generated activity diagram, but the number of action nodes may be exponential in the number of service parameters in the worst case, which depends on the reasoning method in the process of service composition. In our present platform, the number of services and parameters involved is relatively limited, and the search scope is not large for a specific request even if we use a simple reasoning method for services. Thus, the algorithm is tractable given the present environment we have. In addition, the algorithm can generate all the feasible composition solutions. If one needs to produce one solution only, a polynomial-time algorithm can be easily obtained by some minor modifications of the algorithm, since the number of available services is finite (e.g., $|\boldsymbol{C}|$), and the length of composite services is limited by $|\boldsymbol{C}|$. There have been some polynomial-time methods for automatic service composition [153,155]. They can be employed here because our method is a higher-level approach that does not specify a concrete reasoning method for services in the process of composition. As a matter of fact, we pay more attention to an idea to take the key factors as user/domain preferences into service composition. The introduction of branch structures is based on user/domain preferences in the requests. In the reasoning process, once the concerned services appear, a branch structure reflecting the user preference will be introduced after the truth value of a concerned condition is acquired. For a specific request, if there exist composite solutions that contain branch structures to reflect the user preference based on the available services, they can be constructed by this method. In addition, the introduction of branch structures does not increase the overall complexity of the approach.

## 6.4 WEB SERVICE COMPOSITION WITH PARALLEL STRUCTURES

In the process of service composition, if some component services participating in a composite service can be executed in parallel, we should seek the maximal parallelism in their execution. This can improve the efficiency of composite service execution in a distributed and parallel computing environment such as cloud computing. Conventionally, these component services that can be executed in parallel are arranged in a sequence in a feasible solution. As an undesired side effect, this leads to a number of feasible solutions that include the same collection of component services. The only difference among them is the execution order of these services. Since they are actually the same, such methods likely increase the solution cost and complexity, and contribute to low efficiency of the composite service. Take the "treating a stroke patient" composite service in Figure 6.2 for example. By existing methods such as References [152–154], $4! = 24$ feasible solutions will be derived. They are virtually identical and the only difference is the execution order of services *Physi_Info_Acquir*, *Envir_Info_Acquir*, *Subj_Feel_Acquir*, and *E_M_R*. Moreover, any one of the solutions has its execution time equal to the sum of execution time of all the four services, while with parallel processing, the total execution time rests with the slowest time among the four services as shown in Figure 6.2. It should be noted that when a single-processor computer is used to execute the services, the results will be identical.

Generally speaking, identifying all the possible parallel cases of component services is usually very difficult in service composition. However, when we consider this problem inside an enterprise, the situation becomes more manageable. In our platform, we present a few simple rules and adopt some techniques to support parallel structures when composing services.

We introduce the concept of *layer* first. In the process of service composition, starting from the initial state, after every step of reasoning we can obtain a set of newly executable services. We call these services at the same layer. Those states that are associated with services at the same layer are also called states at the same layer, and elements of each state set are in the form of propositions, and thus we call this type of layers proposition layers. Then we define a binary mutual exclusion (BME) relation between services. Two services at a same layer in a process of service composition are mutually exclusive if no valid solutions could possibly contain both of them. Identifying such relationships can help construct parallel structures.

We notice and record BME relationships by two simple rules. Specifically, there are two ways in which services $WS_1$ and $WS_2$ at a given layer are marked to be mutually exclusive.

**BME 1**. If either of the services disables a precondition of the other.

**BME 2**. If their preconditions are marked to be mutually exclusive in their corresponding higher proposition layer.

Two propositions $p$ and $q$ in a proposition layer are marked to be mutually exclusive if any of the services that generates proposition $p$ is mutually exclusive with any that generates $q$. Preconditions of a service mentioned in the two rules specify the conditions that must be true in order for an agent to execute the service.

With these two rules, we can identify parallel component services to a certain extent. We give an identification rule as follows.

**P-Rule**. The services that are not marked to be mutually exclusive of each other in the same service layer can be executed in parallel.

With this parallelism identification rule in hand, we can easily identify the parallel cases and introduce parallel structures through extending our previous algorithms. Here, the state *S* related to an action node is a set of propositions. Especially, input and output parameters are expressed in the form of *know(x)* for convenience and scalability, which represents that the agent *knows* the parameters of a service. However, we do not guarantee finding all the parallel situations in the process of service composition; instead, what we find is similar to one-step parallel cases. This can be demonstrated by an illustrating scenario, which is taken from Reference [152]. Given an online shopping scenario, we need to choose three of the available services, namely, *SearchProduct, OrderProcessing*, and *AccountQuery*. Only input and output parameters of them are given for simplicity. The input sets of these three services are {*ProductName*}, {*ProductCode, ProductQuantity*}, and {*Account-Number, AccountPassword*}, while their output sets are {*ProductCode, ProductPrice, ProductDescription*}, {*OrderInformation, Payment*}, and {*AccountBalance*}, respectively. The available inputs are {*Product-Name, ProductQuantity, AccountNumber, AccountPassword*}.

In Figure 6.5, the activity diagram fragments of service composition for this example are illustrated. We show three cases. Figure 6.5a shows previous methods that do not consider parallelism [152–154]. Figure 6.5b is obtained by using the proposed method. Figure 3 is the ideal solution for this example, but no existing systematic method can lead to this solution yet. This solution would be better than Figure 6.5b if the execution of *SearchProduct* is faster than that of *AccountQuery*.

Even though the proposed method neither guarantees to identify all the parallel situations in the process of service composition, nor leads to the ideal solution in general cases, the efforts are meaningful to advance the-state-of-the-art of WSC.

## 6.5 DEMONSTRATIONS AND RESULTS

### 6.5.1 WSC Example in PHISP

In PHISP, we can provide personalized customization and active recommendation of health care services for the general public, which can be achieved through service composition according to the user's health status information and personalized demands. Moreover, for three types of specific diseases, namely, cerebral apoplexy, coronary

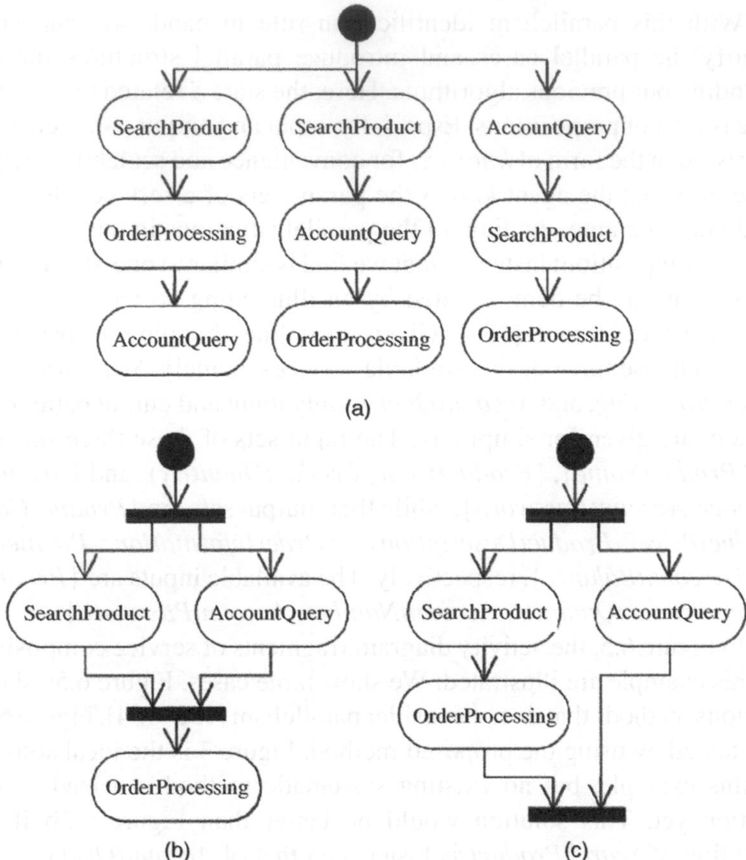


**Figure 6.5** Activity diagram fragments of service composition for an online shopping scenario.

heart disease, and diabetes, we establish their related decision-making library and remote medical care system, respectively, so as to provide intelligent health care services for individuals.

As an illustrating example, we consider a male stroke patient as a user of the health care service platform PHISP. Suppose that he makes a request for his physical health status monitoring and the corresponding health care services. The activity diagram representation of a solution that the platform provides is shown in Figure 6.2.

In this solution, four services can be invoked firstly. They are physiological information acquisition service (*Physi_Info_Acqui*), environmental information acquisition service (*Envir_Info_Acqui*), subjective feeling acquisition service (*Subj_Feel_Acqui*), and electronic medical records service (*E_M_R*). They are not marked to be mutually exclusive to each other, and hence can be executed in parallel. *Physi_Info_Acquir* service can acquire some general physiological signals such as body temperature, blood pressure, saturation of blood oxygen, electrocardiogram, and some special physiological signals for cerebral apoplexy, such as cerebral blood flow perfusion information, brain wave, and blood vessel elasticity information. *Envir_Info_Acquir* service can acquire temperature, humidity, air pressure, and other environmental information. *Subj_Feel_Acquir* service can acquire the user's subjective feelings, food intake, and so on, where the information is often provided by the patient from the terminal. *E_M_R* service can read the patient's medical history information. Based on such information, the cerebral apoplexy-oriented data analysis and diagnosis service (*Cere_Apop_Analy_Diagno*) can analyze the data according to a variety of models, like an analysis model of blood vessel elasticity. Combining the analytic results with EMR information of the patient, the personal health risk assessment service (*Health_Risk_Assess*) assesses the patient's risk level (RL). There are three cases of results: RL = 0 or in normal condition; RL = 1 or having some signs of disease; and RL = 2 or ill. According to different risk levels, there are different processes as determined by domain preferences and practical needs. When RL = 0, the personal health guidance service (*Health_Guid*) is executed next to provide some suggestions and other health guidance. When RL = 1, warn the patient first by the personal health real-time warning service (*Real_Time_Warn*), and then enforce all-round intervention and instruct the patient to deal with the case by means of the all-round intervention service (*All_Round_Interven*). When RL = 2, alarm his hospital and doctor directly by the emergency alarm service (*Emerg_Alarm*), acquire the patient's location information by the geographic information service (*Geograph_Info*), and then activate emergency service (*Activ_Emerg*).

Through this service composition example, it is clear that WSC techniques supporting both branch and parallel structures are required for successful and efficient composition of services. It should be noted that the use of artificial intelligence-based planning methods would not be able to generate the choice structure in the lower part of Figure 6.2; and the traditional technique would generate 24 solutions, each of which has the same, lengthy execution time. Such composite services in the worst case can be four times slower than the one as generated by the proposed method.

### 6.5.2 Implementation of PHISP

We have designed and constructed a medical and health care platform in collaboration with many universities and medical institutions, such as Peking University People's Hospital, Zhejiang University, Huazhong University of Science and Technology, Wuhan University Medicine School, and Shantou University Medical College. It has been used to provide teaching, research, medical treatment, and health care services for college students and teachers, researchers, medical professionals, and ordinary people.

The platform is constructed using the national CNGI-CERNET2 backbone network, which is the test platform for the next generation of Internet technology (i.e., IPv6) in China. By cooperating with the central server, our medical platform can fully exploit the resources and memory space in each network node in the IPv6 wired and wireless network. The CNGI-CERNET2-based platform breaks the function restriction of a traditional medical platform. By exploiting the advantages of IPv6, the system can guarantee reliable and high-speed data communications over wired and wireless networks, which is one of the most effective means to solve the problems caused by the current network technology of the medical industry.

The platform can also satisfy diverse user needs including the medical and health care needs of ordinary people, and provide them with various resources and services. For cerebral apoplexy, coronary heart disease, and diabetes, we have set up several analysis models, and diagnostic and decision-making systems, which can provide remote medicalcare services. A large number of universities and institutes have joined the CNGI-CERNET2 network in China. The platform can thus provide convenient information communication and comprehensive, up-to-date medical information for the users in all these universities and institutes with the IPv6 network. In addition, it can meet the needs of an online cooperative diagnosis and first-aid program for the hospitals located in different places. Figure 6.6 shows the home page of our health care platform.

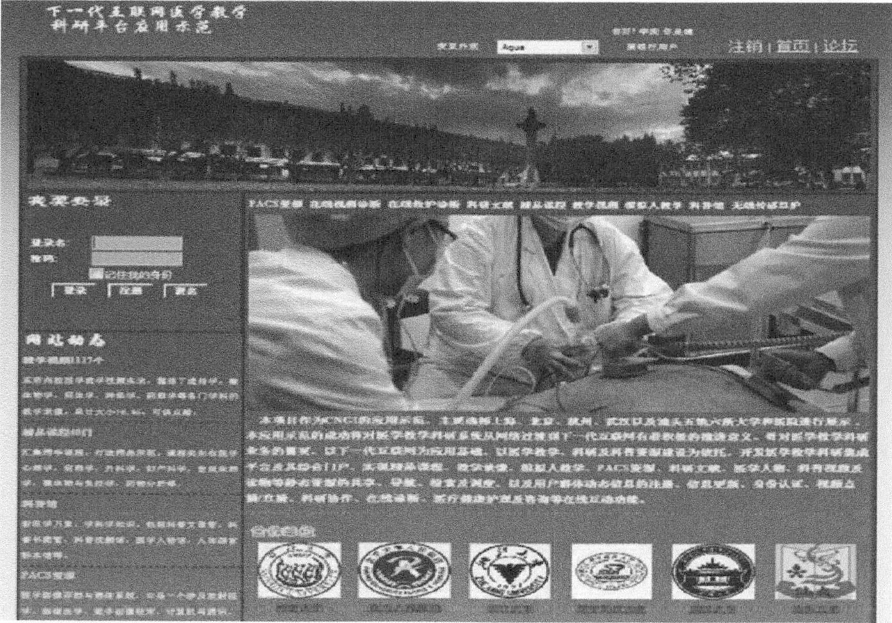


**Figure 6.6** The homepage of the PHISP system.

The current prototype system that has been partially implemented is still in the testing stage. Presently, it is mainly used for teaching and research. The implementation of this platform is a long-term process.

## 6.6 SUMMARY

In the field of medical treatment and health care, existing work including projects, researches, software products, and standards, mainly focuses on digitization for hospitals or medical institutions within organizations. However, few efforts are directly geared toward patients, their families, and other general users. With the rapid development of information and communication technologies and the changing of medical and health care service models, creating various public-oriented health care service systems has become a growing trend. In this chapter, we present such a system, i.e., Public-oriented Health care Information Services Platform (PHISP). It supports personal health information management, personal health risk assessment and guidance, dynamic personal health monitoring and real-time early warning, active recommendation of personalized medical treatment, active seasonal disease warning, and other health care services for individuals. Moreover, for some specific diseases, the platform can provide remote medical care services.

SOA principles are used to guide the system design, and Web service technologies are adopted as the computation infrastructure. In the platform, most functional modules are packaged as services. To realize the personalized customization and active recommendation of health care services for individuals, while providing them with intelligent health information management, several key techniques for service composition are integrated in the platform. Branch and parallel structures are introduced into the process models of composite services. These structures allows a composition to meet users' diverse and personalized needs in changing application environments.

In our implemented platform, some functions and services require improvements. For example, for specific diseases, we adopt some relatively simple data analysis models, and diagnostic and decision-making systems. The present medical and health care platform is still a research and demonstration system. For large-scale commercial applications, much more work is needed. Further improvement and optimization of the proposed composition methods supporting branch and parallel structures are future avenue of research, which may involve learning from work on automatic program synthesis with different control structures.

CHAPTER 7

# Scientific Workflows Enabling Web-Scale Collaboration

Service-oriented architecture (SOA) promises to evolve the Web from an information hub to a machine-to-machine collaboration platform. In science, where rapid and accurate communication is often vital to progress, adopting SOA approaches can bring about "service-oriented science." Biomedical research is one field that benefits from Web-scale collaboration using SOA. The effort to virtualize resources as services in service-oriented science can foster an ecosystem that facilitates scientific investigation in a Web-scale manner. However, a healthy service ecosystem requires more than interoperability: it needs users willing to both use existing services and develop and publish a steady stream of new ones. Thus, we require tools that facilitate service development, publication, discovery, and composition.

Scientific workflow tools that can compose and orchestrate services are an approach for meeting these two requirements and thus sustain the service ecosystem. First, scientists usually achieve scientific explorations using complex and distributed procedures. If scientific workflow tools help them discover services that meet their needs and compose those services in a desired sequence with a lighter programming burden, they will be more willing to use this ecosystem. Second, user-created

*Business and Scientific Workflows: A Web Service-Oriented Approach*, First Edition.
Edited by Wei Tan and MengChu Zhou.

workflows that represent "best practices" for scientific experimentation can also be wrapped as services and published for others to use. In this way, users not only consume but also contribute to the system.

This chapter starts with an introduction to the data deluge phenomenon in science, and specifically in biological science. Then, we present the paradigm of service-oriented science (SOS) in which Web services are virtual access points to data and computational resources. We present Cancer Grid (caGrid) as a case study of an SOS platform, which has been developed under the Cancer Biomedical Informatics Grid (caBIG) program sponsored by the US National Cancer Institute. In Section 7.2, we discuss the requirements for developing scientific workflows for caGrid and explain how we fulfill these requirements by leveraging and enhancing existing software tools. The caGrid Workflow Toolkit, an extension to the Taverna workflow system, is designed and implemented to ease building and running caGrid workflows. Besides the overall design and technical details of caGrid Workflow Toolkit, we also present some real-life and service-based scientific workflows at the end of this chapter.

## 7.1 SERVICE-ORIENTED INFRASTRUCTURE FOR SCIENCE

### 7.1.1 Service-Oriented Scientific Exploration

#### *The Fourth Paradigm*

Scientific investigation has entered the age of *data-intensive science*, or *e-Science*. In January 2007, Jim Gray summarized the four science paradigms chronologically, namely empirical, theoretical, computational, and data-intensive (e-Science). Here, we briefly explain each paradigm by giving some examples. More information can be found in the book [74].

- *Empirical.* Galileo's observational astronomy that leads to the telescopic confirmation of the phases of Venus, and the discovery of the four largest satellites of Jupiter (1500s–1600s).
- *Theoretical.* Kepler's laws of planetary motion (1600s) and Newton's laws of Motion (late 1600s) are representative.

- *Computational.* Numerical simulations of earthquake, tsunami, and other natural disasters (1900s).
- *Data-Intensive (e-Science).* The cyber-infrastructure and LHC Computing Grid to support the CERN Large Hadron Collider [156] where LHC stands for Large Hadron Collider and CERN stands for European Organization for Nuclear Research.

In the data-intensive paradigm, scientists are facing an enormous increase in raw data from various resources such as telescopes, instruments, sensor networks, accelerators, and supercomputers. Here, we give a few examples only. In 2010, ATLAS and the three other main detectors at the LHC produced 13 petabytes of data [75]. *PubMed,* a database of references and abstracts on life sciences and biomedical topics, contained 21 million entries as of July 2011 [157]. The *2011 Nucleic Acids Research Database Issue and the online Molecular Biology Database Collection* [76] lists 1330 carefully selected molecular biology databases among which, *GenBank,* the US NIH DNA sequence database, contained more than 286 billions of entries for more than 380,000 organisms as of August 2010 [77]. This *data deluge* [158] calls for a uniformed and virtualized access method for all these data and the computational resources to analyze them.

### Service-Oriented Science

Compared to e-Science, or data-driven science, the concept of service-oriented science (SOS) proposed by Professor Ian Foster in 2005 has a similar connotation but more specifically focuses on using SOA as the underlying infrastructure integrating data and computation capabilities. Figure 7.1 illustrates the infrastructure and application scenarios of SOS.

SOS infrastructure provides the common facilities to integrate data (such as DNA sequences, astronomical images, and particle physics data), instruments (such as electron microscopes, accelerators, and space telescopes), and computational resources (such as computer clusters and cloud computing platforms). These common facilities are shared by all the services just like the power grid is shared by all power generators. The key facilities include the following:

- *Virtualization.* It uses standard protocols, such as HTTP, SOAP, and REST, to wrap heterogeneous data, instruments, and

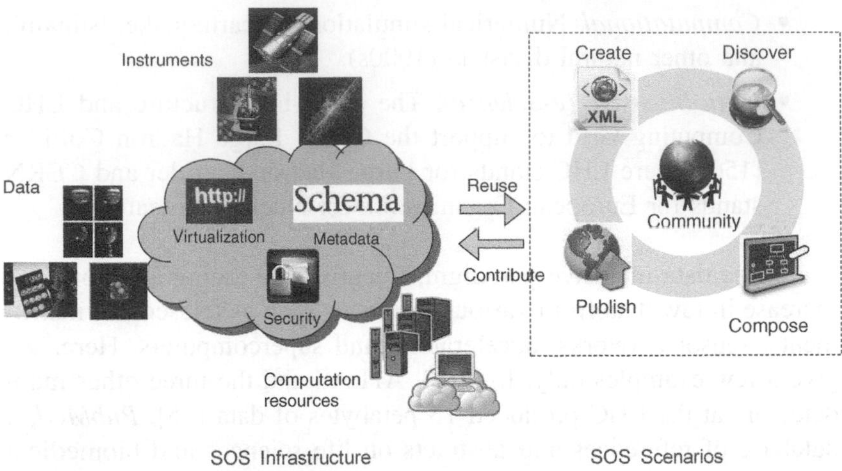


**Figure 7.1** The infrastructure and application scenarios of service-oriented science.

computational resources into uniformed interfaces, such that users can access them without owning or even knowing their internal workings.

- *Security*. Privacy, integrity, authentication, and authorization are key issues in accessing virtualized services. The infrastructure needs to have a mechanism to explicitly define security policies and enforce them during run-time.
- *Metadata*. SOS encourages sharing and collaboration in a multi-disciplinary and cross-institutional manner, such that scientists can obtain data and computation from the Web instead of the lab and undertake experiments at a Web scale. Therefore, it is important that users understand not only the syntax but also the semantics of the services.

On top of the aforementioned infrastructure, SOS applications usually need to create, discover, compose, and publish services and also provide community support. We will explain them one by one.

- *Create*. We have to create Web services wrapping data, program, instruments, and computation resources. There are open-source software libraries such as Apache Axis [159] and CXF [160]. As we have mentioned, scientific applications usually have special requirements such as metadata and security, and therefore, more specialized build-time and run-time software tools are needed to create services and execute them. Currently, several toolkits, such as Globus Toolkit [161] and a package offered by OMII-UK project [162], are available to address this need.

- *Discover.* Being aware of services of interest and choosing which one(s) to use is not a trivial task since SOS exists in a Web-scale ecosystem in which many organizations provide many services. Users may not know these services' URLs or functions and semantics. Because the scientific community is too autonomous to share a common terminology, without domain knowledge it is impossible to determine a service's exact semantics using its syntax. An SOS ecosystem must establish an agreed-on vocabulary and use it to annotate services, such that users can discover them with less ambiguity. Currently, there exist several semantics-based service annotation and discovery mechanisms, and most of them rely on W3C's Resource Description Framework (RDF) [19].
- *Compose.* Due to the diversified purposes and approaches that scientists have, few Web services alone can fulfill the requirement of an *in-silico* experiment. Instead, services often need to be composed and orchestrated in a given sequence, which is called a scientific workflow. Taylor et al. [72] give a comprehensive survey of the existing standards and tools for scientific workflows.
- *Publish.* To foster a service ecosystem, scientists should be not only users but also contributors to SOS. They can either expose the resources (data, programs, instruments, computers, etc.) they own as services, or publish a composite service that invokes multiple services. A composite service, usually in the form of a scientific workflow, can represent a novel experimental routine that is a new intellectual property to SOS. This use-and-publish paradigm is also changing the way people publish their results. Currently, a couple of tools including Trident [163] have provided Microsoft Word plug-ins so that scientists can embed a workflow in a research paper and rerun them to reproduce the experimental results.
- *Community.* By performing tasks such as *creating*, *discovering*, *composing*, and *publishing*, scientists can greatly benefit from

community experience through which they can share data, services, workflows, and the knowledge obtained by doing experiments. We will further discuss this issue in Chapter 8.

Projects that embrace the idea of SOS and adopt a Web service-based infrastructure include myGrid [164,165], caBIG/caGrid [166], CardioVascular Research Grid (CVRG) [167], and BIRN [168]. In the next subsection, we use caGrid as a case study of SOS.

### 7.1.2 Case Study: The Cancer Grid (caGrid)

The Cancer Biomedical Informatics Grid (caBIG) program [169] sponsored by the US National Cancer Institute (NCI) is an open-source, open-access information network enabling the cancer community to share data and knowledge, and eventually accelerating the discovery of new cancer treatment methods. Initiated in 2004, caBIG as of 2011 had more than 2,300 program participants from over 700 institutions. Its tool inventory includes over 40 software tools in the areas such as clinical trials, biospecimens, imaging, infrastructure, and vocabularies. Its tools and technologies are used or evaluated by 15 countries [170].

caGrid is the underlying service-oriented infrastructure of caBIG, and is built on the Globus Toolkit Grid middleware. caGrid mainly consists of the core infrastructure, the services created and managed by this infrastructure, and the research community hosting and using these services.

*caGrid core infrastructure* uses Globus Toolkit version 4 as the service-based middleware, and adopts Web Services Resource Framework (WSRF) [161]. WSRF is an extension to the Web service standard stack by addressing the specific concerns of Grid services such as stateful services, state management, and resource lifecycle management. Using WSRF, the carefully designed core infrastructure contains components such as metadata, service discovery and index, security, and an integrated development environment (IDE) to design a Web service with these enhanced, caGrid specific features, for example, metadata, index, and security.

*caGrid services*, created and managed by the core infrastructure, are virtualized access points of data and analytical resources related to cancer detection, diagnosis, treatment, and prevention. They can be classified into two categories: data resources that are exposed as *data*

**Figure 7.2** The map of caGrid taken from caGrid portal (http://cagrid-portal.nci.nih.gov/), on July 31, 2011.

*services* and computational applications that are exposed as *analytical services*. The former typically include human biospecimens, entrez genes, and microarray, while the latter include sequence alignment, clustering, and classification. Most of the caGrid services are accessible by all researchers without any security requirement, while some services limit their access to users with certain privilege. As shown in Figure 7.2, as of July 31, 2011, caGrid hosted 60 plus data services and 50 plus analytical ones.

*caGrid community* includes more than 100 organizations it connects, including many NCI-designated cancer centers and members of the NCI Community Cancer Center Program. It stores thousands of microarray experiments, pathways, and genes.

## 7.2 SCIENTIFIC WORKFLOWS IN SERVICE-ORIENTED SCIENCE

### 7.2.1 Scientific Workflow: Old Wine in New Bottle?

#### *Scientific Workflows in a Nutshell: Automate, Audit, and Reuse*

Workflow technologies, which are originated in the area of office automation and aim to better manage document flow among multiple users, ensure the correct sequence of processing events and maintain the processing track [171]. Workflows have been extended to automate business processes both inside and across enterprises, and have found growing attention in the grid community, showing the power of parallel computation, scientific investigation, and job flow management [72,73]. This book specifically focuses on the domain of biological science where Web-based services have provided scientists with the access to various data and computation resources, whereas, in general, scientific workflows can contain other types of tasks such as invocations to local and remote applications.

Today, the number of available Web services has grown significantly. BioCatalogue [172], a curated catalogue of life science Web services, has collected more than 1400 services from over 100 providers, and a 2006 paper [173] reported 3000 publicly available services in molecular biology. With the help of workflow technologies, scientists can build a model of their data pipelines integrating distributed data and analytic resources, automate these data pipelines that were previously

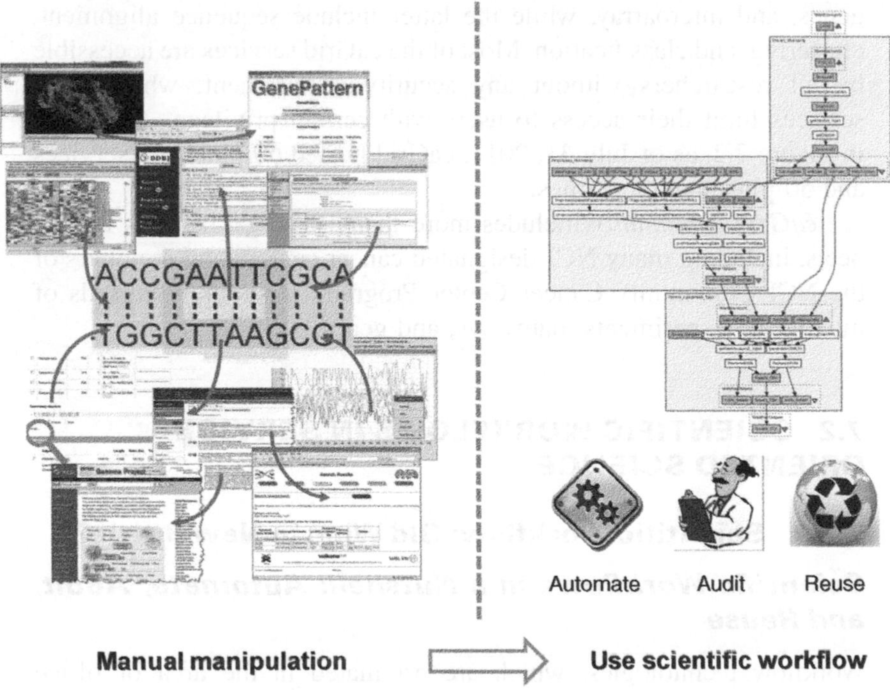


**Figure 7.3** Scientific workflow in biological and biomedical sciences.

performed manually, and leverage this platform to make their exploration trackable and reproducible.

*Scientific workflow*, as a marriage of workflow technologies and domain science, is a specialized form of a workflow designed specifically to compose and execute a series of computational or data manipulation applications in science. In this chapter and the next one, we use biological science as an exemplary domain and focus on Web service-based workflow systems.

- *Automate.* To achieve a fully functional data pipeline, scientists used to switch among browsers, copy from one Web page, convert the obtained data, and paste it to another one. Scientific workflow systems allow them to build a flow model of their data processing pipeline, typically using a graph or script. This flow model will integrate multiple steps including invocations to Web services and other facilitating steps. Each service receives data from previous steps, and facilitating steps provide utilities such as reading data from external sources and data format transformation. Once a flow model is built, its execution is handled by a workflow engine. As a result, scientists no longer need to switch from browsers and software tools, record the intermediary and final results, and do the data transformation manually.
- *Audit.* During the execution of a scientific workflow, the workflow system also keeps track of the data involved, through all transformations, analyses, and interpretations. This audit information, also referred as data *lineage* or *provenance* [174], is of paramount importance to ensure the validity and reproducibility of the experiments undertaken. This audit feature provided by a scientific workflow system makes it a favorable constituent in the increasingly popular electronic laboratory notebook systems [175].
- *Reuse.* Scientific workflows enable reuse in two different scenarios. In the first one, a workflow template can be instantiated for many times, each with a different input, or a parameter setting, or both. This scenario, usually called input-and-parameter-sweep, is quite common in biological experiments where a routine needs to be tried using different specimens and under various settings.

In the second scenario, a workflow that embeds the best practice of one experiment can be shared with the community. For example, a lymphoma diagnosis workflow built and shared by one researcher can be used by another for the purpose of breast cancer analysis.

## *Taverna versus BPEL: Not an Old Wine in New Bottle*

Currently, there are many scientific workflow systems available and the well-edited book [72] provides a summary of them. Among them, many systems are designed for either only composing Web services or providing support to compose services. They include Askalon [176], Kepler [177], GPEL [178], OMII-UK [179], Taverna [180], Triana [181], and Trident [163]. Each of them provides a graph-based interface for service composition, with an underlying workflow metamodel. The workflow metamodels used by these service-based systems are either adopted from industry standard or homegrown.

GPEL and OMII-UK adopt the industry standard languages WS-BPEL. WS-BPEL is an XML-based specification that describes the behavior of a business process composed of Web services, and the workflow itself is also exposed as a Web service. Originally designed for business workflows, BPEL is also embraced by the scientific community. Obviously, adopting industry standard like BPEL can bring some advantages such as rigorously defined model syntax and semantics, readily available software tools, and portability of workflow specifications. However, a distinction can be made between workflow languages designed for business processes and those for scientific pipelines. This distinction arises from the different nature of business and scientific applications. Business workflows present the routines inside or between enterprises, and therefore, comprehensive control-flows embodying business rules, process integrity (including transaction and compliance), and human involvement are the major concerns. Scientific workflows present the experiments conducted by scientists, and therefore, fast data processing and scheduling of computing resources are the major concerns.

To deal with the unique features of scientific workflows, Askalon, Kepler, Taverna, Triana, and Trident have devised their own workflow metamodels. Due to the diversified and specific concerns addressed by these homegrown models, it is difficult to provide a comprehensive comparison between them and BPEL. Instead, we pick up a representative, i.e., Taverna that is used by the aforementioned caGrid project, and compare it with BPEL.

Developed in the UK by the myGrid consortium, Taverna is an open-source workbench for the design and execution of scientific workflows. Aiming primarily at the life science community, its main goal is to make the design and execution of workflows accessible to researchers who are not necessarily experts in Web services and programming. A Taverna workflow consists of a graph of activities that represent Web services or other executable components. Activities receive their inputs from input ports and produce outputs to output ports. An arc in the graph connects an output port of one activity to an input port of another, and thus, it specifies a data dependency. Workflows are specified using a visual language and executed according to a dataflow computation model [182]. Taverna also provides a plug-in architecture such that additional applications, for example, caGrid infrastructure management and services, can be populated to it, as discussed later in Section 7.2.2 *caGrid Workflow Toolkit*.

We choose BPEL and Taverna as representatives for business and scientific workflow languages, respectively, for the following reasons. Firstly, they are typical and widely used in business and scientific domains, respectively. BPEL is the *de facto* standard for business workflows and adopted by IBM, Microsoft, Oracle, SAP, and so on. On the other hand, Taverna is used by many organizations and in various areas including life science, astronomy, and chemistry. Secondly, Taverna and BPEL have a historical connection. Taverna originally supported a subset of WSFL [183] which is an ancestor of BPEL. Therefore, from this comparison, we can find out how two languages from the same origin evolve to serve different purposes. Last but not least, in caGrid, we use both BPEL and Taverna. Thus, we have gained sufficient first-hand experience in comparing them.

Although BPEL and Taverna share some common modeling elements, these come as a result of different design motivations, which account for different programming styles. BPEL is designed for the interactions among business partners that expose their functions via service interfaces and for facilitating their *interoperability*. The major motivation for the design of Taverna, on the other hand, is to streamline the *dataflow* among services, scripts, and other applications.

A BPEL process is *control-flow-driven* because it contains full pledged control primitives to describe the complex business logic. In contrast, a Taverna workflow is *dataflow-driven*, that is, a workflow graph describes data dependencies instead of control dependencies. Therefore, a BPEL workflow is executed according to the control structure, while a Taverna workflow's tasks are activated when data, rather than control, reach them. In a scientific domain, such a dataflow paradigm has the advantage that system-level issues such as task scheduling and parallelization are completely transparent to designers, as parallelism is specified implicitly through data dependencies.

This dataflow versus control-flow difference also leads to the distinction in how parallelism is handled in BPEL and Taverna. In BPEL, a set of parallel tasks need to be explicitly specified using the *<Flow>* or *<ForEach>* constructs. In contrast, a scientific workflow often needs to deal with large datasets that are expressed using collection data structure such as arrays or lists. The Taverna dataflow model permits the execution of a task on each element of an input list, without explicitly adding a parallel construct. Since data parallelism in a scientific workflow can be overwhelming, this feature, referred to as *implicit iteration* of tasks over lists, can not only make the workflow compact but also exploit system-level concurrency and pipelined execution.

In addition, in a business workflow, *transactional property* is critical to the correctness of a business transaction. In case of failure, the system has to roll back to a consistent state. BPEL provides a rich set of primitives to keep the process itself as well as participant services in a consistent state upon process failure. In BPEL, faults are caught by fault handlers and processed there with some compensation for the work already accomplished, to keep the business logic in a consistent state. Taverna embodies a functional programming style, which assumes side effect-freeness of involving functions (i.e., activities). With this assumption, Taverna handles failures in a straightforward way, that is, it asks the failed activities to retry (or try a substitute). This assumption is reasonable because a large majority of services, for example, most caGrid services, are stateless and side effect-free, being concerned simply with either data querying or data processing. If such services fail to yield a result, Taverna can simply retry them or resort to a substitute.

Table 7.1 summarizes the comparison results between BPEL and Taverna. Some examples and additional discussions can be found in

**Table 7.1** Comparison of BPEL and Taverna

| | BPEL | Taverna |
|---|---|---|
| Driving factor in design | 1. Interoperability of business processes<br>2. Link multiple partners<br>3. Recoverability | 1. Extensible invocation scheme<br>2. Pipeline processing of data<br>3. Reproducibility |
| Activities in model | Basic and structure activities | Data processing units with input/output ports |
| Semantics of links | Transfer of control | Transfer of data |
| Data definition | Explicitly defined (global variables) | Implicit defined (activities' input/output) |
| Data initialization | Complex data types need to be explicitly initialized | Implicitly initialized |
| Control logic | Fully fledged: sequence, conditional, parallel, event-triggered, and so on | Limited: sequential, parallel, and conditional |
| Parallel execution | Explicitly defined using <flow> or <ForEach> operators | Implicit iteration |
| Fault handling | Throw-catch, compensation handler to ensure transaction properties | Retry and substitution, assuming no side effect |

[184]. This comparison reveals that scientific workflows (using Taverna as an example) do have unique characteristics compared to their business counterparts, thereby deserving special attention.

Our experience in using both Taverna and BPEL as the candidate solutions for caGrid illustrates that:

- BPEL offers a comprehensive set of primitives to model workflows of all flavors (control-flow oriented, dataflow oriented, and event-driven), with full features (process logic, data manipulation, event and message processing, fault handling, etc.). As an imperative language, BPEL offers fine control and close communication to workflow engines. BPEL is capable of handling dataflows, although in some cases, the modeling experience is cumbersome and tedious.
- Taverna provides a compact set of primitives that eases the modeling of dataflows. Its functional programming framework makes many routine tasks invisible to the programmer such that users can focus on specifying "what to do" instead of "how to do them." The workflow engine handles routine tasks such as variable initialization, parallel execution through implicit iteration, and pipelined execution.

After a pilot study on both Taverna and BPEL, caGrid decided to use Taverna to orchestrate its services, thanks to its aforementioned advantages in dataflow modeling. Despite this fact, no rational user will argue against the superiority of BPEL for certain tasks. Different tasks will result in demand for different types of workflow languages and systems.

## 7.2.2 caGrid Workflow Toolkit

### *Motivation*

caGrid project selected Taverna as its workflow execution system of choice due to its integration with Web service technology and support for a wide range of Web services, plug-in architecture to cater for easy integration of third-party extensions, and a broad user base within the bioinformatics/biomedicine community [185]. The caGrid Workflow Toolkit, an extension to the Taverna workflow system, is designed and implemented to ease building and running caGrid workflows. It provides users with support for various phases in using workflows: service discovery, composition and orchestration, data access, and secure service invocation, which have been identified by the caGrid community as challenging tasks in a multi-institutional and cross-discipline domain.

1. *Service discovery*—where to find services that are relevant to the scientific investigation of a user.
2. *Data access*—what kind of data (data types) can be obtained from a given service and how to transfer data from and to it.
3. *Service interaction*—how to invoke services and maintain session information in multistep interactions.
4. *Security enforcement*—how to enforce authentication and authorization in service invocations and privacy and integrity in data transfers.
5. *Knowledge sharing*—how to share workflows with the community, how to find out what other researchers in the field are doing, and how to leverage the best practice from them.

We have followed two principles in the design and development of the toolkit. First, instead of reinventing the wheel, we have adopted the software tools that are widely used by the life science community, namely Taverna and myExperiment [186]. We have improved these tools by offering more advanced features in the form of plug-ins that make caGrid infrastructure accessible from Taverna. Second, we have worked closely with scientists from caBIG to fulfill their needs, while making our tool applicable to any user community that embraces a similar service infrastructure.

### Implementation of caGrid Workflow Toolkit

Figure 7.4 shows the architecture of the caGrid Workflow Toolkit. The solid rectangle in the middle consists of the five components that are extensions to Taverna. The components in dashed rectangles are modules in caGrid infrastructure and myExperiment. They are numbered in accordance with the toolkit's components to prescribe the interactions in between. *Service discovery* component locates the

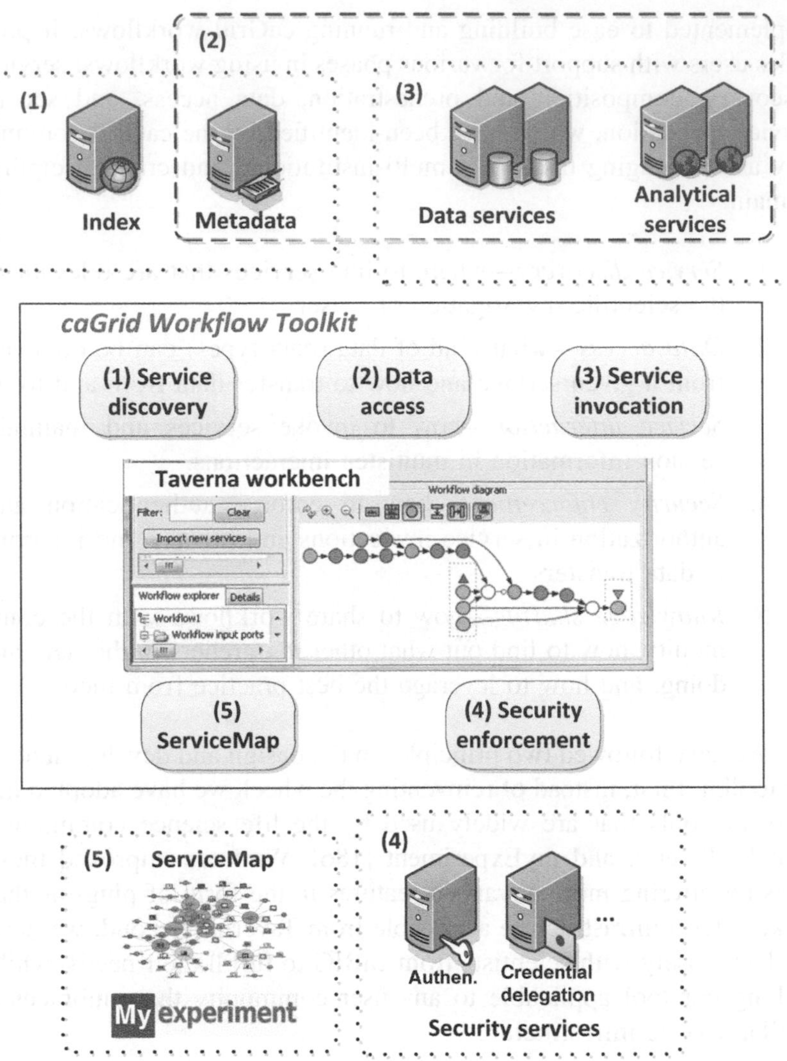


**Figure 7.4** caGrid workflow toolkit [187].

caGrid services by querying *Index Service*, which is the centralized service registry of caGrid and the *Metadata Service*, which defines the data types used by all caGrid services. *Data access* component provides: (1) a GUI to build query clauses against data service, and (2) a data transfer utility to move files from and to services. *Service invocation* enables the stateful interactions with services. *Security enforcement* ensures the privacy, integrity, authentication, and authorization in services invocation and data transfer. The last component *ServiceMap* shares workflows to myExperiment and uses best practices in myExperiment to recommend service and workflow snippets to users.

Taverna Workbench provides an extensible framework to interact with various executables, in our case, caGrid services. The caGrid Workflow Toolkit containing caGrid-specific extensions can be downloaded and installed in Taverna Workbench by pointing its *Plug-in Manager* to http://software.cagrid.org/taverna2/. Please note that the caGrid Workflow Toolkit components in Figure 7.4 correspond to only five physical plug-ins: *caGrid-activity*, *cql-builder*, *caGrid-transfer-activity*, *cds-activity*, and *service-map*. This is because the layout of Figure 7.4 gives a more abstract and easy-to-follow illustration of the features the toolkit offers. However, in the actual software implementation, we need to comply with the Taverna plug-in infrastructure that results in spreading the logical functionality to plug-ins. The correspondence between the logical components and the actual Taverna plug-ins is explained in Table 7.2. Figure 7.5 shows the four plug-ins (except *service-map* that is to be covered in Chapter 8) in a Taverna service panel.

**Table 7.2** Correspondence Between Logical Components and Taverna Plug-Ins

| Components | Taverna plug-ins | Notes |
|---|---|---|
| Service discovery | caGrid-activity | caGrid-activity plug-in contains a service discovery tool |
| Data access | cql-builder | A GUI to build CQL clauses |
| | caGrid-transfer-activity | An activity to transfer files between services and clients |
| Service interaction | caGrid-activity | caGrid-activity plug-in takes care of stateful service invocation |
| Security enforcement | caGrid-activity | caGrid-activity plug-in takes care of secured service invocation |
| | cds-activity | An activity to delegate credential |
| ServiceMap | Service-map | See Chapter 8 for more details |

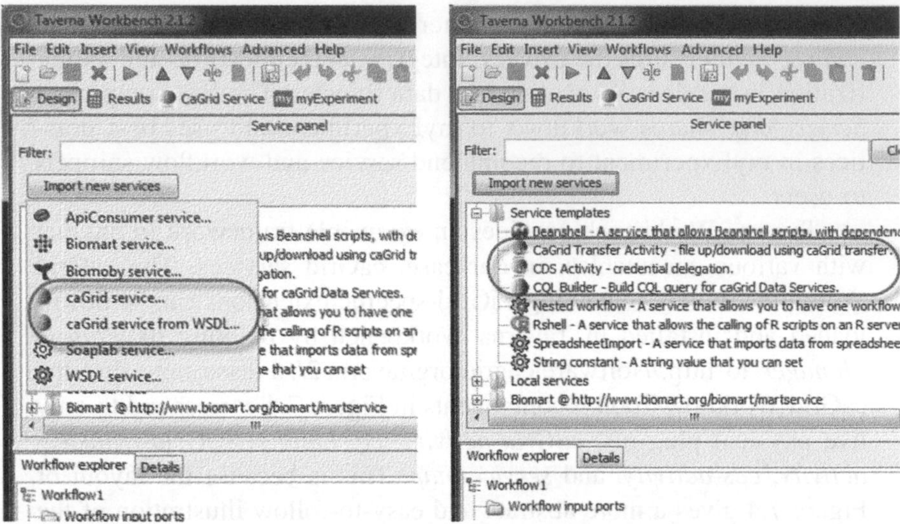


**Figure 7.5** Four plug-ins in Taverna service panel. The four plug-ins in caGrid workflow toolkit are as follows: caGrid-activity (*caGrid service . . .* and *caGrid service from WSDL . . .*) for service discovery, invocation, and security enforcement; cql-builder (*CQL Builder*) for the visualized construction of CQL clause to query data services; caGrid-transfer-activity (*caGrid Transfer Activity*) for file transfers between clients and services; and cds-activity (*CDS Activity*) for credential delegation.

**Service Discovery.** In a typical service-oriented infrastructure such as caGrid, the address of a service of interest is not usually known to the end users. This makes the task of locating appropriate services a challenge for users, given the fact that caGrid now comprises more than 100 services storing different data or providing varied analysis capabilities, which are deployed at geographically distributed institutions.

On top of the Globus Index Service [188], caGrid provides the mechanism to discover services of interest by querying a live service registry. All the caGrid services are required to publish the metadata that describe their functionality using WSRF. This information is aggregated in the registry Index Service and used to find out information about the currently running services and their current WSDL addresses. Clients can then query this aggregated information using standard WSRF operations.

The services' descriptive metadata include service name, WSDL, hosting research center, operations with associated data types, and the semantic annotation on the aforementioned metadata, as shown

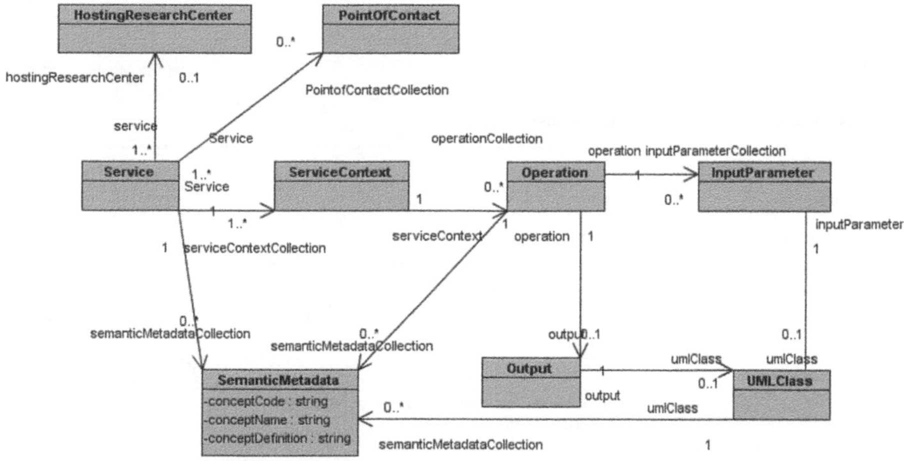


**Figure 7.6** caGrid service metadata.

in Figure 7.6. The service discovery component locates caGrid services by querying Index Service. It provides three types of querying methods leveraging caGrid's metadata and indexing infrastructure:

1. String-based querying performs free text searching in service descriptions. For example, one can search for services whose descriptions contain string "*array*."
2. Property-based querying performs search towards predefined service properties, for example, to locate services *hosted* by *NCICB* that stands for the NCI Center for Bioinformatics, or whose *name* is *CaArraySvc*.
3. Semantic-based querying. caGrid uses an ontology called NCI Enterprise Vocabulary Services (EVS) to annotate services and their associated data. A vocabulary item in EVS is called a *Concept*, and the *Concept Code* is used to uniquely identify it. A semantic-based approach allows users to locate services that are annotated with some concept code, for example, *C44282* representing concept *Microarray*.

Consider a service discovery example in Figure 7.7, to search services whose description contains *array*, hosted by *NCICB*, and annotated with concept code *C44282*.

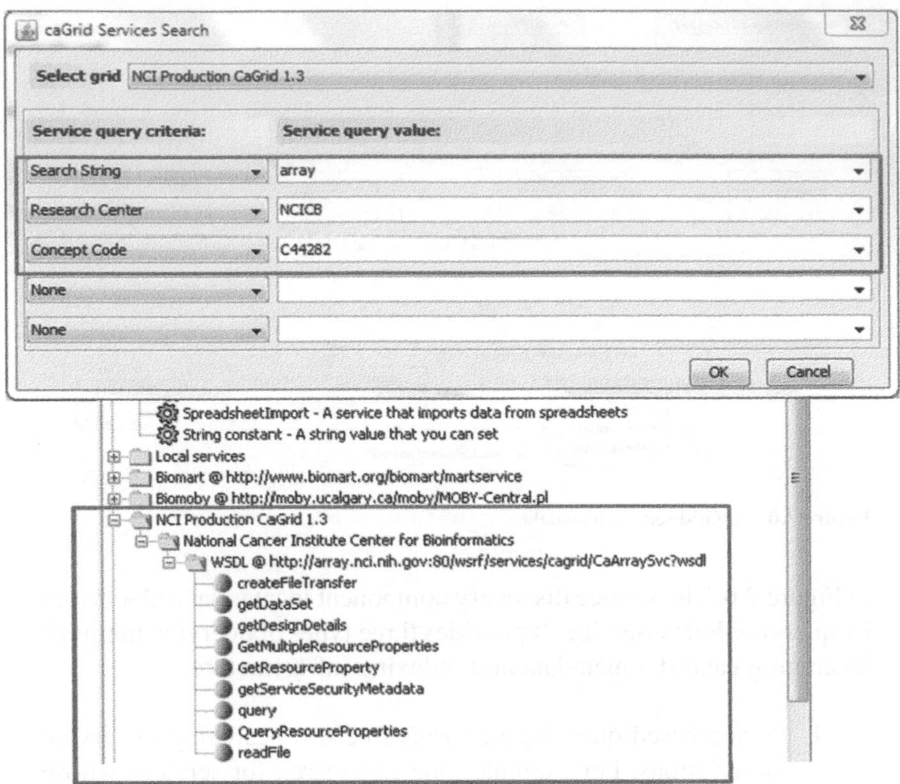


**Figure 7.7** Service discovery GUI and the result. Search services whose description contains *array*, hosted by *NCICB*, and annotated with concept code *C44282*.

**Data Access.** caGrid Data Service [189] is used to share cancer research data. caGrid data services implement an object-oriented virtualization on top of the backend data source. Based on this virtualization, data items can be searched by their object classes, properties, and association relations. caGrid also defines an XML-based object-oriented query language called caGrid Query Language (CQL) for the querying purpose. The data access component provides a GUI to build CQL queries against data services, and users can browse the data object model graph and build a CQL clause easily without knowing its syntax.

Another feature offered by the data access component is the data transfer tool called caGrid transfer. It leverages the caGrid transfer utility to move files between services and clients using the HTTP protocol, without embedding them in SOAP messages. In practice, we have found this more efficient, since it avoids data serialization or deserialization and saves much memory on both client and server sides.

**Service Invocation.** caGrid services use WSRF extension to enable stateful communications with clients. The *service invocation* component implements WSRF specification such that it can interact with services in a stateful manner. This feature is extremely useful in a multistep interaction with a service, which is quite common in scientific applications. For example, a scientist submits a dataset to a caGrid service to run a computation-intensive task. Since the computation usually takes some time in the backend system, a result cannot be returned in a synchronous manner. In this case, the service chooses to synchronously return an EPR (End Point Reference) that identifies the service interaction. At a later time, scientists use the EPR as a handler to query the status of the task that they submitted earlier and obtain the result when it is ready. The WSRF implementation on the server side uses the EPR to identify the instance of the service and return the specific result data appropriately. The issuance and management of an EPR is handled by the Globus toolkit and the service invocation component, and is transparent to users.

**Security Enforcement.** Security is an important aspect in biomedical applications. Scientists want to ensure the privacy, integrity, authentication, and authorization in the sharing of data and computation resources in a multi-institutional environment. For example, scientists may constrain the access to their data to certain organizations or groups of users (authentication and authorization); they may want to access their data in an encrypted way such that no other people can intercept the content (privacy); they may also want an assurance that the data the recipient receives are exactly the same as those sent by the sender (integrity). All these issues have been addressed by the Grid Security Infrastructure (GSI) [190] in the Globus toolkit. GSI leverages public key infrastructure (PKI) and X.509 certificates [188] to address these security requirements.

caGrid uses the Grid Authentication and Authorization with Reliably Distributed Services (GAARDS) [191] as an extension to the GSI, to provide services and tools for the administration and enforcement of security policies in caGrid. The *security enforcement* component as shown in Figure 7.4 allows users to log into caGrid, obtain a grid credential from the Authentication Service, store it locally, and use it for subsequent service invocations for the lifetime of the credential (effectively achieving single sign-on by this means). In addition to this single-sign-on feature, the security enforcement component also allows credential delegation such that a service can act on behalf of a user. For example, the Federated Query Processor (FQP) service can use a delegated credential from a user, query multiple data services on the user's behalf, aggregate the results, and forward them back to the user.

**ServiceMap.** myExperiment is a sister project of Taverna and a Web-based collaborative platform for sharing workflows and related research objects such as data items, papers, and software bundles. The *ServiceMap* component simply uses myExperiment Web site to publish the workflows [192] built and used by the caGrid community. These workflows contain detailed descriptions of what the workflows are set to achieve and instructions on how to use them, for example, what data to use as input. They also embed knowledge on how to use individual services as well as how to orchestrate multiple services into a fully fledged data pipeline. In the next section, we will give some exemplary caGrid workflows. A more important feature of ServiceMap (to be discussed in more detail in Chapter 8) is to provide service composition assistance such as recommending service(s) and/or operation chain(s) that are of interest to users.

Several other Taverna extensions for specific uses exist such as CDK-Taverna [193] and an R-extension [194]. The former is an extension to access a cheminformatics library called CDK, while the latter allows users to submit a statistical calculation job to a remote R server. The caGrid extension of Taverna is implemented from the perspective of services computing, thereby enabling users to access a broad range of remote services in a more standard, secure, and scalable manner. In this way, scientists can greatly improve their productivity by accessing powerful information provision tools and automating their data analysis, without knowledge of, or control over, the internal workings of those tools. In addition to caGrid services, we have successfully applied the caGrid Workflow Toolkit in other projects that use the similar service technology stack, for example, the Cardio-Vascular Research Grid (CVRG).

### 7.2.3 Exemplary caGrid Workflows

This section shows two caGrid Workflows we have created and uploaded to myExperiment. The first workflow is a simple task, that is, querying and fetching microarray data; while the second one is a fully fledged routine with real scientific value, that is, lymphoma type prediction. For all the caGrid workflows and other Taverna ones, users are encouraged to visit the link http://www.myexperiment.org/search?query=cabig&type=workflows. All caGrid workflows are modeled in a graphical way and organized into meaningful modules, such that they can easily be reused out of the box or be modified and repurposed.

#### *Workflow 1: Access to caArray Data Using cql-builder and caGrid-transfer*

caArray [195] is an open-source, Web and programmatically accessible microarray data management system developed by caBIG. Since it acquires, disseminates, and aggregates a large volume of cancer-related array data, cancer researchers in caBIG frequently start their *in-silico* investigation by querying and retrieving data from caArray and subsequently analyze them using tools and services on and off the caGrid.

Figure 7.8 shows a workflow that queries all the files related to a microarray experiment and selects and downloads some of them. The input of the workflow is the identifier of the microarray experiment (*experiment_id*) of interest. Within the CQL builder (*CQL_Builder*), a complex CQL clause is built, querying all the caArray file objects associated with this experiment as shown via the CQL builder GUI and the criteria editing dialog in Figure 7.9. A user can then pick up one or several caArray files (*extract_a_file*), create a download session (*createFileTransfer*), and use the caGrid-transfer-activity plug-in (*caGrid_Transfer_Activity*) to download files to a local directory. The output is the name of the downloaded file (*resultFile*). From now on, we only mention the key activities/services in a workflow, and those that are not mentioned may be local activities doing data transformations, XML manipulations, and so on.

In the CQL builder GUI (the upper dialog of Figure 7.9), users can choose which service to query by giving the service's URL, and then, its object-oriented data model is populated and ready to be selected. Users can select one of them (*gov.nih.nci.caarray.domain.file.CaArrayFile*)

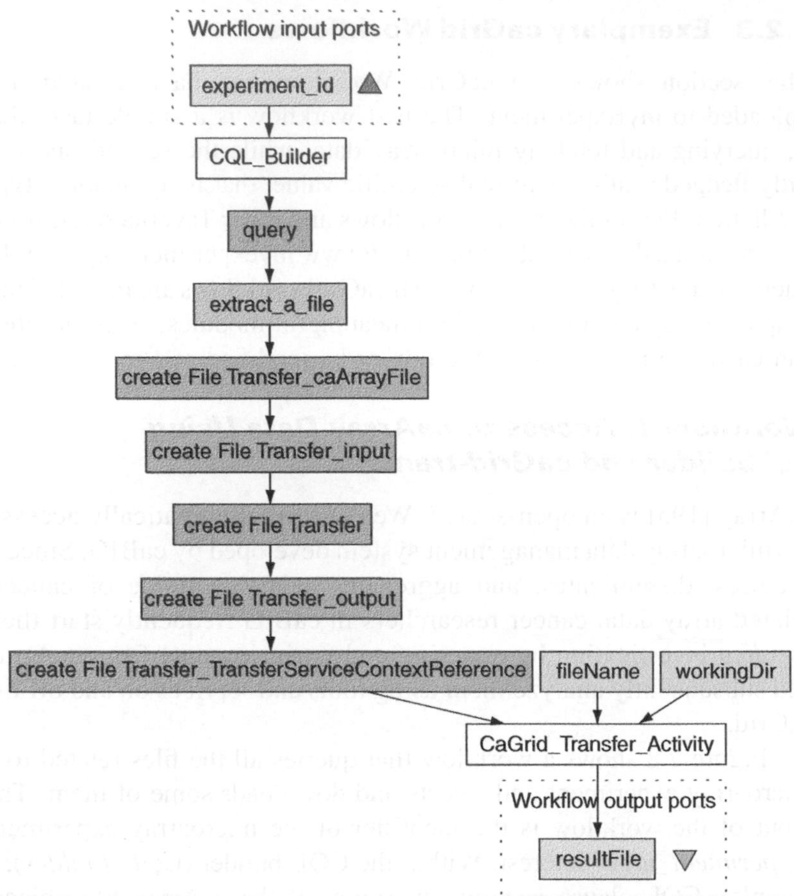


**Figure 7.8** Query caArray data service and retrieve files [196]. CQL_Builder provides a GUI to build a complex CQL clause querying caArray files. caGrid_Transfer_Activity downloads files to a local directory using caGrid transfer utility.

and edit the criteria clause (the GUI to edit query criteria is shown in the lower part of Figure 7.9).

### Workflow 2: Lymphoma Type Prediction

Here, we describe a real-life workflow built for caBIG users to illustrate a fairly complex scenario. The workflow enables cancer diagnosis based on microarray analysis [197]. As shown in Figure 7.10, the workflow

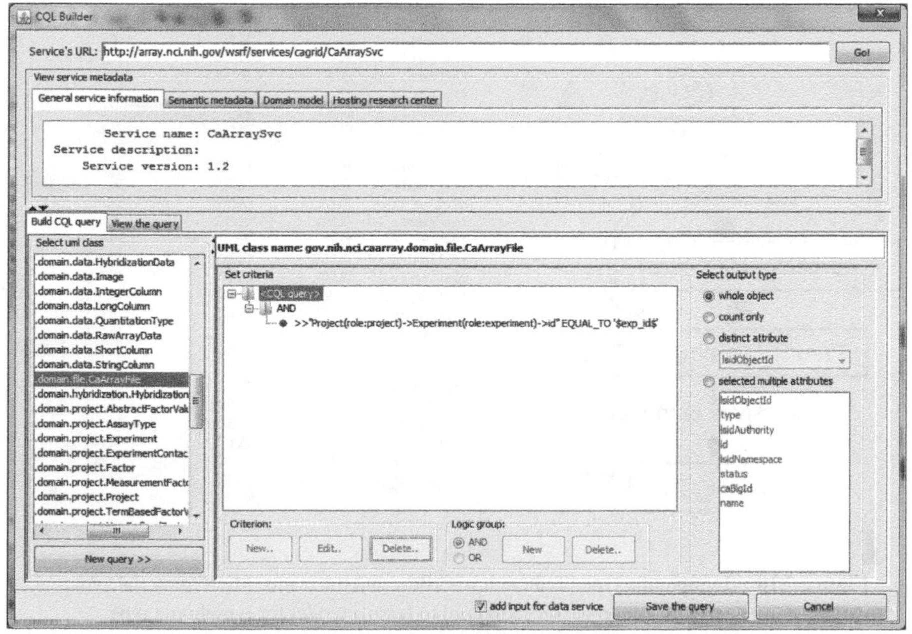


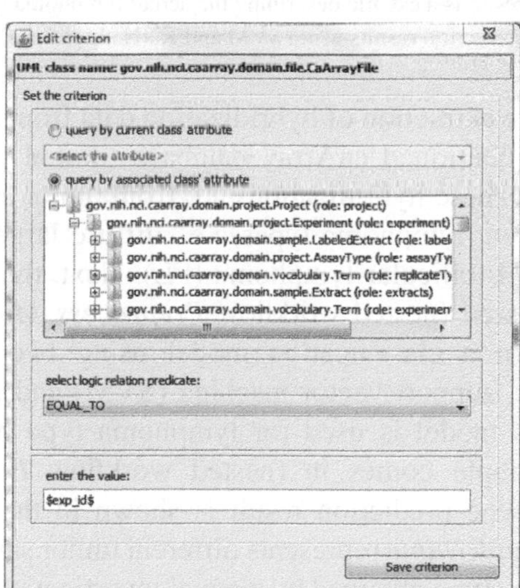


**Figure 7.9** CQL builder to construct CQL querying clause to caArray service. CQL Builder dialog provides a GUI to build a complex CQL clause querying data services. The Edit criterion dialog is used to build querying criteria in CQL.

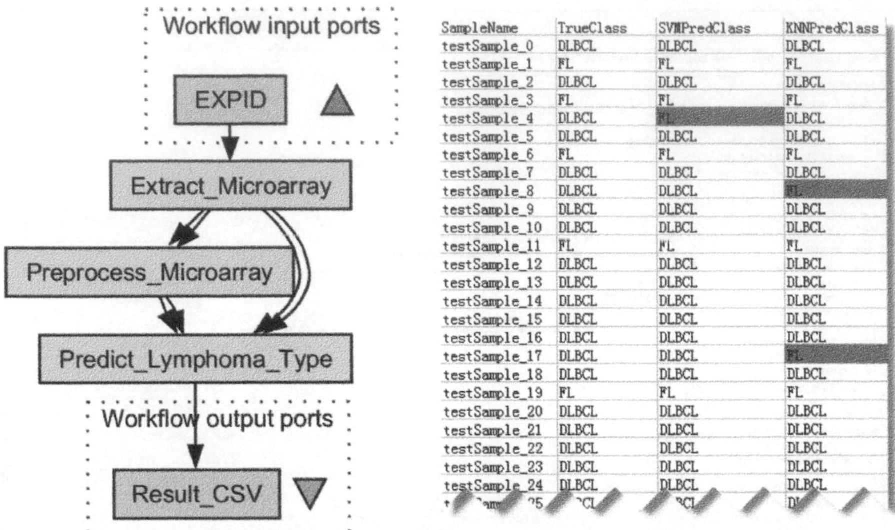


| SampleName | TrueClass | SVMPredClass | KNNPredClass |
|---|---|---|---|
| testSample_0 | DLBCL | DLBCL | DLBCL |
| testSample_1 | FL | FL | FL |
| testSample_2 | DLBCL | DLBCL | DLBCL |
| testSample_3 | FL | FL | FL |
| testSample_4 | DLBCL | FL | DLBCL |
| testSample_5 | DLBCL | DLBCL | DLBCL |
| testSample_6 | FL | FL | FL |
| testSample_7 | DLBCL | DLBCL | DLBCL |
| testSample_8 | DLBCL | DLBCL | FL |
| testSample_9 | DLBCL | DLBCL | DLBCL |
| testSample_10 | DLBCL | DLBCL | DLBCL |
| testSample_11 | FL | FL | FL |
| testSample_12 | DLBCL | DLBCL | DLBCL |
| testSample_13 | DLBCL | DLBCL | DLBCL |
| testSample_14 | DLBCL | DLBCL | DLBCL |
| testSample_15 | DLBCL | DLBCL | DLBCL |
| testSample_16 | DLBCL | DLBCL | DLBCL |
| testSample_17 | DLBCL | DLBCL | FL |
| testSample_18 | DLBCL | DLBCL | DLBCL |
| testSample_19 | FL | FL | FL |
| testSample_20 | DLBCL | DLBCL | DLBCL |
| testSample_21 | DLBCL | DLBCL | DLBCL |
| testSample_22 | DLBCL | DLBCL | DLBCL |
| testSample_23 | DLBCL | DLBCL | DLBCL |
| testSample_24 | DLBCL | DLBCL | DLBCL |

**Figure 7.10** Lymphoma type prediction workflow and the result. Microarray data are extracted from caArray, preprocessed, and used to learn a model for lymphoma type prediction. The result is a csv file describing the actual lymphoma type of each tumor sample and the prediction results using SVM and KNN algorithms, respectively.

starts with the extraction of hybridization data from a given experiment in the aforementioned caArray database (nested workflow *Extract_Microarray*).These hybridizations are from tumor samples that belong to two different lymphoma types, i.e., diffuse large B-cell lymphoma (DLBCL) and follicular lymphoma (FL). Next, the hybridization data are preprocessed (nested workflow *Preprocess_Microarray*) and then used to learn a classification model using two machine learning methods, i.e., support vector machine (SVM) and *K*-nearest neighbor (KNN). This model is used for lymphoma type prediction when an unknown sample comes in (nested workflow *Predict_Lymphoma_Type*). The type prediction result is shown in the right part of Figure 7.10. *SampleName* represents different tumor samples; *TrueClass* is the lymphoma type obtained by manual investigation (and is considered to be accurate); and *SVMPredClass* and *KNNPredClass* represent the types predicted by SVM and KNN, respectively. Prediction errors are highlighted. While Figure 7.10 shows the skeleton of the lymphoma workflow by condensing the nested workflows, Figure 7.11 gives a detailed view with nested workflows expanded.

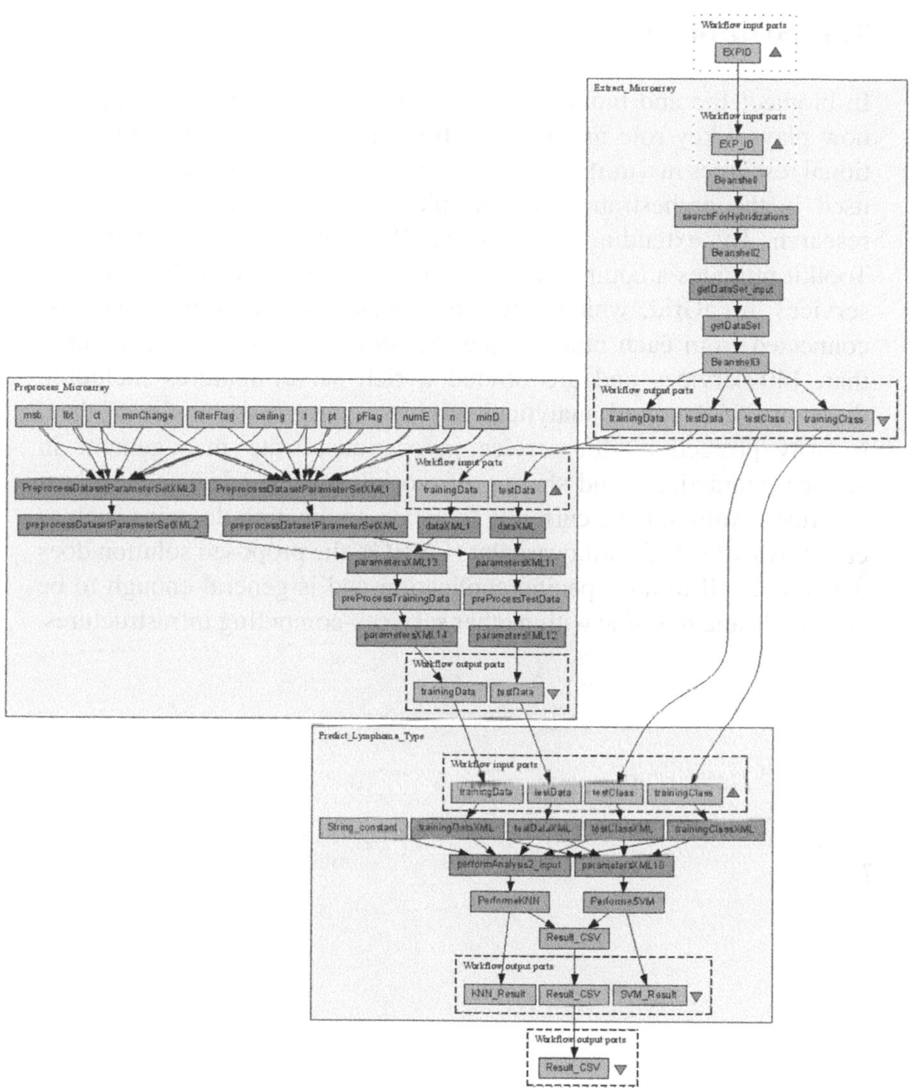


**Figure 7.11** The complete lymphoma type prediction workflow [198].

## 7.3 SUMMARY

In biomedicine and bioinformatics, services computing infrastructure now plays a key role in the integration of various data and computational resources in a uniform manner. Workflow technologies are widely used in the orchestration of multiple services to facilitate *in-silico* research. By extending the Taverna Workbench, caGrid Workflow Toolkit provides a comprehensive solution to compose and coordinate services in caGrid, which would otherwise remain isolated and disconnected from each other. Using the toolkit, users can access more than 140 services and are offered a rich set of features including discovery of data and analytical services, query and transfer of data, security protections for service invocations, state management in service interactions, and sharing of workflows, experiences, and best practices. Although we currently focus on application domains such as cancer (caBIG) and cardiovascular (CVRG), the proposed solution does not limit itself to any specific application and is general enough to be applicable and reusable within other services-computing infrastructures.

CHAPTER 8

# Network Analysis and Reuse of Scientific Workflows

In Chapter 7, we have discussed how Web services and scientific workflows can integrate heterogeneous resources, streamline data processing, and eventually foster the Web-scale collaboration. Given the software tools (caGrid Workflow Toolkit, for example) facilitating services access and workflow composition, however, scientists still hesitate to exploit the existing services/workflows. One major reason is that usually they are unaware of the existence of them, not to mention how to reuse the best practices [187]. As a consequence, scientists are not able to effectively incorporate the best practices and tailor them when they need to build a workflow for their own experiments.

One solution to this challenge is to introduce the social network (SN) concept into scientific workflows. This chapter addresses the issue of network analysis and reuse of scientific workflows in a why–what–how approach.

*Why*. First, we review the advances in the social network technology and its impact on science. Through a survey on social network services (SNSs) for scientists, we find that social networks not only

*Business and Scientific Workflows: A Web Service-Oriented Approach*, First Edition.
Edited by Wei Tan and MengChu Zhou.

have changed the way through which people communicate but also can promote collaboration in a scientific community.

*What*. We then present a network analysis on myExperiment [199], an online biological workflow repository. By examining the relationship between workflows and services, we reveal the current usage pattern of services in scientific workflows, and how can this knowledge be extracted to facilitate and promote their reuse.

*How*. Based on a network-based model called ServiceMap, we aim to provide a global positioning system (GPS)-like support to: (1) help domain scientists better understand various usage patterns of the existing services; and (2) provide a system-level support to recommend possible service compositions.

The dataset and experiment used in this chapter are from myExperiment, but the principles and methods employed are equally applicable to other service-based workflow systems.

## 8.1 SOCIAL COMPUTING MEETS SCIENTIFIC WORKFLOW

Social computing is about using computational systems to support social behavior. Its emergence can be seen as a joint force of technology and social changes. Social network services (SNSs) [200], as a popular form of social computing, has profoundly changed the way through which people communicate and share interest. Online SNSs, such as Google+, Twitter, Facebook, and LinkedIn, have all provided innovative and pervasive means to connect people across various borders. These stories make both business and scientific communities regard the social network (SN) as a means to further improve their computing infrastructure.

Advances in social network techniques have gained momentum to impact the major Internet-based computing paradigms, including the widely adopted services computing. Currently, social networks connects people or groups who expose similar interests or features. In services computing, a social network can connect not only people and organizations but also other entities such as software components, Web-based services, data resources, and workflows. More importantly, it can record, trace, and visualize the interactions among people and nonhuman artifacts. By this means, people can accumulate the *wisdom of crowds* [201] and summarize them into best practices. For example, users can identify trusted service providers or partners to share resources by examining the interaction patterns among Web services, users, and providers. myExperiment is such a social network encouraging the sharing of bioinformatics Web services and processes, and eventually inspiring collaborative scientific exploration. We will look into myExperiment in more detail later in this section.

Social networks and services computing are both hot topics in the broad scope of Internet computing. Researchers and technologists have started to put attention on combining the power of both. In this section, we first survey the existing social network services for scientists, and then review the research work in this area.

## 8.1.1 Social Network Services for Scientists

The success of Facebook and LinkedIn demonstrates that the power of the Web can not only foster but also capitalize on a personal network. SNSs, both for the general public and specifically for the scientific community, are changing scientists' communication and experimental practice, thanks to the enhanced interaction and collaboration capability brought by SNSs. This section surveys the existing SNSs that are currently used by scientists. We classify them by using two criteria: *level of generality* and *ability to execute*. In the level of generality dimension, we distinguish an SNS for *general* and *specific* purposes; in the ability to execute dimension, we distinguish *informative* and *executable* SNSs. An SNS is executable if one can run computation on it.

### *SNS of the General Purpose*

*Informative*. General-purpose SNSs such as Facebook and LinkedIn have been harnessed by the scientific community to cultivate communication and collaboration [202]. For example, major scientific associations such as the American Association for the Advancement of Science (AAAS) and the Institute of Electrical and Electronics Engineers (IEEE) have set up groups on both Facebook and LinkedIn. In these major community groups and many smaller ones, members can share research progress, search for jobs, and seek collaborations.

*Executable.* Besides these informative SNSs, many Web sites provide open and collaborative platforms to search executable Web services, and even to execute computation. This category includes

- *Seekda* (http://webservices.seekda.com/), a Web services search engine.
- *Yahoo Pipes* (http://pipes.yahoo.com/), a composition tool to build data mashups that aggregate Web feeds, Web pages, and other contents.
- *Amazon EC2* (http://aws.amazon.com/ec2/), Amazon Elastic Compute Cloud, a cloud computing service provided by Amazon. It allows users to rent virtual computers to run their own applications in a pay-as-you-go manner.

### SNS for the Research-Specific Purpose

*Informative.* There are various SNS sites for academia, for example, CiteULike (http://www.citeulike.org/), Connotea (http://www.connotea.org/), Microsoft Academic Search (http://academic.research.microsoft.com/), Arnetminer (http://arnetminer.org/), and Nature Network (http://network.nature.com/). These Web sites are based on author–publication–citation network and can be used to identify connections among authors, publications, and research topics. Nature Network also provides facilities such as blogs, forums, and groups.

There are also SNS sites for specific communities, such as life scientists (prometeonetwork, http://prometeonetwork.com/), doctors (doctors.net.uk, http://www.doctors.net.uk/), and physicians (sermo, http://www.sermo.com/; within3, https://www.within3.com/). These sites provide not only general SNS functionality such as news feed, e-mail, and forum but also community-specific ones such as online training, e-learning, and access to digital libraries. There are also SNS sites with an even narrower audience, such as EcoliWiki (http://ecoliwiki.net/) and WikiPathways (http://www.wikipathways.org/) to annotate bacteria and biological pathways, respectively.

*Informative–Executable.* Many sites go beyond just bringing people together. Instead, they enable researchers to share data and protocols. The protocols describe the methodologies to conduct experiments and obtain data. We put them into the *informative–executable* category because they reflect laboratory routines but are not executable by themselves. Web sites in this category include the following:

- Protocol repository for multiple disciplines, such as Protocol Exchange (http://www.nature.com/protocolexchange/) and Protocolpedia (http://www.protocolpedia.com/).
- Protocol repository for specific disciplines, such as iPlant (http://www.iplantcollaborative.org/) and OpenWetWare (http://openwetware.org/) for biology.

*Executable*. Some research-specific purpose SNSs are computation-oriented to a certain degree. In other words, they facilitate the sharing of executable computational components. The UK myGrid team has provided a suite of Web sites for various purposes, including[1] the following:

- *myExperiment* (http://www.myexperiment.org/). A curated registry of scientific workflows and associated research objects.
- *BioCatalogue* (http://www.myExperiment.org/). A curated registry of life science Web services.
- *MethodBox* (http://www.methodbox.org/). A site to share datasets, methods, and scripts.

Besides the myGrid family, Globus Online [203] is an online service that facilitates the moving of large quantities of data from one place to another, which is common in data-centric scientific computing; Galaxy [204] provides a Web server to share and execute workflows in life science; caGrid introduced in Chapter 7 offers a service-oriented Grid infrastructure and workflow toolkit for cancer research; and nanoHub [205] provides a nanotechnology research gateway hosting not only user groups and tutorials but also simulation tools.

A list of the aforementioned SNSs for scientists is shown in Figure 8.1. Each SNS is positioned based on its relative level of generality (the $x$-axis) and ability to execute (the $y$-axis).

[1] Find more details about myExperiment and family at the next bullet "myExperiment: an SNS for the Service-Oriented Science."

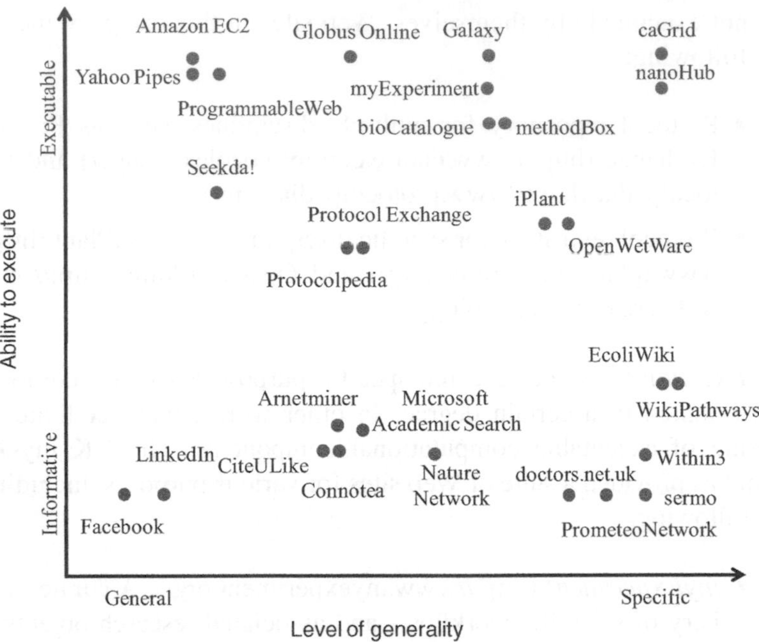


**Figure 8.1** SNS for scientists[2].

## *myExperiment: an SNS for the Service-Oriented Science*

myExperiment is a social Web site sharing scientific workflows and research objects that are closely related to them [206,207]. The project is directed by Professor David De Roure at the University of Oxford and Professor Carole Goble at the University of Manchester. The Web site was launched in 2007 and as of September, 2011 it had over 3000 members, 200 groups, 1000 workflows (from various workflow systems, mostly notably Taverna), 300 files, and 100 packs. myExperiment has a Representational State Transfer (REST) application programming interface (API) to access its publicly available dataset.

myExperiment can be considered as a *Facebook of scientists.* Instead of sharing status, news, and photos with friends, myExperiment

[2] Some online services included in this figure, for example, Amazon EC2, Globus Online, Galaxy, and caGrid, are arguably SNSs by themselves. However, we still list them here because they all provide an opencollaborative environment that is very close to an SNS and can rapidly evolve toward that direction.

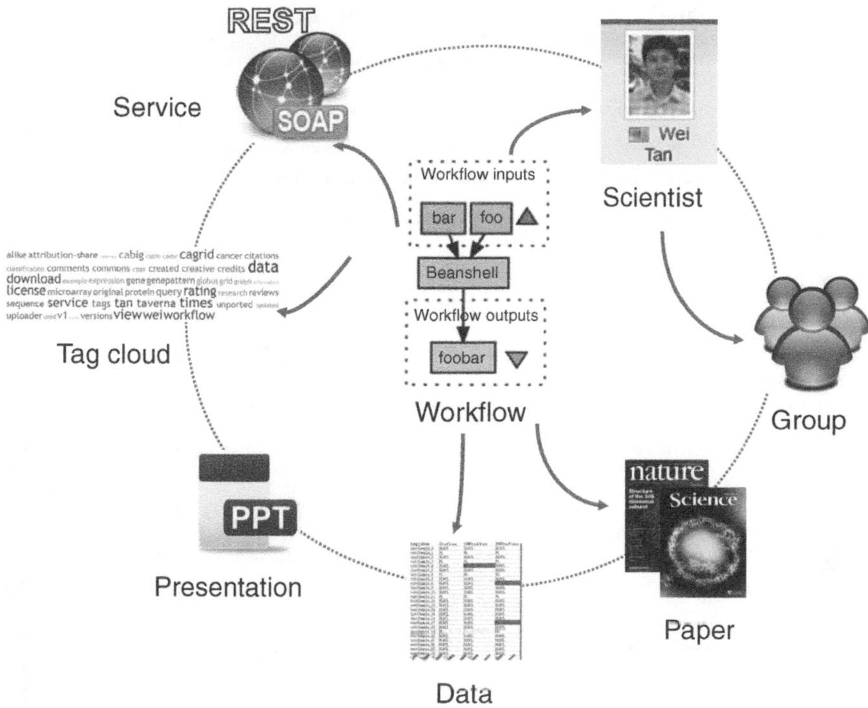


**Figure 8.2** Conceptual model of myExperiment social network.

users share scientific workflows and other research objects, such as ratings, metadata (e.g., tag cloud), data, and papers, with their professional network. Figure 8.2 shows the interactions among myExperiment research objects. *Workflows* are created and uploaded by *scientists* who belong to different *groups*. Workflows comprise Web *services*, annotated by a *tag cloud*, use *data*, and cite or cited by *papers/presentations*. Note that there exist other relations among objects, which we do not explicitly specify in the figure. For example, one scientist may share credit on a workflow, data item, or paper, with his/her peer scientist; while a paper may refer to a dataset. Figure 8.3 is an excerpt of a myExperiment Web page showing how the lymphoma type prediction workflow, introduced in Chapter 7, correlates with tag cloud, input and output data, citations, author's social network, and so on.

Being a part of the myGrid project in the United Kingdom, myExperiment has two sister projects, that is, BioCatalogue and

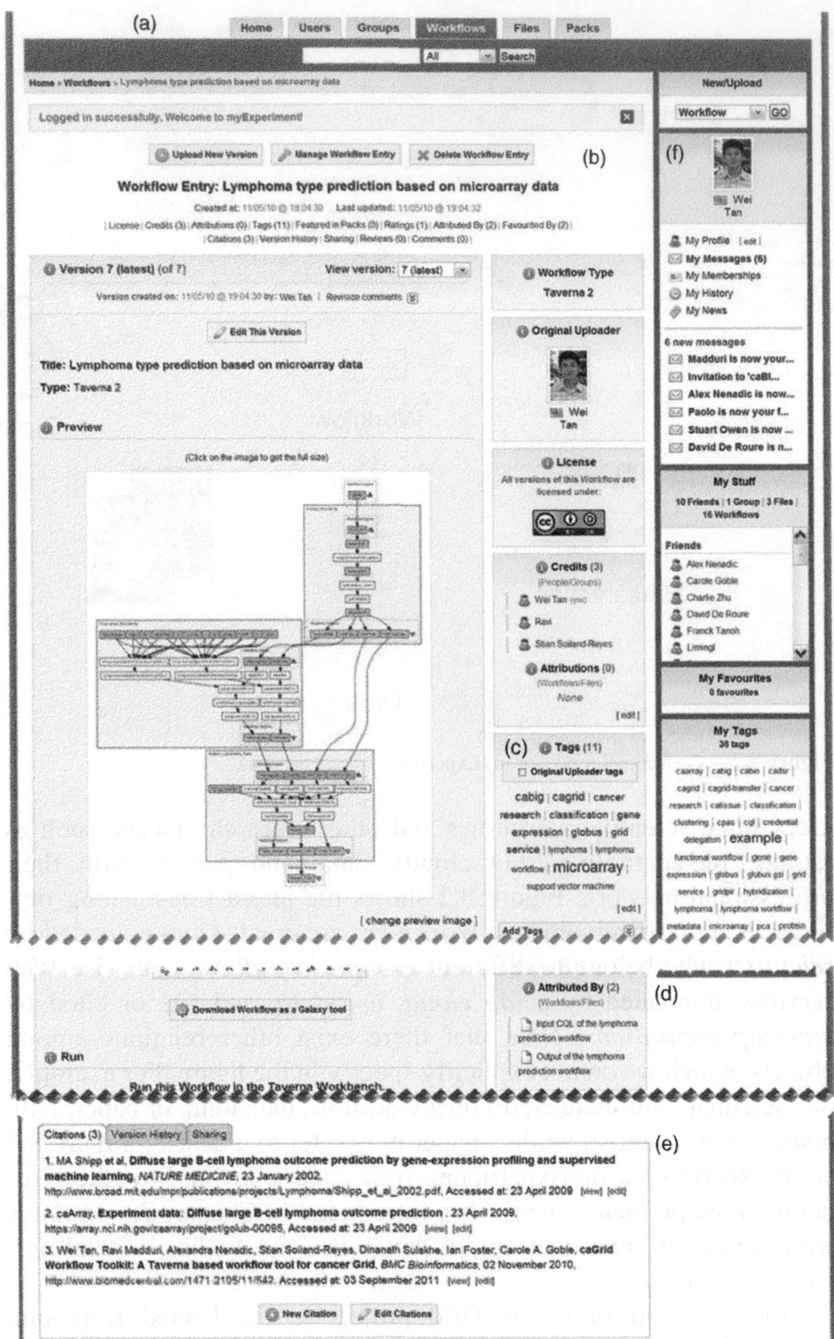
(a)
Home
Users
Groups
Workflows
Files
Packs
All
Search
Home » Workflows » Lymphoma type prediction based on microarray data
Logged in successfully, Welcome to myExperiment!
Upload New Version
Manage Workflow Entry
Delete Workflow Entry
(b)
Workflow Entry: Lymphoma type prediction based on microarray data
Created at: 11/05/10 @ 19:04:30 Last updated: 11/05/10 @ 19:04:32
| License | Credits (3) | Attributions (0) | Tags (11) | Featured in Packs (0) | Ratings (1) | Attributed By (2) | Favourited By (2) |
| Citations (3) | Version History | Sharing | Reviews (0) | Comments (0) |
Version 7 (latest) (of 7)
View version: 7 (latest)
Version created on: 11/05/10 @ 19:04:30 by: Wei Tan | Revision comments
Edit This Version
Title: Lymphoma type prediction based on microarray data
Type: Taverna 2
Preview
(Click on the image to get the full size)
[ change preview image ]
Download Workflow as a Galaxy tool
Run
Run this Workflow in the Taverna Workbench...
Workflow Type
Taverna 2
Original Uploader
Wei Tan
License
All versions of this Workflow are licensed under:
Credits (3)
(People/Groups)
Wei Tan (you)
Ravi
Stan Soiland-Reyes
Attributions (0)
(Workflows/Files)
None
[ edit ]
(c)
Tags (11)
Original Uploader tags
cabig | cagrid | cancer research | classification | gene expression | globus | grid service | lymphoma | lymphoma workflow | microarray | support vector machine
[ edit ]
Add Tags
Attributed By (2)
(Workflows/Files)
Input CQL of the lymphoma prediction workflow
Output of the lymphoma prediction workflow
(d)
New/Upload
Workflow
GO
(f)
Wei Tan
My Profile [ edit ]
My Messages (6)
My Memberships
My History
My News
6 new messages
Madduri is now your...
Invitation to 'caBI...
Alex Nenadic is now...
Paolo is now your f...
Stuart Owen is now ...
David De Roure is n...
My Stuff
10 Friends | 1 Group | 3 Files | 16 Workflows
Friends
Alex Nenadic
Carole Goble
Charlie Zhu
David De Roure
Franck Tanoh
Limingl
My Favourites
0 favourites
My Tags
36 tags
caarray | cabig | cabio | cadsr | cagrid | cagrid-transfer | cancer research | catissue | classification | clustering | cpas | cql | credential delegation | example | functional workflow | gene | gene expression | globus | globus gsi | grid service | gridpir | hybridization | lymphoma | lymphoma workflow | metadata | microarray | pca | protein
Citations (3)
Version History
Sharing
(e)
1. MA Shipp et al, Diffuse large B-cell lymphoma outcome prediction by gene-expression profiling and supervised machine learning, NATURE MEDICINE, 23 January 2002, http://www.broad.mit.edu/mpr/publications/projects/Lymphoma/Shipp_et_al_2002.pdf, Accessed at: 23 April 2009 [view] [edit]
2. caArray, Experiment data: Diffuse large B-cell lymphoma outcome prediction , 23 April 2009, https://array.nci.nih.gov/caarray/project/golub-00095, Accessed at: 23 April 2009 [view] [edit]
3. Wei Tan, Ravi Madduri, Alexandra Nenadic, Stan Soiland-Reyes, Dinanath Sulakhe, Ian Foster, Carole A. Goble, caGrid Workflow Toolkit: A Taverna based workflow tool for cancer Grid, BMC Bioinformatics, 02 November 2010, http://www.biomedcentral.com/1471-2105/11/542, Accessed at: 03 September 2011 [view] [edit]
New Citation
Edit Citations

MethodBox. BioCatalogue is a curated registry of life science Web services. It provides various annotations on services (input and output data, user defined tags, etc.) and continuously monitors their availability and reliability. MethodBox is a social network site to share datasets, methods, and scripts. The three projects, being complementary to one another, offer a collaborative environment where scientists can publish and share their knowledge.

### 8.1.2 Related Research Work

#### *Mining Software Repositories in Software Engineering*

Nowadays there are many open-source software projects that maintain their code and artifact repositories in Web sites such as Apache (www.apache.org), GitHub (github.com), Google Code (code.google.com), and SourceForge (sourceforge.net). These repositories contain not only the source code of a software but also its historical changes (i.e., versioning), bugs/issues, documentation, mailing lists, and people interaction embedded in aforementioned artifacts. Using data mining methods [208] such as association rule mining, clustering, classification, and network analysis, many tedious software engineering tasks can be partially or fully automated (Figure 8.4). These tasks include the following [209,210]:

- *API Suggestion.* Based on the frequent API sequence mined from repositories, we can suggest the next API to use during coding.
- *Duplicate Bug Identification.* Based on the text clustering results, we can identify duplicate bugs in the issue tracking system.
- *New Task/Issue Assignment.* Based on the history of task fulfillment and classification results, we can assign a programmer with required expertise to take a new task.

---

**Figure 8.3** Excerpt of a myExperiment workflow Web page (http://www.myexperiment.org/workflows/746.html) showing (a) various research objects; (b) a lymphoma type prediction workflow and its component services; (c) tags on this workflow; (d) other objects related to this workflow (the sample input and output files, in this case); (e) citations of this workflow; and (f) the user's profile and social network (messages, groups, friends, etc.).

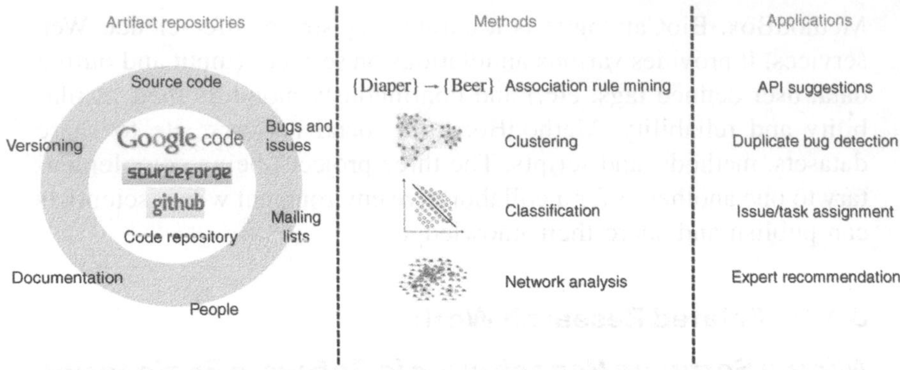


**Figure 8.4** Mining software repositories.

- *Expert Recommendation.* Based on people communication records, we can recommend a person with certain expertise and within a requestor's social network.

CodeBook, a project from Microsoft Research, builds a social network-oriented platform over code [211]. The CodeBook social network maintains a directed graph connecting programmers to reusable work artifacts such as work item, source code, files, and test results. Within the directed graph, a regular language reachability algorithm is devised such that Codebook can answer queries involving transitive connections.

## Process Mining and Social Software in Workflow Management

Process mining [212], originally proposed by Professor Wil M. P. van der Aalst, is a technique combining business process management (BPM) and knowledge discovery. Its major aim is to extract knowledge from event logs recorded by an enterprise information system. The knowledge to extract includes the underlying process structure that generates the events, and the data and social structures associated with it. More recently, Professor Aalst has proposed a framework named TomTom4BPM [213,214] that adopts process mining technique for various purposes, such as comparing the actual process execution with premodeled ones and dynamically navigating during process exceptions. There are some studies related to process mining, such as deriving patterns from past usage data to predict the most likely next step in building visualization pipelines [215], and case-based reasoning in finding a similar workflow and using it to suggest the next component to be included in a workflow [216].

The interplay of social software and BPM is receiving more attention [217–219]. Different from a pure, traditional software system, the BPM system is more human-centric and involves much collaboration. Therefore, it is natural that BPM can leverage the power of social software for various purposes such as personal networking, cross-task information sharing, and intra-workflow collaboration.

### *Social Network and Services Computing*

Maamar et al. [220,221] point out that Web service-based SOA falls short of its potential because it does not incorporate the interaction with peer services or users, ignores the past usage and can neither self-evolve nor self-organize. They also argue that weaving social network elements into Web services can stimulate the collaboration, competition, and substitution of services, and eventually foster a better service ecosystem. myExperiment and BioCatalogue, as mentioned in Chapter 7 and earlier in this chapter, are also examples that combine a social network with services computing. In the following two sections of this chapter, we will discuss how we analyze the service network in myExperiment, derive its metrics, and use them to assist service composition.

## 8.2 NETWORK ANALYSIS OF MYEXPERIMENT

### 8.2.1 Network Model at a Glance

We downloaded myExperiment workflows via its REST API on August 23, 2010. We analyzed the structure of each Taverna workflow serialized in an XML-based format. We found that (a) 347 of the workflows contained at least one Web service and (b) altogether there were 241 unique services. Because our goal was to identify the current usage pattern of services in workflows, we focused on these 347 workflows and 241 services.

Figure 8.5 illustrates the overall approach of this network analysis. After downloading the myExperiment workflows, we abstract them by

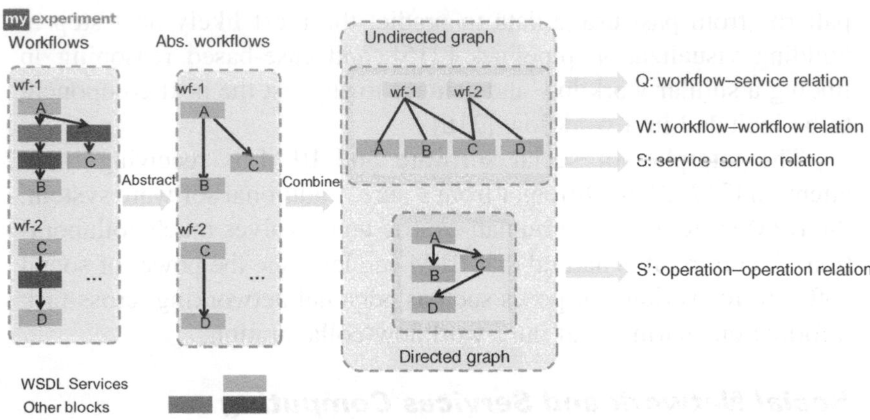


**Figure 8.5** The network analysis of the myExperiment workflows.

removing non-Web (i.e., WSDL based) services, such as local beanshells and XML manipulating blocks, while maintaining the data flows between services. Afterwards, these abstract workflows are combined into two disjoint networks (graphs): an undirected *workflow–service network* and a directed *operation network*. In the former, nodes are either workflows or services and edges represent the inclusive relations between them, that is, a workflow $i$ is connected to a service $j$ if $i$ consists of $j$. In the latter, nodes are operations in services, and a directed edge represents a data link between two operations in some workflow. More details regarding the myExperiment workflow set, how networks are built and analyzed can be found in [222].

From the workflow–service network, we derive two additional networks: a *workflow–workflow network* in which two workflows are connected if they comprise services in common and a *service–service network* in which two services are connected if they appear in some workflow together. We use Pajek [223], a widely used social network analysis tool, to produce all the three graphs. Table 8.1 summarizes the metrics of the myExperiment dataset and we will further explain them later.

## 8.2.2 Undirected Network

We parse the myExperiment workflows to create the workflow–service relation $Q$, formalized as an $m \times n$ matrix, where $m$ is the number of

**Table 8.1** Overview of the myExperiment Workflow Dataset

| Metrics | Value |
|---|---|
| Taverna workflows with at least one Web service | 347 |
| Unique services | 241 |
| Operations | 283 |
| Average services per workflow | 2.05 |
| Average workflows per service | 2.96 |
| Average collaborators per service | 4.40 |
| The largest component of service–service network | 47% |

workflows, that is, $m = 347$, and $n$ is the number of services, that is, $n = 241$:

$Q = [q_{ij}]$, $0 \le i \le m$, $0 \le j \le n$, where

$q_{ij} = 1$ if workflow $i$ contains service $j$.

We derive two more relations, $W$ and $S$, from $Q$ as follows:

$W = Q \cdot Q^{\mathrm{T}} = [w_{ij}]$, $0 \le i, j \le m$, where

$w_{ij}$ = the number of services shared by workflows $i$ and $j$ and $w_{ii}$ = the number of services in workflow $i$; and

$S = Q^{\mathrm{T}} \cdot Q = [s_{ij}]$, $0 \le i, j \le n$, where

$s_{ij}$ = the number of workflows where both services $i$ and $j$ are invoked and $s_{ii}$ = the number of workflows where service $i$ is invoked.

### *Relation Q*

$Q$ represents the 347 workflows that contain services. In the visualization of $Q$ shown in Figure 8.6, diamonds represent workflows, circles represent services, and an edge between a diamond and a circle indicates that the workflow calls the service. We have performed the statistical analysis of $Q$, with the results summarized in Figure 8.7. Most workflows contain few services (more than 200 out of 347 workflows invoked only one service); and only a few workflows contain more than

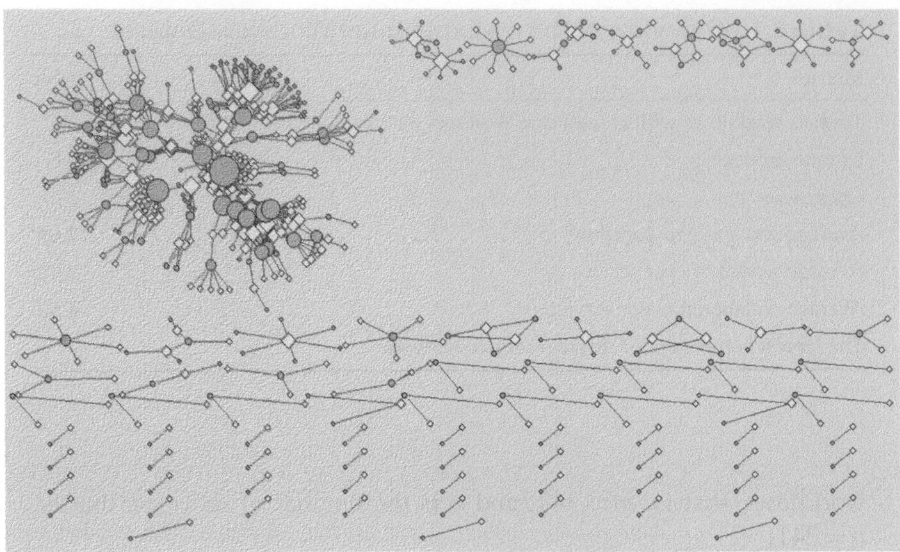

**Figure 8.6** Workflow–service relation $Q$ with degree centrality visualized.

five. On average, each workflow that we consider consumes 2.05 services. Meanwhile, most services participate in only a few workflows. Fifty percent of services participate in a single workflow only. There are a few utility services called by more than 10 workflows. On average, each service participates in 2.96 workflows.

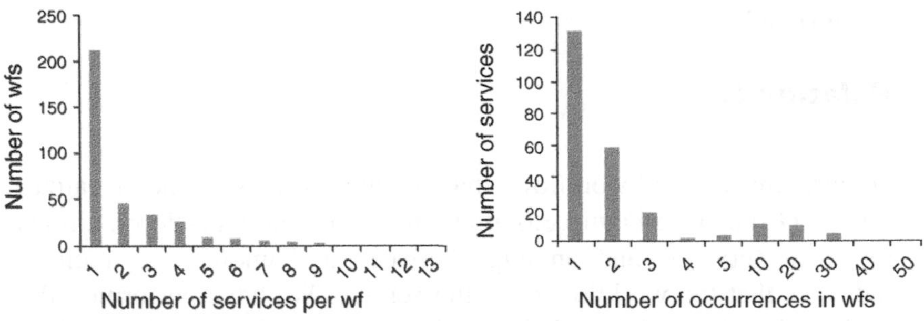


**Figure 8.7** Histogram of the number of services per workflow and the number of occurrences in workflows per service where wf stands for workflow.

From the dataset, we seek to identify (1) frequently used services and (2) workflows that invoke more services. We, therefore, configure Pajek such that node size represents its degree centrality or popularity—that is, the larger a node is, the more nodes it connects to. The larger circles in Figure 8.6 imply that more workflows use the services; the larger diamonds imply that the workflows use more services.

### Relation W

In the social network analysis, a *clique* [223] is a maximal complete subgraph of three or more nodes, all of which are directly connected to one another. It usually represents an interest group whose members tend to have more homogeneous opinions and share more common traits. In workflow–workflow relation *W*, two workflows (nodes) are connected if they invoke common services. Therefore, a clique in *W* refers to a group of workflows that invoke common services. In other words, the group of workflows comprising a clique may share some common goals or requirements.

Figure 8.8 is a visualization of *W* wherein each node represents a workflow, the node's size connotes the number of services used, and the thickness of an edge indicates the number of services shared by the

**Figure 8.8** Visualization of workflow–workflow relation W. The dense areas indicate cliques.

two workflows at both ends. We only show a workflow that at least shares one service with one peer workflow, to guarantee that there is no isolated node in Figure 8.8. The dense areas are cliques of workflows sharing common utility services. Overlapped cliques may also imply some common interests or goals.

### *Relation S*

A workflow may be viewed as a recipe documenting how services collaborate to fulfill a scientific experiment's requirement. Therefore, service–service relation *S* can be seen as a collaboration network among services—that is, services appearing in the same workflow collaborate with one another.

Figure 8.9 highlights the betweenness of the largest component of *S* while neglecting other parts that are disconnected to this component. In Figure 8.9, the size of a node is proportional to its betweenness centrality; an edge's thickness is proportional to the number of workflows that share the two services on its ends.

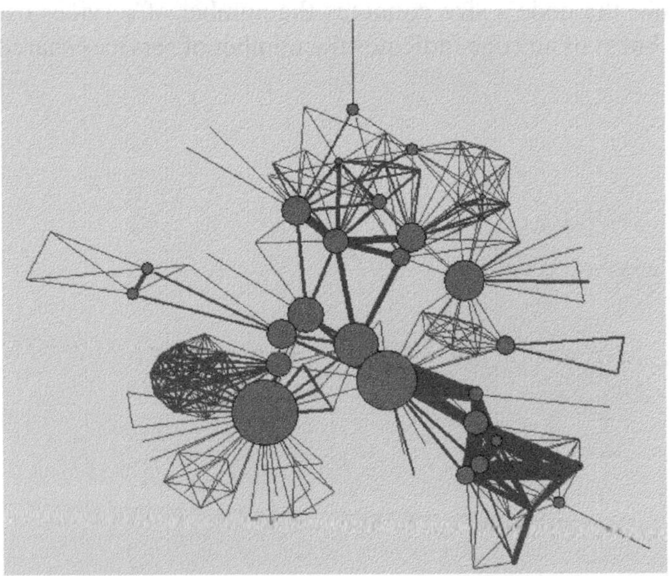

**Figure 8.9** The largest component of service–service relation *S* with betweenness centrality visualized.

In the social network analysis, a *component* is a set of network nodes connected by some relationship such that they are strongly connected. This largest component in relation *S* (which consists of 241 services) has 113 services and therefore covers 47% of all services. This indicates that many services in the myExperiment function individually rather than work together to form a linked research community.

In *S*, it is straightforward to see that a service with high degree centrality collaborates with more peer services in all workflows. The average degree centrality of a service in *S* is 4.4, which indicates that on average a service collaborates with 4.4 peers in myExperiment. Meanwhile, a service with high betweenness centrality as highlighted in Figure 8.9 indicates that service collaborations are more likely to go through it—that is, it has more control over the information flow between services.

### 8.2.3 Directed Graph

To study finer-grained collaboration among services in our dataset, we zoom in on *S* to the operation level. We derive a directed relation *S*′, as shown in Figure 8.10, by examining the invocation relations among

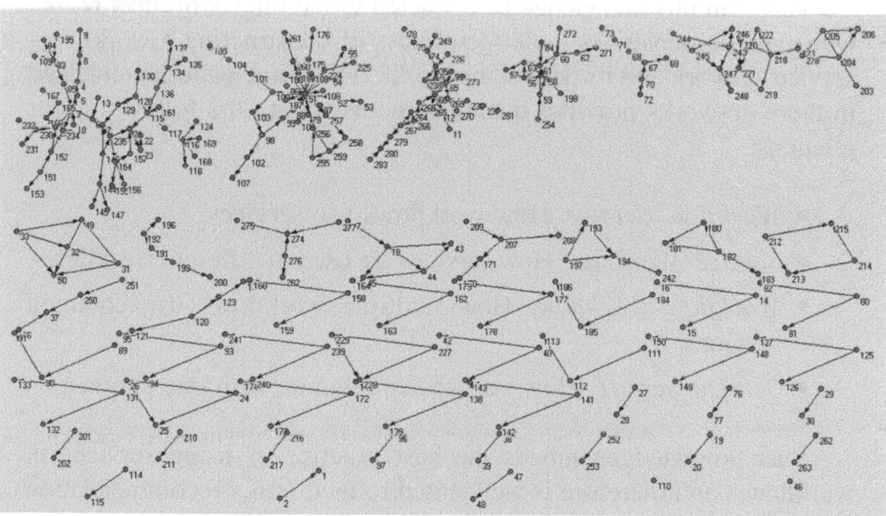

**Figure 8.10** Visualization of operations invocation network *S*′. Operations are grouped into weakly connected components called clusters.

283 operations in 241 services. Nodes are operations in services, and a directed edge represents a data link between two operations in some workflow.

Based on $S$ and $S'$, we can define two levels of collaboration among services. The collaboration relationship among services invoked in the same workflow in $S$ is *weak*. Compared to $S$, $S'$ contains the operation-level information of both intra- and inter-workflow invocation sequences. Thus, a *strong* collaboration relationship between two services implies a direct operation invocation between them in some workflow.

### 8.2.4 Summary of Findings

The network analysis of scientific workflows in the myExperiment repository reveals the current usage pattern of services in scientific workflows. It shows that the use of life science services is low in myExperiment workflows, and only a couple of utility services are frequently used in many workflows. Meanwhile, many services used in myExperiment workflows function individually without collaborating with each other. In summary, current service reuse in scientific workflows is unsatisfactory.

How can this knowledge be extracted to facilitate workflow reuse? Our work demonstrates the effectiveness of constructing a workflow–service network and its derived networks. The usage pattern embedded in these networks provides quantitative answers to the following four relations:

- *Workflow–Service*. How workflows use services.
- *Service–Workflow*. How services are used in different workflows.
- *Workflow–Workflow*. How multiple workflows use common services.
- *Service–Service*. How services collaborate with one another.

Such knowledge embeds the best practice of using services in workflows, and therefore is well suited to feed into a recommendation system to facilitate services-oriented workflow reuse. In the next section, we will discuss how to use the information, derived in this section, to provide map and GPS-like assistance to service composition.

## 8.3 SERVICEMAP: PROVIDING MAP AND GPS ASSISTING SERVICE COMPOSITION IN BIOINFORMATICS

The wide use of Web services and scientific workflows has enabled bioinformaticians to reuse experimental resources and streamline data processing in a Web-scale manner. This section presents a follow-up work of the network analysis on myExperiment as discussed in the previous one. The motivation comes from two common questions proposed by scientists: (1) Given the services that I plan to use, what are other services usually used together with them? and (2) Given two or more services I plan to use together, can I find an operation chain to connect them based on others' past usage? Aiming to provide a system-level GPS-like support to answer the two questions, we present ServiceMap [224], a network model established to study the best practice of service use. We propose two approaches over the ServiceMap: association rule mining and relation-aware, cross-workflow searching. Our approaches are validated by the real-life data obtained from the myExperiment repository. Empirical statistics of the constructed service network are also reported.

### 8.3.1 Motivation

Our experience in the caBIG project has revealed two questions that domain scientists frequently ask when they try to exploit external Web services in building a scientific workflow:

> *Q1*: Given the services I plan to use, what are the other services often used together with them, by other scientists?
>
> *Q2*: Given two or more services I want to use together, can I find an operation chain, which is already used by others, to connect them?

Q1 is usually raised when scientists obtain some data or analytical capabilities wrapped and exposed as services. Since they are new to the services, they intend to know how their peer scientists use them together with other services of which they may or may not be aware. Besides, due to the explorative nature of scientific workflows, incorporating a newly found service with known ones may lead to new investigation ideas. For example, assume that scientists used to use a statistical analysis service with a microarray service, to find the significantly expressed genes in some tissue. However, they are unaware of a newly developed gene pathway service that is able to show interactions among genes. If they can be prompted that their peer scientists frequently use the pathway service together with the statistical one, they know that from the microarray data they already have, they can identify not only significant genes but also their interaction patterns.

Q2 is usually asked when a scientist's experimental procedure is too complex. In the microarray experiment mentioned in the last paragraph, scientists know that they need to obtain data out of a microarray service, analyze them in another statistic service, and then retrieve pathway information. However, such a procedure may be much more complex than its literal description: querying data, setting up connection, and downloading a large volume of data can take multiple steps; data need to be cleaned before shipping to the statistic service; access to the pathway service needs a special security mechanism, and so on. In this case, they want to know the exact sequence in which these service operations are chained together by others.

For the better understanding of Q1 and Q2, we also list two questions, that is, Q1′ and Q2′, which are frequently asked to a map or GPS system.

*Q1′*: What other places do people who visit these places also visit? and

*Q2′*: What is the best route between two places?

Questions Q1 and Q2 are clearly similar to Q1′ and Q2′, respectively. If we make an analogy between (1) service operations and places in a map, and (2) scientific workflows (or service compositions) and streets/routes in a map, we can easily conclude that the questions asked by scientists resemble those that can be solved by a map or GPS system (i.e., to recommend places to visit or find a route between two places). This analogy inspires us to take a further step from our previous network analysis of myExperiment by building a service network and associated facility to address Q1 and Q2, just like how a map/GPS system addresses Q1′ and Q2′ (Figure 8.11).

ServiceMap

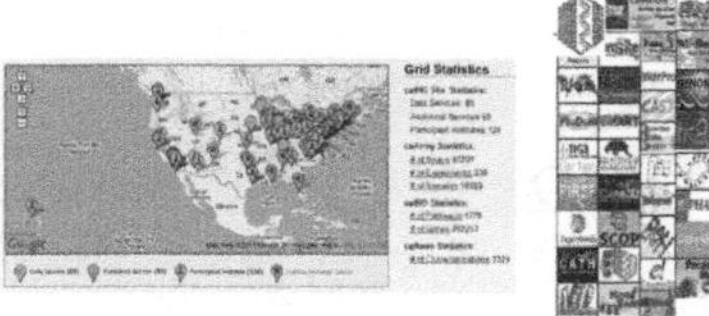

Map and GPS systems

*Q1*: what other services do people who use these services also use?

*Q2*: what is an operation chain between two services/operations?

*Q1'*: what other places do people who visit these places also visit?

*Q2'*: what is a route between two places?

**Figure 8.11** The analogy between ServiceMap and Map/GPS systems.

## 8.3.2 ServiceMap Approach

As mentioned earlier, Q1 and Q2 are not isolated but raised in different stages in an *in-silico* experiment. Q1 is usually raised when an experiment is at its conceptual level, and scientists need to figure out the available resources to leverage. Q2 is raised in a later stage when the routine of an experiment needs to be concretized at the operational level. It is also a common practice to iterate over these two stages due to the explorative nature of bioinformatics experiments. Inspired by this requirement from multiple user communities including caBIG, we present ServiceMap as a framework to address both Q1 and Q2, in a holistic manner.

As illustrated in Figure 8.12 , ServiceMap leverages the two disjoint networks, that is, an undirected *workflow–service network* and a directed *operation network*, both derived in the network analysis as shown in Section 8.2.

In the undirected workflow–service network, nodes are either workflows or services, and edges represent the inclusive relations between them. In the directed operation network, nodes are operations in services, and a directed edge represents a data link between two operations in some workflow. While Section 8.2 focuses on how to build and calculate the metrics of these networks, ServiceMap focuses on algorithms on these networks to answer Q1 and Q2. A brief summary of these algorithms is as follows. To answer Q1, we derive the frequent item sets and association rules in the workflow–service network, and recommend relevant services in a given context, that is, existing services in a

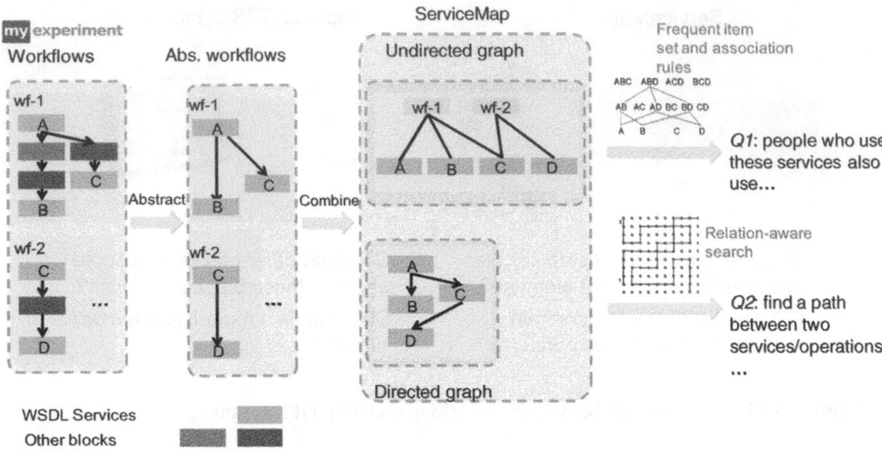


**Figure 8.12** A ServiceMap approach.

workflow. To answer Q2, we propose a relation-aware, cross-workflow search method to identify an operation chain that connects two services and is composed by fragments from individual workflows.

### 8.3.3 What Do People Who Use These Services Also Use?

Here we present the ServiceMap approach to address Q1: *What do people who use these services also use?*

We adopt the well-known association rule mining method to formulate and solve this problem. Here, we only highlight the skeleton of our approach. More details regarding association rule mining can be found in [208]. We use an open-source data-mining tool Weka [225] to calculate frequent item sets and association rules.

**Step 1: Treat Services as *Items*.**

$S = \{s_1, s_2, \ldots, s_m\}$ is the set of services in all myExperiment workflows $W$ (to be defined later).

**Step 2: Treat Workflows as *Transactions*.**

$W = \{w_1, w_2, \ldots, w_n\}$ is the set of workflows in myExperiment. Each workflow consists of a subset of services from $S$.

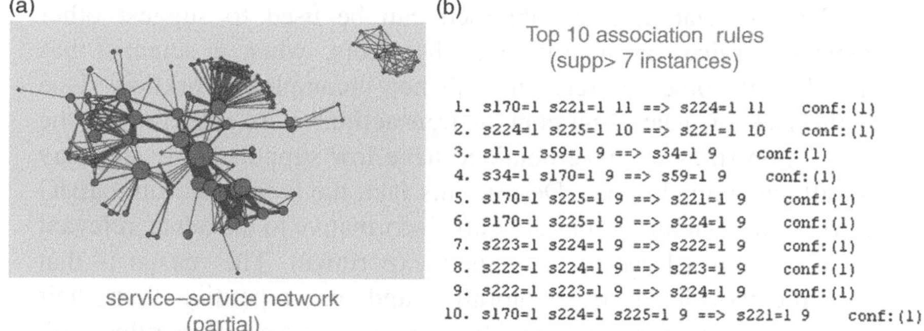

(a)
service–service network
(partial)
(b)
Top 10 association rules
(supp> 7 instances)
1. s170=1 s221=1 11 ==> s224=1 11 conf:(1)
2. s224=1 s225=1 10 ==> s221=1 10 conf:(1)
3. s11=1 s59=1 9 ==> s34=1 9 conf:(1)
4. s34=1 s170=1 9 ==> s59=1 9 conf:(1)
5. s170=1 s225=1 9 ==> s221=1 9 conf:(1)
6. s170=1 s225=1 9 ==> s224=1 9 conf:(1)
7. s223=1 s224=1 9 ==> s222=1 9 conf:(1)
8. s222=1 s224=1 9 ==> s223=1 9 conf:(1)
9. s222=1 s223=1 9 ==> s224=1 9 conf:(1)
10. s170=1 s224=1 s225=1 9 ==> s221=1 9 conf:(1)


**Figure 8.13** Services frequently used together and the association rules.

### Step 3: Calculate Frequent Item Sets.

Since the number of transactions ($n = 347$) is relatively small in the context of 241 items, we do not have any large frequent set. The maximum support for any item set $X \subseteq S$ and $|X| \geq 2$ is only 5.5% (i.e., 19 transactions).

### Step 4: Calculate Association Rules.

This step is to find the set of all association rules, each in the form of $X \Rightarrow Y$, $X, Y \subseteq S$, $X \cap Y = \varnothing$, such that both supp($X$) and conf $(X \Rightarrow Y) = \frac{\text{supp}(X \cup Y)}{\text{supp}(X)}$ are significant enough.

Figure 8.13a illustrates a portion of the service–service network. Nodes are services and an edge between them means that they are used together in one workflow. Node size represents how many workflows in which this service appears and edge width represents how many workflows in which these two services appear together. It gives an intuitive view of which services are used together frequently. Figure 8.13b illustrates the 10 association rules with the highest confidence value and has more than seven supporting workflows. See the first line as an example.

$$1.\, s170 = 1\, s221 - 111 \Rightarrow s224 = 1\, 11\, \text{conf} : (1)$$

This line indicates that when services *s170* and *s221* show up together in a workflow, *s224* will show up for sure (with confidence value 1). There are 11 supporting transactions (workflows).

The association rules obtained can be used to suggest other relevant services frequently used by peers, when a scientist has already put some services into his/her incomplete workflow. Due to the lack of a large number of transactions (i.e., workflows), the association rules we have obtained have low support value and may not all make much sense. Despite this fact, the feedback from caBIG users shows that these rules are quite informative to introduce relevant services from a large set into their experiment. The reason is that scientific workflows are explorative and less repetitive than their business counterpart, and therefore even the association rules with low support are noteworthy. Some users have told us that they are enthusiastic of the services recommended to them, in terms of generating innovative data and unexpected results.

### 8.3.4 What is an Operation Chain Between Services/Operations

Now we present the ServiceMap approach to address Q2: *Given two or more services I want to use together, what is a path between them?*

Current scientific artifact repositories such as BioCatalogue [172] and myExperiment typically adopt keyword-based search. The idea is to index an entity as a vector of keywords and use the TF–IDF (term frequency–inverse document frequency) algorithm [226] to measure the weight of each keyword. Methods have recently been developed to search substructures in a tree- or graph-like structure [227] or over nested workflows [228]. These approaches suffer from two limitations. First, each result comes from a single document. For example, two workflows cannot be concatenated as a result, even by doing that you can chain two services. Second, sequential relationships cannot be established between keywords. For example, one can search for a workflow containing both services *foo* and *bar*, but cannot define the order of their appearance.

To answer Q2, we make use of the directed *operation network* $S'$ in which nodes represent operations in services, and a directed edge represents a data link between two operations in an abstract workflow. $S'$ can be seen as a directed map in which service operations are places, and workflows are routes connecting them.

### *Motivation for Relation-Aware and Cross-Workflow Search*

We propose to use network $S'$ and explore a relation-aware and cross-workflow search technique. Before diving into details, let us take an example to explain how $S'$ supports such a search. A typical question in bioinformatics is that "Given a DNA sequence, can I first find similar ones from *WU-BLAST* and then compare them with those from *ClustalW2*?" Note that *WU-BLAST* and *ClustalW2* are two popular sequence alignment services. To answer this question, we can leverage the relation-aware search to find candidate workflows that start from some operation in *WU-BLAST* and end with some operation in *ClustalW2*. The question can be thus rewritten into the following query:

$$search\ workflow\ where\ WU\text{-}BLAST \rightarrow ClustalW2$$

It is quite likely that in the repository there is not a single workflow that contains an operation chain starting from *WU-BLAST* and ends at *ClustalW2*. In this case, the result should be a new workflow concatenating snippets from several existing ones. We use the largest cluster in $S'$ to demonstrate this idea. This cluster, which is in the top-left of Figure 8.10, is enlarged and shown in Figure 8.14 with the name of each node (i.e., operation) in it. Operations 116, 117, 168, and 169 belong to service *WU-BLAST*; 128 and 130 belong to service *ClustalW2*. Two paths <169, 116, 117, 119, 128, 130> and <168, 116, 117, 119, 128, 130> are two

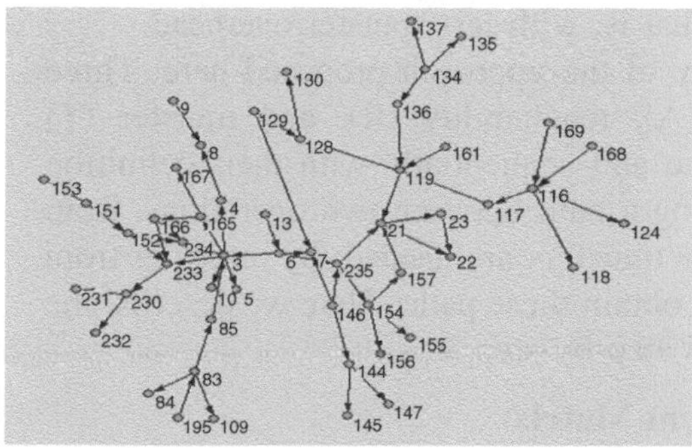

116 WSWUBlast.wsdl#runWUBlast
117 WSWUBlast.wsdl#getIds
119 WSDbfetch.wsdl#fetchBatch
128 WSClustalW2.wsdl#runClustalW2
130 WSClustalW2.wsdl#checkStatus
168 WSWUBlast.wsdl#getPrograms
169 WSWUBlast.wsdl#getDatabases

**Figure 8.14** Obtain a service chain between two operations.

candidate paths satisfying the search criterion. Based on the scientist-side context, for example, the DNA sequence at hand, the first candidate workflow will be suggested in which the data format matches operation 169's input. The resulting routine actually is a concatenation of three snippets, each of which is from a myExperiment workflow.

This example demonstrates that $S'$ allows us to discover global relations spread in multiple workflows and originally not easy to identify. Our experience working with caBIG community shows that this feature is quite useful for scientists to explore best practices from multiple colleagues and combine their experiment snippets into a more comprehensive one.

## *Method for Relation-Aware and Cross-Workflow Search*

Here we describe the method for the relation-aware and cross-workflow search. For simplicity Q2 is formulated as follows: given two operations $o_i$ and $o_j$, a set of workflows $W$ and the derived operation network $S'$, how to find a path in $S'$ that connects $o_i$ and $o_j$ and meets a certain criterion, for example, it should cross the least number of workflows.

The crossing-the-least-workflow criterion is reasonable because each time when two snippets from two workflows are to be concatenated, additional tuning such as data transformation and security enforcement are needed. Therefore, a path crossing fewer workflows is more desirable. Again, if we make this analogy that operations are stops in a public transportation system and a workflow is a bus/subway route connecting multiple stops, we prefer a path between two stops, which crosses fewer routes, that is, with less transfer overhead.

Figure 8.15 is a summary of the approach proposed here. Three matrices, that is, adjacent (A), reachability (R), and transfer (T) matrices are calculated offline and sequentially with their definition to be given later. When finding a path between two operations, from matrix $T$, we know how many transfers are needed; by referring from matrix $T$ back to $R$ and $A$, we obtain these paths. Here we describe the method shown in Figure 8.15 step-by-step.

**Step 1: Calculate an Adjacent Matrix.**

$W = \{W_1, W_2, \ldots, W_n\}$ is the set of workflows we extract from myExperiment.

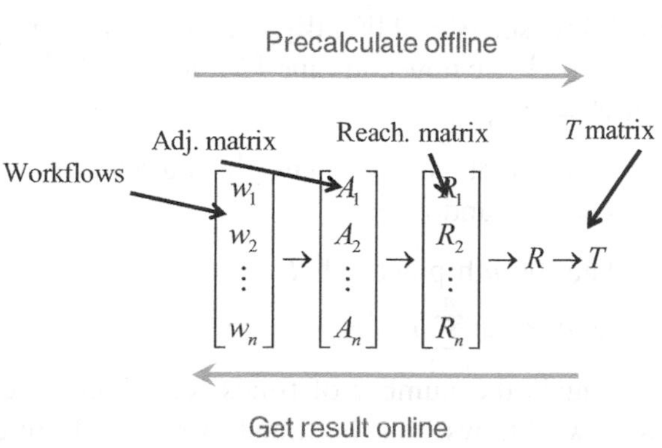


**Figure 8.15** Obtain the least transfer route between two operations.

$W_i = (O_i, E_i)$ in which $O_i$ is the set of (service) operations in $W_i$ and $E_i$ is the set of edges among these operations.

$A_i : O_i \times O_i \to \{0, 1\}$ is the *adjacent matrix* of $W_i$. That is, given $o_{ik}, o_{ij} \in O_i$, element $[k,j]$ of $A_i$ is defined as $A_{ikj} = 1$ if $o_{ik}$ has a link to $o_{ij}$ in $W_i$ and 0 otherwise.

$A_i$ can be directly obtained from $W_i$. Based on the adjacent matrix, we can derive the reachability matrix of each workflow.

**Step 2: Calculate a Reachability Matrix.**

$R_i : O_i \times O_i \to \{0, 1\}$ is the *reachability matrix* of $W_i$.

Given $o_{ik}, o_{ij} \in O_i$, element $[k,j]$ of $R_i$ is defined as $R_{ikj} = 1$ if $o_{ik}$ can reach $o_{ij}$ in $W_i$ and 0 otherwise.

$R_i$ cannot be directly obtained from $W_i$. Instead, it can be calculated from matrix $A_i^*$:

$A_i^* = A_i + A_i^2 + \cdots + A_i^{m_i-1}$ ($m_i$ is the dimension of $A_i$)

$$R_{ikj} = \begin{cases} 1 & \text{if } A_{ikj}^* > 0 \\ 0 & \text{otherwise} \end{cases}$$

$R_i$ represents the reachability relations between any two operations in $W_i$, and by aggregating them we can examine the reachability relations among operations in a global, cross-workflow perspective, that is, in $S'$.

Given the workflow set $W = \{W_1, W_2, \ldots, W_n\}$ and the operation set $O = \{o_1, o_2, \ldots, o_m\}$, we now combine $\{R_1, R_2, \ldots, R_n\}$ into an aggregated relation $R = [r_{ij}]_{m \times m}$:

$r_{ij} = \sum_k \{R_{kij} = 1\}$, that is, $r_{ij}$ equals the number of workflows in which $o_i$ can reach $o_j$, and $r_{ii} = 0$.

We then calculate the $n$th power of $R$:

$$R^n = \left[r_{ij}^n\right]_{m \times m} \text{ and } r_{ij}^n = \sum_{k=1}^{n} r_{ik}^{n-1} r_{kj}$$

Therefore, $r_{ij}^n$ equals the number of times for which $o_i$ can reach $o_j$ by traversing $n$ workflows, that is, transferring $n-1$ times. Now we know for each given operation pair, the existence of a directed chain that crosses a certain number of workflows and connects these two operations.

**Step 3: Calculate a Transfer Matrix.**

At the beginning of Section 8.3.4, we emphasize that we want a service chain *crossing the least workflows*, the way passengers want an itinerary crossing the least routes (i.e., with the least transfers). To achieve that goal, we need to introduce another transfer matrix $T$.

Given $m$ operations and $n$ workflows:

$T = [t_{ij}]_{m \times m} : t_{ij} = \{\min k \in \{1, 2, \ldots, n\} \text{s.t.} \, r_{ij}^k > 0\}$ if such $k$ exists, and 0 otherwise.

$T$ reveals the least transfer distance between two given operations. By definition, $t_{ij} - 1$ is the number of transfers through which $o_i$ can reach $o_j$. If $t_{ij} = 0$, there is no path between them crossing the available workflows.

**Step 4: Calculate Transfer Paths.**

If $t_{ij} = k \geq 2$, at least $k-1$ transfer is needed for any path from $o_i$ to $o_j$. The least transfer path spans over $k$ workflows that can be denoted $\{w_1, w_2, \ldots, w_k\}$. Then this path can be denoted $o_i \xrightarrow{w_1} o_{q_1} \xrightarrow{w_2} \cdots \xrightarrow{w_{k-1}} o_{q_{k-1}} \xrightarrow{w_k} o_j$ in which two adjacent operations

```
1  obtainLeastTransferPath(tMatrix, i, j){
2       pathList = null;
3       //i cannot reach j by any transfer
4       if(tij==0){
5           return null;
6       }
7       //i can reach j by a direct route,
8       //i.e., i can reach j in some workflow, return i->j
9       else if (tij==1){
10          return i->j;
11      }
12      //tij>=2, find a node k that can be directly reached by i
13      else{
14          forEach k s.t. (tik==1&&tkj==tij-1){
15              p = i->k;
16              newPathList = concatenatePaths(p,
17                          obtainLeastTransferPath(tMatrix, k, j));
18              forEach path in newPathList{
19                  pathList.add(path);
20              }
21          }
22          return pathList;
23      }
24 }
```

**Figure 8.16** Algorithm to obtain least transfer paths between two operations.

are in the same workflow, that is,

$$t_{iq_1} = t_{q_1q_2} \cdots = t_{q_{k-2}q_{k-1}} = t_{q_{k-1}j} = 1$$

Such a path (or paths) can be found by using the recursive algorithm shown in Figure 8.16.

*Line 1*: Given $T$ and $< o_i, o_j >$, find a service chain between $o_i$ and $o_j$ with the least transfer.

*Line 2*: Initiate the resulting path set to null.

*Lines 4–6*: $t_{ij} = 0$ means $i$ cannot reach $j$ by any transfer.

*Lines 9–11*: $t_{ij} = 1$ means $i$ can reach $j$ without any transfer; find the workflow in which $i$ can reach $j$, and obtain the service chain in it.

*Lines 13–21*: $t_{ij} \geq 2$ means $i$ can reach $j$ with at least one transfer; find an immediate node $k$ that $i$ can reach, and connect it with a least transfer path from $k$ to $j$.

*Line 24*: Return the resulting path list.

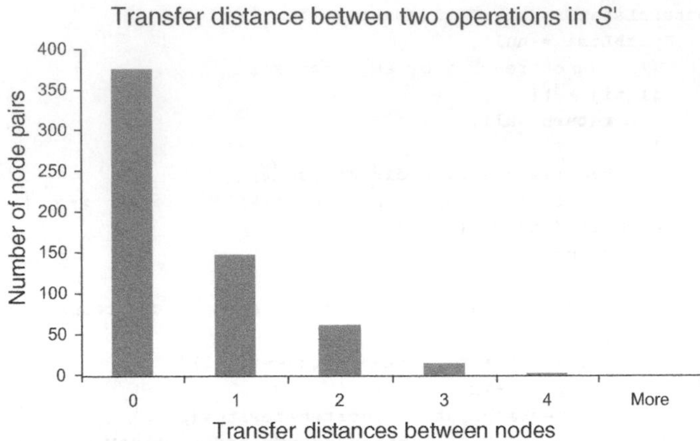


**Figure 8.17** Least transfer distance histogram of myExperiment workflows.

### 8.3.5 An Empirical Study

Given the matrix-based approach described in Section 8.3.4, we calculate the least transfer distances and transfer paths between any pair of service operations invoked in the same myExperiment workflow set obtained on August 23, 2010. As a reminder here, it contains 347 workflows, 241 services, and 283 operations. Figure 8.17 is the histogram showing the least transfer distances between any pair of nodes representing 283 operations in $S'$, that is, $283 \times 283 = 80{,}089$ node pairs. 375 pairs of operations can reach each other without any transfer, that is, they are connected within a single workflow. 147 operation pairs are reachable via 1 transfer; and 61 and 14 pairs are reachable via 2 and 3 transfers, respectively. Only 2 pairs of operations are reachable via 4 transfers; and there is no path with more than 4 transfers between any two operations.

In contrast to a public transportation system, the reachability among the operations is obviously sparse: only $375 + 147 + 61 + 14 + 2 = 599$ out of 80,089 operation pairs are reachable (about 0.75%); if two nodes are not reachable within 4 transfers, they are not reachable at all. The sparseness is due to two major reasons. First, bioinformatics services/operations cannot be arbitrarily connected because they have different usage scenarios by nature. Second, the services in the myExperiment workflows largely function individually rather than collaboratively, as discussed in Section 8.2.2. Although the myExperiment workflow set only illustrates a subset of the usage of the bioinformatics services, our experiment does reveal the necessity of increasing the reusability and collaboration among bioinformatics services.

## 8.4 SUMMARY

In this chapter, we have discussed the issue of the network analysis and reuse of scientific workflows in a why–what–how sequence.

*Why*. We have first reviewed the advances in social network technology and especially its impact on science. Through a survey on social network services for scientists, we find that a social network has not only changed the way through which people do personal networking and information sharing but also promoted collaboration in a scientific community to the next level.

*What*. We have then applied social network analysis methods to mine and analyze the myExperiment workflow repository, focusing on service usage patterns. The results indicate that services are currently reused in an *ad hoc* style instead of a federated manner. This observation suggests a need to help domain scientists dynamically locate related services and workflows and reuse successful processes to attain their research purposes.

*How*. Based on a network-based model, we have presented a ServiceMap framework, equipped with association rule mining and matrix-based search algorithms, to provide a GPS-like support for two types of service search queries: (1) Given a service I plan to use, what other services are usually used together? and (2) Given several services I want to use together, can I find an operation chain to connect them, based on others' past usage?

CHAPTER 9

# Future Perspectives

Recent years have witnessed the emergence, maturity, and wide application of service-oriented architecture (SOA). Meanwhile, building business and scientific workflows in SOA has become an important means for service reuse and process management. To fill the gap between the academic research and the real-life applications, we have discussed in this book several service composition methods and their applications in business, scientific, and medical service systems.

This book has provided a detailed discussion about why Web service and service-based workflow technologies are essential in both business and scientific domains. It has presented some fundamental methods such as Petri nets and social network analysis methods to advance the theory and applications of workflow design and Web service composition. It has also presented real applications of the developed theory and methods to such platforms as personalized healthcare and biomedical grids. With a perspective from both academia and industry, we hope that this book would provide insights to researchers and practitioners, and stimulates peers in this field to solve many more problems of their interest and concern.

On one hand, after more than one decade research and development, there are still many challenges to tackle while bringing the workflow technology and services computing together, especially in a rapidly evolving IT environment. On the other hand, the emergence of new computing paradigms, especially cloud computing and social computing, has shed some light on more collaborative, intelligent, and big-data-aware

*Business and Scientific Workflows: A Web Service-Oriented Approach*, First Edition.
Edited by Wei Tan and MengChu Zhou.

research and development. Here, we discuss a few open and exciting issues in this field.

## 9.1 WORKFLOWS IN HOSTING PLATFORMS

The success of cloud computing has put the SaaS (software as a service) model in the ascendant. SaaS is a software delivery model in which application and associated data are hosted on the cloud, and users access the software using a thin client such as a Web browser. Hosting workflow systems using SaaS has several advantages. First, like any other middleware, workflow management systems are complex to design, deploy, and manage; moreover, they need to scale out to cope with sudden workload surge. These features make it desirable to provision a workflow system in a SaaS manner.

Second, a benefit that is specific to workflow is that workflow-as-a-service can enable the sharing of best practices. Current approaches to service composition are generally used in isolated standalone applications. Developers cannot leverage any existing knowledge, and the experience they have gained through the composition practice is neither accumulated nor shared among people who undertake similar tasks. Think of this alternative: in a hosted workflow platform when users are to compose a new workflow, they can see similar workflows already completed and contributed by others. During composition, they can get context-aware assistance such as which services to use, in what sequence, and even whom to consult for questions.

Third, SaaS has been the model for many enterprise software packages/tools such as CRM and ERP, while the workflow technology is usually embedded in them. The trend to run workflows in hosting platforms such as cloud is also triggered by business process outsourcing (BPO) where the operations of specific business processes are outsourced to a third-party service provider. Nowadays, such workflow systems are provided by major vendors such as Amazon, Salesforce, and IBM.

We would like to envision the future of hosted workflow systems by making an analogy to Apple's App Store that is arguably the most successful business mode in IT industry nowadays. In App Store users browse and shop various applications, download and use them in devices such as iPhone and iPad. These applications when in use usually need to access cloud-hosted data (contents to be delivered to users, such as user profile, location information, and social media). In the envisioned hosted workflow system, when business consultants or engineers want to design a new business process, they go to an online marketplace (similar to App Store) to shop for services including atomic services and composite ones built through workflows. Instead of downloading applications to the client side, they compose these services and deploy the resulting workflow, both in a hosting environment. The hosted workflow engine will coordinate the execution of the workflow by invoking services in a predefined sequence and provide a management interface to the users. By this means, they can enjoy the advantages brought by the hosting environment, such as management simplicity, elasticity, and pay-per-use economy.

## 9.2 WORKFLOWS EMPOWERED BY SOCIAL COMPUTING

The proliferation of social network Web sites, such as Twitter, Facebook, and Wikipedia, has provided a great means to connect people who share interests and activities across various borders. These success stories make business and scientific communities regard a social network as a means for further improvement of their computing infrastructure. Advances in social-network techniques have gained the momentum to impact the major Internet-based computing paradigms including services computing. Currently, social networks connect people and groups who expose similar interests or features. In services computing, they can connect not only people and organizations, but also other artifacts such as software components, Web services, data, and workflows. More importantly, social networks can record, trace, and visualize complex relations among people and artifacts, as well as accumulate the wisdom of crowds, which has a profound technical and social impact. For example, by examining interaction patterns among services, users, and providers, one can identify trusted or reputable service providers or partners to share resources. ProgrammableWeb (http://www.programmableweb.com/) and myExperiment are two social network sites that share Web services and processes, in business and scientific domains, respectively. Some preliminary work has been done by leveraging social network analysis in services computing, as discussed in Chapter 8 as an example, and we expect more advances in this direction in the near future.

## 9.3 WORKFLOWS MEETING BIG DATA

There is a soaring quantity of information, also known as the data deluge, in business, government, and science. In business, Wal-mart transaction databases are estimated to contain more than 2.5 petabytes of data [229], growing at a fast pace with customer behavior and preferences, and market trends data. In the military, US Air Force drones collected around 24 years' worth of video footage over Afghanistan and Iraq in 2009, and the amount was supposed to be 30 times as many in 2011 [229]. In science, in 2010 the detectors at the Large Hadron Collider (LHC) facility at CERN produced 13 petabytes of data [75]. Moreover, sensor, social media, mobile, and location data are growing at an unprecedented speed. In parallel to their fast growth, data are also becoming increasingly semi-structured and diversified.

This astonishing growth and diversity in data have profoundly affected the way people process and make sense of them. How the workflow technology should evolve for accessing, assembling, analyzing, and acting upon big data remains a big challenge. At build-time, we need to investigate what needs to be changed in a workflow meta-model, to describe a workflow that gathers, organizes, and processes a large volume of data (structured, semi-structured, and unstructured). Data are going to be the first-class citizen in workflows. At run-time, a workflow engine needs to interact with the underlying computation infrastructure (cloud or on-premise clusters) and data processing mechanisms such as MapReduce [230]. The collaborative interplay among the three, that is, workflow, data, and computation infrastructure, is vital to enable the low-latency and high-throughput analytics on big data.

The novel applications of SOA to help build business, scientific, and medical workflows promise higher-level service reuse and better process management for research organizations and business enterprises. The area requires much work to be performed by not only academic researchers but also industrial developers and practitioners. This book has presented some of the recent research and development results that shall help move the application of SOA a step forward. It calls for more efforts into novel service composition methods and their applications in business, scientific, and medical services and software systems.

## 9.4 EMERGENCY WORKFLOW MANAGEMENT

Incidents, disasters, and catastrophes cause social disruptions to human life and significant damage to natural and technological systems [231]. The recent years have witnessed more and more of them including the very recent one, hurricane "Sandy" affecting the eastern America especially the states of New York and New Jersey. Therefore, emergency workflow management becomes increasingly important. Such workflows must be able to grow or shrink to cope with frequent changes of the course of actions dictated by unexpected incidents. This is totally different from traditional business and scientific workflows where once they are established, users just execute them repeatedly without the necessity of frequent modifications [232]. The need for making many *ad hoc* changes to emergency workflows calls for the on-the-fly verification of the correctness of the evolving workflows [233–235]. The second difference lies in the difference of users. The emergency workflow users are predominantly volunteer-based. In the event of a typical emergency, many volunteers are called on to respond to an incident. They may not have a good understanding of workflows, not to mention the underlying principles that are used to build them. Therefore, an emergency workflow must be designed in such an *intuitive* way that inexperienced responders are able to follow and use it [233]. Third, emergency workflows come with a high stake. When an incident occurs, people depend on them to minimize property damage and save as many lives as possible. Therefore, no defects are tolerable in them. The above-mentioned differences pose new challenges to the designers of such emergency workflows. The application of SOA should be a good way to help designers achieve the required flexibility and on-the-fly-verification capability for the correctness of the designed and varying workflows. Lightweight, easy-to-use, and formal methodologies are the most welcomed.

# Abbreviations List

| | |
|---|---|
| **AAAS** | American Association for the Advancement of Science |
| **AI** | Artificial intelligence |
| **Amazon EC2** | Amazon Elastic Compute Cloud |
| **AOP** | Aspect-oriented programming |
| **API** | Application programming interface |
| **BA** | Business analytics |
| **BME** | Binary mutual exclusion |
| **BPEL** | Business Process Execution Language |
| **BPI** | Business process improvement |
| **BPM** | Business process management |
| **BPMN** | Business Process Modeling Notation |
| **BPMS** | Business process management system |
| **BPO** | Business process outsourcing |
| **BPR** | Business process reengineering |
| **BRMS** | Business rule management system |
| **BSN** | Body sensor networks |
| **caBIG** | Cancer Biomedical Informatics Grid |
| **caGrid** | Cancer Grid |
| **CERN** | European Organization for Nuclear Research |
| **CERNET** | China Education and Research Network |
| **CNGI** | China Next Generation Internet |
| **CP** | Configuration process |
| **CPN** | Colored Petri net |
| **CRG** | Communicating reachability graph |
| **CRM** | Customer relationship management |
| **CSCW** | Computer supported cooperative work |
| **CTL** | Computational tree logic |

*Business and Scientific Workflows: A Web Service-Oriented Approach*, First Edition.
Edited by Wei Tan and MengChu Zhou.

| | |
|---|---|
| **CVRG** | CardioVascular Research Grid |
| **DICOM** | Digital Imaging and Communications in Medicine |
| **EHR** | Electronic health record |
| **EMR** | Electronic medical record |
| **EPR** | Endpoint reference |
| **ERP** | Enterprise resource planning |
| **FSM** | Finite state machine |
| **FSP** | Finite state process |
| **GPRS** | General packet radio services |
| **GPS** | Global positioning system |
| **GSI** | Grid Security Infrastructure |
| **GSM** | Global System for Mobile Communications |
| **GUI** | Graphical user interface |
| **HIS** | Hospital information systems |
| **HL7** | Health Level Seven |
| **HTTP** | Hypertext Transfer Protocol |
| **IEEE** | Institute of Electrical and Electronics Engineers |
| **IHE** | Integrating the Healthcare Enterprise |
| **IOPE** | Input, output, precondition and effect |
| **IPv6** | Internet Protocol version 6 |
| **IT** | Information technology |
| **ITIL** | Information Technology Infrastructure Library |
| **JSON** | JavaScript object notation |
| **KNN** | *k*-nearest neighbor |
| **LHC** | Large Hadron Collider |
| **LTL** | Linear temporal logic |
| **MADM** | Multiattribute decision making |
| **MIS** | Management information system |
| **NCI** | National Cancer Institute |
| **NCICB** | NCI Center for Bioinformatics |
| **NIH** | National Institutes of Health |
| **OA** | Office automation |
| **OASIS** | Organization for the Advancement of Structured Information Standards |
| **OWL** | Web Ontology Language |
| **OWL-S** | Web Ontology Language-Service |
| **PACS** | Picture archiving and communication systems |
| **PHISP** | Public-oriented Healthcare Information Service Platform |

| | |
|---|---|
| **PKI** | Public key infrastructure |
| **PPCE** | Processing preference with conditional expression |
| **PPMC** | Processing preference with multiple cases |
| **PPP** | Processing preference with priority |
| **QoS** | Quality of service |
| **REST** | Representational state transfer |
| **SaaS** | Software as a service |
| **SAW** | Simple additive weighting |
| **SC-net** | Service configuration net |
| **SCA** | Service Component Architecture |
| **SCOR** | Supply chain operations reference model |
| **SCP** | Service composition planner |
| **SDG** | Service dependency graph |
| **SDO** | Service Data Objects |
| **SFC** | Service functional configuration |
| **SMTP** | Simple Mail Transfer Protocol |
| **SNS** | Social network service |
| **SOA** | Service-oriented architecture |
| **SOAP** | Simple Object Access Protocol |
| **SSE** | Solution of the state-shift equation |
| **SVM** | Support vector machine |
| **SWF-net** | Service workflow net |
| **TF IDF** | Term frequency-inverse document frequency |
| **TQM** | Total quality management |
| **UDDI** | Universal Description, Discovery, and Integration |
| **UML** | Unified Modeling Language |
| **W3C** | World Wide Web Consortium |
| **WF-net** | Workflow net |
| **WfMC** | Workflow Management Coalition |
| **WS-CDL** | Web Services Choreography Description Language |
| **WSC** | Web service composition |
| **WSDL** | Web Service Definition Language |
| **XML** | Extensible Markup Language |
| **XPath** | XML Path Language |
| **XPDL** | XML Process Definition Language |
| **XSLT** | Extensible Stylesheet Language Transformation |
| **YAWL** | Yet Another Workflow Language |

# References

1. Schulte, W. R. and Y. V. Natis (1996). "Service Oriented" Architectures, Part 1 Gartner, Inc. SPA-00-7426.
2. Erl, T. (2005). *Service-oriented architecture: concepts, technology, and design.* Prentice Hall/Pearson PTR.
3. Erl, T. (2007). *SOA: principles of service design.* Upper Saddle River, NJ, USA, Prentice Hall Press.
4. W3C. "Web Services Architecture." Retrieved January 13, 2011, from http://www.w3.org/TR/ws-arch/.
5. Fayad, M. and D. C. Schmidt (1997). "Object-oriented application frameworks." *Communications of the ACM* **40** (10): 32–38.
6. Hollingsworth, D. (1995). The workflow reference model. *Technical report, Workflow Management Coalition.* TC00-1003.
7. Weske, M. (2007). *Business Process Management: Concepts, Languages, Architectures.* New York, Springer-Verlag.
8. OASIS. "Web Services Business Process Execution Language Version 2.0." Retrieved January 1, 2012, from http://docs.oasis-open.org/wsbpel/2.0/OS/wsbpel-v2.0-OS.html.
9. Davenport, T. H. and J. E. Short (1990). "The new industrial engineering: information technology and business process redesign." *Sloan Management Review.* Summer 1990, **31** (4): 11–27.
10. Hammer, M. (1990). "Reengineering work: don't automate, obliterate." *Harvard Business Review* **68** (4): 104–112.
11. Harrington, H. J. (1991). *Business Process Improvement: The Breakthrough Strategy For Total Quality, Productivity, and Competitiveness.* McGraw-Hill Professional.
12. Harry, M. J. and R. Schroeder (2000). *Six Sigma: The Breakthrough Management Strategy Revolutionizing the World's Top Corporations.* New York, Doubleday.
13. Feigenbaum, A. V. (2002). *Total Quality Management. Encyclopedia of Software Engineering.* John Wiley & Sons, Inc.

*Business and Scientific Workflows: A Web Service-Oriented Approach*, First Edition.
Edited by Wei Tan and MengChu Zhou.

14. Graham, I. (2006). *Business Rules Management and Service Oriented Architecture: A Pattern Language*. England, John Wiley & Sons.
15. Grudin, J. (1994). "Computer-supported cooperative work: history and focus." *IEEE Computer* **27** (5): 19–26.
16. Sumner, M. (2005). *Enterprise Resource Planning*. Upper Saddle River, New Jersey, Prentice Hall.
17. Kohavi, R., N. J. Rothleder, et al. (2002). "Emerging trends in business analytics." *Communications of the ACM* **45** (8): 45–48.
18. W3C. "Extensible Markup Language (XML)." Retrieved January 1, 2012, from http://www.w3.org/XML/.
19. W3C. "Resource Description Framework (RDF)." Retrieved April 1, 2012, from http://www.w3.org/RDF/.
20. json.org. "JSON (JavaScript Object Notation)." Retrieved January 01, 2012, from http://www.json.org/.
21. Curbera, F., M. Duftler, et al. (2002). "Unraveling the Web services web: an introduction to SOAP, WSDL, and UDDI." *IEEE Internet Computing* **6** (2): 86–93.
22. W3C. "SOAP Version 1.2 Specification Assertions and Test Collection (Second Edition)." Retrieved January 8, 2012, from http://www.w3.org/TR/2007/REC-soap12-testcollection-20070427/.
23. Richardson, L. and S. Ruby (2007). *RESTful Web Services*. O'Reilly Media, Inc.
24. W3C. "Web Services Description Language (WSDL) 1.1." Retrieved January 07, 2012, from http://www.w3.org/TR/wsdl.
25. W3C. "OWL-S: Semantic Markup for Web Services " Retrieved July 31, 2011, from http://www.w3.org/Submission/OWL-S/.
26. W3C. "Web Services Choreography Description Language Version 1.0." Retrieved January 1, 2012, from http://www.w3.org/TR/ws-cdl-10/.
27. OASIS. "UDDI Version 3.0.2." Retrieved January 8, 2012, from http://uddi.org/pubs/uddi_v3.htm.
28. W3C. "Web Services Description Language (WSDL) Version 2.0 Part 1: Core Language." Retrieved January 7, 2012, from http://www.w3.org/TR/wsdl20/.
29. mediawiki.org. "The MediaWiki API." Retrieved January 07, 2012, from http://www.mediawiki.org/wiki/API.
30. W3C. "OWL 2 Web Ontology Language " Retrieved July 31, 2011, from http://www.w3.org/TR/owl2-overview/.
31. OMG. "Business Process Model and Notation (BPMN) Version 2.0." Retrieved January 01, 2012, from http://www.omg.org/spec/BPMN/2.0/.
32. OASIS. "OASIS Open Composite Services Architecture." Retrieved April 1, 2012, from www.oasis-opencsa.org.
33. IBM. "IBM Business Process Manager." Retrieved June 26, 2012, from http://www-01.ibm.com/software/integration/business-process-manager/.
34. Oracle. "Oracle SOA Suite." Retrieved April 1, 2012, from http://www.oracle.com/technetwork/middleware/soasuite/overview/index.html.

35. W3C. "Web Services Activity Statement." Retrieved January 13, 2011, from http://www.w3.org/2002/ws/Activity.html.
36. Erl, T. (2004). *Service-oriented architecture: a field guide to integrating XML and web services*. Prentice Hall PTR.
37. Periorellis, P. (2007). *Securing Web Services: Practical Usage of Standards and Specifications*. IGI Global.
38. WfMC (2005). Process Definition Interface– XML Process Definition Language. *Technical report, Workflow Management Coalition*. WFMC-TC-1025.
39. van der Aalst, W. M. P. and K. M. v. Hee (2004). *Workflow Management: Models, Methods, and Systems*. Cambridge, MA, The MIT Press.
40. Berardi, D., D. Calvanese, et al. (2003). Automatic composition of e-services that export their behavior. International Conference on Service Oriented Computing (ICSOC). Trento, Italy, **2910** 43–58.
41. Dang, Z., O. H. Ibarra, et al. (2005). "On composition and lookahead delegation of e-services modeled by automata." *Theoretical Computer Science* **341** (1–3): 344–363.
42. Gerede, E., R. Hull, et al. (2004). Automated composition of e-services: lookaheads. 2nd International Conference on Service Oriented Computing. New York City, NY, USA, 252–262.
43. Ardagna, D. and B. Pernici (2006). "Dynamic web service composition with QoS constraints." *International Journal of Business Process Integration and Management* **1** (4): 233–243.
44. Canfora, G., M. D. Penta, et al. (2005). An approach for QoS-aware service composition based on genetic algorithms. Conference on Genetic and evolutionary computation. Washington, D.C., USA, 1069–1075.
45. Schuller, D., A. Polyvyanyy, et al. (2011). Optimization of complex QoS-aware service compositions. *International Conference on Service Oriented Computing*. Paphos, Cyprus, Springer 452–466.
46. Casati, F. and M. C. Shan (2001). "Dynamic and adaptive composition of e-services." *Information Systems* **26** (3): 143–163.
47. Fensel, D. and C. Bussler (2002). "The Web Service Modeling Framework WSMF." *Electronic Commerce Research and Applications* **1** (2): 113–137.
48. Tan, W., Y. Fan, et al. (2009). "A Petri net-based method for compatibility analysis and composition of web services in business process execution language." *IEEE Transactions on Automation Science and Engineering* **6** (1): 94–106.
49. Benatallah, B., F. Casati, et al. (2005). Developing adapters for Web services integration. International Conference on Advanced Information Systems Engineering (CAiSE). Porto, Portugal.
50. Kongdenfha, W., R. Saint-Paul, et al. (2006). An aspect-oriented framework for service adaptation. *International Conference on Service Oriented Computing (ICSOC)*. Chicago, USA, Springer.

51. Brogi, A. and R. Popescu (2006). Automated Generation of BPEL Adapters. *International Conference on Service Oriented Computing (ICSOC)*. Chicago, USA Springer 27–39.
52. Nezhad, H. R. M., B. Benatallah, et al. (2007). Semi automated adaptation of service interactions. 16th International World Wide Web Conference (WWW). Banff, Canada, 993–1002.
53. Nezhad, H. R. M., G. Y. Xu, et al. (2010). Protocol-aware matching of Web Service interfaces for adapter development. *World Wide Web Conference*. Raleigh, North Carolina, USA, ACM 731–740.
54. van der Aalst, W. M. P. and C. Stahl (2011). *Modeling Business Processes: A Petri Net-Oriented Approach*. Cambridge, MA, The MIT Press.
55. Ouyang, C., E. Verbeek, et al. (2007). "Formal semantics and analysis of control flow in WS-BPEL." *Science of Computer Programming Archive* **67** (2–3): 162–198.
56. Martens, A. (2005). Analyzing Web Service based business processes. *8th International Conference on Fundamental Approaches to Software Engineering*. Edinburgh, UK, Springer, **3442** 19–33.
57. Hinz, S., K. Schmidt, et al. (2005). Transforming BPEL to Petri nets. *International Conference on Business Process Management*. Nancy, France, Springer, 220–235.
58. Bultan, T., J. Su, et al. (2006). "Analyzing conversations of Web services." *IEEE Internet Computing* **10** (1): 18–25.
59. Fu, X., T. Bultan, et al. (2005). "Synchronizability of conversations among Web services." *IEEE Transactions on Software Engineering* **31** (12): 1042–1055.
60. Kazhamiakin, R., M. Pistore, et al. (2006). Analysis of communication models in web service compositions. *15th International Conference on World Wide Web (WWW)*. Edinburgh, Scotland, ACM, 267–276.
61. Baeten, J. C. M. and W. P. Weijland (1991). *Process Algebra*. New York, NY, USA, Cambridge University Press.
62. Foster, H., S. Uchitel, et al. (2003). Model-based verification of Web service compositions. 18th IEEE International Conference on Automated Software Engineering. Montreal, Canada, 152–161.
63. Foster, H., S. Uchitel, et al. (2004). Compatibility verification for Web service choreography. IEEE International Conference on Web Services. San Diego, California, USA, 738–741.
64. Foster, H., S. Uchitel, et al. (2006). Model-based analysis of obligations in Web service choreography. *Advanced International Conference on Telecommunications and International Conference on Internet and Web Applications and Services (AICT/ICIW 2006)*. Guadeloupe, French, IEEE Computer Society, 149.
65. Lucchi, R. and M. Mazzara (2007). "A pi-calculus based semantics for WS-BPEL." *Journal of Logic and Algebraic Programming* **70** (1): 96–118.

66. Kuang, L., Y. Xia, et al. (2010). Analyzing behavioral substitution of Web services based on pi-calculus. IEEE International Conference on Web Services (ICWS). Miami, Florida, USA, 441–448.

67. Chafle, G., S. Chandra, et al. (2005). Orchestrating composite Web services under data flow constraints. IEEE International Conference on Web Services. Orlando, Florida, 211–218.

68. Chafle, G. B., S. Chandra, et al. (2004). Decentralized orchestration of composite web services. *13th International World Wide Web conference*. New York, NY, USA, ACM 134–143.

69. Nanda, M. G., S. Chandra, et al. (2004). Decentralizing execution of composite web services. *19th annual ACM SIGPLAN conference on Object-oriented programming, systems, languages, and applications table of contents*. Vancouver, BC, Canada, ACM Press 170–187.

70. Nanda, M. G. and N. Karnik (2003). Synchronization analysis for decentralizing composite Web services. *ACM Symposium on Applied Computing*. Melbourne, Florida, ACM Press 407–414.

71. Sun, S. X., Z. Qingtian, et al. (2011). "Process-mining-based workflow model fragmentation for distributed execution." *IEEE Transactions on Systems, Man and Cybernetics, Part A: Systems and Humans* **41** (2): 294–310.

72. Taylor, I., E. Deelman, et al., Eds. (2007). *Workflows for e-Science: Scientific Workflows for Grids*. Springer.

73. Tan, W., L. Fong, et al. (2007). BPEL4Job: a fault-handling design for job flow management. *International Conference on Service-Oriented Computing*. Vienna, Austria, Springer, 27–42.

74. Hey, T., S. Tansley, et al. (2009). *The Fourth Paradigm: Data-Intensive Scientific Discovery*. Redmond, Washington, Microsoft Research.

75. Brumfiel, G. (2011). "High-energy physics: down the petabyte highway." *Nature* **469** (7330): 282–283.

76. Galperin, M. Y. and G. R. Cochrane (2011). "The 2011 Nucleic Acids Research Database Issue and the online Molecular Biology Database Collection." *Nucleic Acids Research* **39** (Suppl 1): D1–D6.

77. Benson, D. A., I. Karsch-Mizrachi, et al. (2011). "GenBank." *Nucleic Acids Research* **39** (Suppl 1): D32–D37.

78. Murata, T. (1989). "Petri nets: properties, analysis and applications." *Proceedings of the IEEE* **77** (4): 541–580.

79. Hrúz, B. and M. Zhou (2007). *Modeling and Control of Discrete-Event Dynamic Systems: With Petri Nets and Other Tools*. London, UK, Springer-Verlag.

80. Zhou, M. and K. Venkatesh (1998). *Modeling, Simulation, and Control of Flexible Manufacturing Systems: A Petri Net Approach*. Singapore, World Scientific.

81. van der Aalst, W. M. P. (1998). "The application of Petri nets to workflow management." *The Journal of Circuits, Systems and Computers* **8** (1): 21–66.

82. Jensen, K. and L. M. Kristensen (2009). *Coloured Petri Nets: Modeling and Validation of Concurrent Systems*. New York, Springer-Verlag.
83. Jensen, K. and G. Rozenberg (1991). *High-Level Petri Nets: Theory and Application*. London, UK, Springer-Verlag.
84. David, R. and H. Alla (2005). *Discrete, Continuous, and Hybrid Petri Nets*. Berlin Heidelberg, Springer Verlag.
85. Zhou, M. and N. Wu (2010). *System Modeling and Control with Resource-Oriented Petri Nets*. New York, CRC Press.
86. Milanovic, N. and M. Malek (2004). "Current solutions for Web service composition." *Internet Computing, IEEE* **8** (6): 51–59.
87. Jensen, K. (1995). *Coloured Petri Nets: Basic Concepts, Analysis Methods and Practical Use*, vol. 2, Berlin, Springer-Verlag.
88. Rozenberg, G. (1997). *Handbook of Graph Grammars and Computing by Graph Transformation*. Singapore, World Scientific.
89. West, D. B. (2008). *Introduction to Graph Theory*. Upper Saddle River, NJ, Prentice Hall.
90. Tan, W., Y. Fan, et al. (2010). "Data-driven service composition in enterprise SOA solutions: a Petri net approach." *IEEE Transactions on Automation Science and Engineering* **7** (3): 686–694.
91. Oh, S.-C., D. Lee, et al. (2008). "Effective web service composition in diverse and large-scale service networks." *IEEE Transactions on Services Computing* **1** (1): 15–32.
92. Zimmermann, O., V. Doubrovski, et al. (2005). Service-oriented architecture and business process choreography in an order management scenario: rationale, concepts, lessons learned. Conference on Object Oriented Programming Systems Languages and Applications. San Diego, California, USA, 301–312.
93. Ricken, J. (2007). Top-down modeling methodology for model-driven SOA construction. On the Move to Meaningful Internet Systems 2007: OTM 2007 Workshops. Vilamoura, Portugal, **4805** 323–332.
94. McIlraith, S. and T. Son (2002). Adapting golog for composition of semantic Web services. International Conference on Principles and Knowledge Representation and Reasoning (KR-02). Toulouse, France, 482–493.
95. McDermott, D. (2002). Estimated-regression planning for interactions with Web services. AI Planning Systems Conference (AIPS'02). Toulouse, France, 204–211.
96. Sirin, E., B. Parsia, et al. (2004). "HTN planning for Web Service composition using SHOP2." *Journal of Web Semantics* **1** (4): 377–396.
97. Cardoso, J. and A. Sheth (2003). "Semantic e-workflow composition." *Journal of Intelligent Information Systems* **21** (3): 191–225.
98. Sirin, E., J. Hendler, et al. (2003). Semi-automatic composition of web services using semantic descriptions. 1st Workshop on Web Services: Modeling, Architecture and Infrastructure. Angers, France, 17–24.

99. Narayanan, S. and S. A. McIlraith (2002). Simulation, verification and automated composition of Web services. *Eleventh International World Wide Web Conference*. Honolulu, Hawaii, USA, ACM Press 77–88.

100. Ponnekanti, S. R. and A. Fox (2002). SWORD: a developer toolkit for Web service composition. Eleventh International World Wide Web Conference (Alternate Paper Tracks). Honolulu, Hawaii, USA, 83–107.

101. Williams, A. B., A. Padmanabhan, et al. (2005). "Experimentation with local consensus ontologies with implications for automated service composition." *IEEE Transactions on Knowledge and Data Engineering* **17** (7): 969–981.

102. Kona, S., A. Bansal, et al. (2008). Generalized semantics-based service composition. IEEE International Conference on Web Services. Beijing, China, 219–227.

103. Lecue, F. and A. Delteil (2007). Making the difference in semantic web service composition. Twenty-Second AAAI Conference on Artificial Intelligence. Vancouver, Canada, 1383–1388.

104. Xiong, P., Y. Fan, et al. (2008). "QoS-aware Web service configuration." *IEEE Transactions on Systems, Man and Cybernetics, Part A: Systems and Humans* **38** (4): 888–895.

105. Xiong, P., Y. Fan, et al. (2009). "Web Service configuration under multiple quality-of-service attributes." *IEEE Transactions on Automation Science and Engineering* **6** (2): 311–321.

106. Rao, J. and X. Su (2004). A survey of automated Web service composition methods. First International Workshop on Semantic Web Services and Web Process Composition. San Diego, California, USA, 43–54.

107. Zeng, L. Z., B. Benatallah, et al. (2004). "QoS-aware middleware for Web Services composition." *IEEE Transactions on Software Engineering* **30** (5): 311–327.

108. Staab, S., W. van der Aalst, et al. (2003). "Web Services: been there, done that?" *IEEE Intelligent Systems* **18** (1): 72–85.

109. Carman, M., L. Serafini, et al. (2003). Web service composition as planning. ICAPS Workshop on Planning for Web Services. Trento, Italy.

110. Srivastava, B. and J. Koehler (2003). Web Service composition-current solutions and open problems. ICAPS Workshop on Planning for Web Services. Trento, Italy, 28–35.

111. Aggarwal, R., K. Verma, *et al.* (2004). Constraint driven Web service composition in METEOR-S. IEEE International Conference on Services Computing. Shanghai, China, 23–30.

112. Hull, R. and J. Su (2005). "Tools for composite web services: a short overview." *ACM SIGMOD Record* **34** (2): 86–95.

113. Yellin, D. M. and R. E. Strom (1997). "Protocol specifications and component adaptors." *ACM Transactions on Programming Languages and Systems* **19** (2): 292–333.

114. eBay. "Third Party Checkout." Retrieved June 26, 2012, from http://developer.ebay.com/DevZone/XML/docs/WebHelp/Checkout-Third_Party_Checkout.html.

115. Girault, C. and R. Valk (2003). *Petri nets for systems engineering*. Berlin, Springer-Verlag.

116. Szomszor, M., T. R. Payne, et al. (2006). Automated syntactic mediation for Web Service integration. International Conference on Web Services. Chicago, USA, 127–136.

117. Valmari, A. (1991). Stubborn sets for reduced state space generation. *10th International Conference on Applications and Theory of Petri Nets*. Bonn, Germany, Springer, 491–515.

118. Deng, S., Z. Wu, et al. (2006). Modeling service compatibility with pi-calculus for choreography. 25th International Conference on Conceptual Modeling (ER2006). Tucson, AZ, 26–39.

119. van der Aalst, W. M. P. (2000). "Loosely coupled interorganizational workflows: modeling and analyzing workflows crossing organizational boundaries." *Information and Management* **37** (2): 67–75.

120. Lohmann, N., P. Massuthe, et al. (2006). Analyzing interacting BPEL processes. *4th International Conference on Business Process Management*. Vienna, Austria, Springer, 17–32.

121. Martens, A., S. Moser, et al. (2006). Analyzing compatibility of BPEL processes. International Conference on Internet and Web Applications and Services/Advanced International Conference on Telecommunications (AICT-ICIW '06). Guadeloupe, French Caribbean, 147–147.

122. Hamadi, R. and B. Benatallah (2003). A petri net-based model for web service composition. Australasian Database Conference (ADC). Adelaide, Australia, 191–200.

123. Czarnecki, K. and U. Eisenecker (2000). *Generative Programming: Methods, Tools, and Applications*. Addison-Wesley.

124. Fiadeiro, J. L., A. Lopes, et al. (2006). A formal approach to service component architecture. Third International Workshop on Web Services and Formal Methods (WS-FM). Vienna, Austria, 193–213.

125. Liang, Q. A. and S. Y. W. Su (2005). "AND/OR graph and search algorithm for discovering composite web services." *International Journal of Web Services Research (IJWSR)* **2** (4): 48–67.

126. Zhou, Z. and Z. Duan (2006). Building business processes or assembling service components: reuse services with BPEL4WS and SCA. *4th European Conference on Web Services*. Zurich, Switzerland, IEEE, 138–147.

127. Suzuki, T., T. Kanehara, et al. (1993). On algebraic and graph structural properties of assembly Petri net. *IEEE International Conference on Robotics and Automation*. Atlanta, Georgia, USA, IEEE, 507–514.

128. Dantzig, G. B. (1963). *Linear Programming and Extensions*. Princeton, NJ, Princeton University Press.

129. Hwang, C. L. and K. L. Yoon (1981). *Multiple Attribute Decision Making: Methods and Applications*. New York, Springer.

130. Ma, J., Z. P. Fan, et al. (1999). "A subjective and objective integrated approach to determine attribute weights." *European Journal of Operational Research* **112** (2): 397–404.

131. Deif, A. (1986). *Sensitivity Analysis in Linear Systems*. New York, Springer.

132. Karakoc, E., K. Kardas, et al. (2006). A workflow-based Web service composition system. *IEEE/WIC/ACM International Conference on Web Intelligence and International Agent Technology Workshops*. Hong Kong, IEEE 113–116.

133. Xiong, P. and Y. Fan (2006). A QoS-aware UDDI model for web services discovery. Asia Pacific Symposium on SSME. Beijing, China, 121–123.

134. springsource.org. "The Spring Framework." Retrieved June 17, 2012, from http://www.springsource.org/.

135. Fan, Y. (2001). *Fundamentals of Workflow Management Technology*. New York, Springer.

136. Li, J., Y. Fan, et al. (2004). "Performance modeling and analysis of workflow." *IEEE Transactions on Systems, Man and Cybernetics, Part A: Systems and Humans* **34** (2): 229–242.

137. Li, Z. W. and M. C. Zhou (2004). "Elementary siphons of Petri nets and their application to deadlock prevention in flexible manufacturing systems." *IEEE Transactions on Systems, Man and Cybernetics, Part A: Systems and Humans* **34** (1): 38–51.

138. Menasce, D. A. (2002). "QoS issues in Web services." *IEEE Internet Computing* **6** (6): 72–75.

139. Ran, S. (2003). "A model for web services discovery with QoS." *ACM SIGecom Exchanges* **4** (1): 1–10.

140. Perryea, C. A. and S. Chung (2006). Community-based service discovery. IEEE International Conference on Web Services. Chicago, USA, 903–906.

141. Liu, Y., A. H. Ngu, et al. (2004). QoS computation and policing in dynamic web service selection. International World Wide Web conference on Alternate track papers & posters. New York, 66–73.

142. Ardagna, D. and B. Pernici (2005). Global and local QoS constraints guarantee in Web service selection. IEEE International Conference on Web Services. Orlando, USA, 805–806.

143. Jurca, R., B. Faltings, et al. (2007). Reliable QoS monitoring based on client feedback. International World Wide Web Conference. Banff, Canada, 1003–1011.

144. Huang, C. L., C. C. Lo, et al. (2006). "Reaching consensus: a moderated fuzzy web services discovery method." *Information and Software Technology* **48** (6): 410–423.

145. Lamparter, S., A. Ankolekar, et al. (2007). Preference-based selection of highly configurable Web services. International World Wide Web Conference. Banff, Canada, 1013–1022.

146. Gao, Y., B. Zhang, et al. (2005). Optimal selection of web services for composition based on interface-matching and weighted multistage graph. International Conference on Parallel and Distributed Computing, Applications and Technologies. Dalian, China, 336–338.
147. Gao, A. Q., D. Q. Yang, et al. (2005). Web service composition using integer programming-based models. IEEE International Conference on e-Business Engineering. Beijing, China, 603–606.
148. Garfinkel, R. and G. L. Nemhauser (1972). *Integer programming*. New York, John Wiley & Sons.
149. Yan, J., Y. Yang, et al. (2006). "SwinDeW-a p2p-based decentralized workflow management system." *IEEE Transactions on Systems, Man and Cybernetics, Part A: Systems and Humans* **36** (5): 922–935.
150. Wohlstadter, E., S. Tai, et al. (2004). GlueQoS: middleware to sweeten quality-of-service policy interactions. International Conference on Software Engineering. Edinburgh, United Kingdom, 189–199.
151. Guo, H., D. Zhang, et al. (2006). An optimized peer-to-peer overlay network for service discovery. IEEE Symposium on Computers and Communications. Sardinia, Italy, 82–87.
152. Wang, P., Z. Ding, et al. (2011). "Automated web service composition supporting conditional branch structures." *Enterprise Information Systems* to be published. [Online]. Available: http://dx.doi.org/10.1080/17517575.2011.584132.
153. Oh, S. C., D. Lee, et al. (2007). "Web service planner (wspr): an effective and scalable web service composition algorithm." *International Journal of Web Services Research (IJWSR)* **4** (1): 1–22.
154. Rao, J., P. Küngas, et al. (2006). "Composition of semantic web services using linear logic theorem proving." *Information Systems* **31** (4–5): 340–360.
155. Zheng, X. and Y. Yan (2008). An efficient syntactic web service composition algorithm based on the planning graph model. IEEE International Conference on Web Services. Beijing, China, 691–699.
156. WLCG. "The World Wide LHC Computer Grid." Retrieved July 30, 2011, from http://lcg.web.cern.ch/LCG/.
157. PubMed. "PubMed." Retrieved April 1, 2012, from http://www.ncbi.nlm.nih.gov/pubmed/.
158. Bell, G., T. Hey, et al. (2009). "Beyond the data deluge." *Science* **323** (5919): 1297–1298.
159. apache.org. "Apache Axis." Retrieved July 30, 2011, from http://axis.apache.org/.
160. apache.org. "Apache CXF." Retrieved July 30, 2011, from http://cxf.apache.org/.
161. Foster, I. (2006). "Globus toolkit version 4: software for service-oriented systems." *Journal of Computer Science and Technology* **21** (4): 513–520.
162. OMII-UK. "Open Middleware Infrastructure Institute." Retrieved April-01-2012, from http://www.omii.ac.uk/.

163. Barga, R., J. Jackson, et al. (2008). The trident scientific workflow workbench. *IEEE International Conference on eScience*. Indianapolis, IN, USA, IEEE 317–318.
164. Stevens, R. D., A. J. Robinson, et al. (2003). "myGrid: personalised bioinformatics on the information grid." *Bioinformatics* **19** (Suppl 1): i302–i304.
165. Goble, C., K. Wolstencroft, et al. (2007). Knowledge discovery for biology with Taverna: producing and consuming semantics in the Web of Science. *Semantic Web: Revolutionizing Knowledge Discovery in the Life Sciences*. C. J. O. Baker and K.-H. Cheung, editors Springer US, 355–395.
166. Saltz, J., T. Kurc, et al. (2008). "e-Science, caGrid, and translational biomedical research." *IEEE Computer* **41** (11): 58–66.
167. cvrg.org. "The CardioVascular Research Grid (CVRG)." Retrieved April 1, 2012, from http://cvrgrid.org/.
168. Helmer, K. G., J. L. Ambite, et al. (2011). "Enabling collaborative research using the Biomedical Informatics Research Network (BIRN)." *Journal of the American Medical Informatics Association* **18** (4): 416–422.
169. Von Eschenbach, A. C. and K. Buetow (2006). "Cancer informatics vision: caBIG™." *Cancer informatics* **2**: 22–24.
170. caBIG. "caBIG: cancer Biomedical Informatics Grid." Retrieved July 31, 2011, from http://cabig.cancer.gov.
171. Georgakopoulos, D., M. Hornick, et al. (1995). "An overview of workflow management: from process modeling to workflow automation infrastructure." *Distributed and parallel Databases* **3** (2): 119–153.
172. Bhagat, J., F. Tanoh, et al. (2010). "BioCatalogue: a universal catalogue of web services for the life sciences." *Nucleic Acids Research* **8** (Suppl 2): W689–W694.
173. Hull, D., K. Wolstencroft, et al. (2006). "Taverna: a tool for building and running workflows of services." *Nucleic Acids Research* **34** (Web Server issue): W729–W732.
174. Davidson, S. B. and J. Freire (2008). Provenance and scientific workflows: challenges and opportunities. *ACM International Conference on Management of Data (SIGMOD)*. Vancouver, Canada, ACM, 1345–1350.
175. Martin, C. J., M. H. Haji, et al. (2009). "A user-orientated approach to provenance capture and representation for in silico experiments, explored within the atmospheric chemistry community." *Philosophical Transactions of the Royal Society A: Mathematical, Physical and Engineering Sciences* **367** (1898): 2753–2770.
176. Siddiqui, M. and T. Fahringer (2010). *Grid Resource Management: On-Demand Provisioning, Advance Reservation, and Capacity Planning of Grid Resources*. Springer.
177. Ludäscher, B., I. Altintas, et al. (2006). "Scientific workflow management and the Kepler system." *Concurrency and Computation: Practice and Experience* **18** (10): 1039–1065.

178. Slominski, A. (2007). Adapting BPEL to scientific workflows. *Workflows for e-Science: Scientific Workflows for Grids*. I. J. Taylor, E. Deelman, D. B. Gannon, and M. Shields, editors, Springer, 208–226.

179. Chen, L., W. Emmerich, et al. (2009). Grid Services Orchestration with OMII-BPEL. *Grid computing: infrastructure, service, and applications*. L. Wang, W. Jie and J. Chen, editors CRC Press 191–222.

180. Oinn, T., M. Greenwood, et al. (2006). "Taverna: lessons in creating a workflow environment for the life sciences." *Concurrency and Computation: Practice and Experience* **18** (10): 1067–1100.

181. Churches, D., G. Gombas, et al. (2006). "Programming scientific and distributed workflow with Triana services." *Concurrency and Computation: Practice and Experience* **18** (10): 1021–1037.

182. Sroka, J., J. Hidders, et al. (2010). "A formal semantics for the Taverna 2 workflow model." *Journal of Computer and System Sciences* **76** (6): 490–508.

183. van der Aalst, W. M. P. (2003). "Don't go with the flow: Web services composition standards exposed." *IEEE Intelligent Systems* **18** (1): 72–76.

184. Tan, W., P. Missier, et al. (2010). "A comparison of using Taverna and BPEL in building scientific workflows: the case of caGrid." *Concurrency and Computation: Practice and Experience* **22** (9): 1098–1117.

185. Tan, W., I. Foster, et al. (2008). "Combining the Power of Taverna and caGrid: Scientific Workflows that Enable Web-Scale Collaboration." *IEEE Internet Computing* **12** (6): 61–68.

186. Roure, D. D., C. Goble, et al. (2009). "The design and realisation of the myExperiment Virtual Research Environment for social sharing of workflows." *Future Generation Computer Systems* **25** (5): 561–567.

187. Tan, W., R. Madduri, et al. (2010). "CaGrid Workflow Toolkit: a taverna based workflow tool for cancer grid." *BMC Bioinformatics* **11**: 542.

188. Sotomayor, B. and L. Childers (2006). *Globus Toolkit 4: Programming Java Services*. Morgan Kaufmann.

189. Saltz, J., S. Oster, et al. (2006). "caGrid: design and implementation of the core architecture of the cancer biomedical informatics grid." *Bioinformatics* **22** (15): 1910–1916.

190. Welch, V., F. Siebenlist, et al. (2003). Security for Grid services. 12th IEEE International Symposium on High Performance Distributed Computing. Seattle, WA, USA, 48–57.

191. Langella, S., S. Hastings, et al. (2008). "Sharing data and analytical resources securely in a biomedical research grid environment." *Journal of the American Medical Informatics Association* **15** (3): 363–373.

192. myExperiment.org. "myExperiment–caBIG Workflows." Retrieved July 31, 2011, from http://www.myexperiment.org/search?query=cabig&type=workflows.

193. Kuhn, T., E. Willighagen, et al. (2010). "CDK-Taverna: an open workflow environment for cheminformatics." *BMC Bioinformatics* **11**: 159.

194. Li, P., J. Castrillo, et al. (2008). "Performing statistical analyses on quantitative data in Taverna workflows: an example using R and maxdBrowse to identify differentially-expressed genes from microarray data." *BMC Bioinformatics* **9**: 334.

195. Bian, X., J. Klemm, et al. (2009). Data submission and curation for caArray, a standard based microarray data repository system. *3rd International Biocuration Conference*. Berlin, Germany, Nature Publishing Group.

196. myExperiment.org. "myExperiment -Query caArray Data Service and Retrieve files." Retrieved July 31, 2011, from http://www.myexperiment.org/workflows/1254.

197. Shipp, M. A., K. N. Ross, et al. (2002). "Diffuse large B-cell lymphoma outcome prediction by gene-expression profiling and supervised machine learning." *Nature Medicine* **8** (1): 68–74.

198. myExperiment.org. "myExperiment - Lymphoma Type Prediction Workflow." Retrieved July 31, 2011, from http://www.myexperiment.org/workflows/746.

199. Goble, C. A., J. Bhagat, et al. (2010). "myExperiment: a repository and social network for the sharing of bioinformatics workflows." *Nucleic Acids Research* **38** (Web Server issue): W677–W682.

200. boyd, d. m. and N. B. Ellison (2007). "Social network sites: definition, history, and scholarship." *Journal of Computer-Mediated Communication* **13** (1): 210–230.

201. Surowiecki, J. (2004). *The Wisdom of Crowds: Why the Many Are Smarter Than the Few and How Collective Wisdom Shapes Business, Economies, Societies, and Nations*. Doubleday Books.

202. Gewin, V. (2008). "The new networking nexus." *Nature* **451** (7181): 1024–1025.

203. Foster, I. (2011). "Globus online: accelerating and democratizing science through cloud-based services." *IEEE Internet Computing* **15** (3): 70–73.

204. Goecks, J., A. Nekrutenko, et al. (2010). "Galaxy: a comprehensive approach for supporting accessible, reproducible, and transparent computational research in the life sciences." *Genome Biology* **11** (8): R86.

205. Klimeck, G., M. McLennan, et al. (2008). "nanohub.org: advancing education and research in nanotechnology." *Computing in Science & Engineering* **10** (5): 17–23.

206. Bechhofer, S., D. D. Roure, et al. (2010). Research objects: towards exchange and reuse of digital knowledge. *First International Workshop on the Future of The Web for Collaborative Science (FWCS2010)*. Raleigh, NC, USA, Nature Precedings.

207. Roure, D. D. (2010). "e-Science and the Web." *IEEE Computer* **43** (5): 90–93.

208. Tan, P. N., M. Steinbach, et al. (2006). *Introduction to Data Mining*. Boston, Pearson Addison Wesley.

209. Xie, T., S. Thummalapenta, et al. (2009). "Data mining for software engineering." *IEEE Computer* **42** (8): 55–62.

210. Martin, R., W. Robert, et al. (2010). "Recommendation systems for software engineering." *IEEE Software* **27**: 80–86.

211. Begel, A., K. Y. Phang, et al. (2010). Codebook: discovering and exploiting relationships in software repositories. *32nd ACM/IEEE International Conference on Software Engineering*. Cape Town, South Africa ACM 125–134.

212. van der Aalst, W. M. P. (2011). *Process Mining: Discovery, Conformance and Enhancement of Business Processes*. New York, NY, USA, Springer-Verlag.

213. van der Aalst, W. (2009). TomTom for business process management (TomTom4BPM). *21st International Conference on Advanced Information Systems Engineering (CAiSE)*. Amsterdam, The Netherlands, Springer, 2–5.

214. van der Aalst, W. M. P. (2009). Using process mining to generate accurate and interactive business process maps. *International Business Information Systems Workshops*. Poznan, Poland, Springer, 1–14.

215. Koop, D., C. E. Scheidegger, et al. (2008). "VisComplete: automating suggestions for visualization pipelines." *IEEE Transactions on Visualization and Computer Graphics* **14** (6): 1691–1698.

216. Chinthaka, E., J. Ekanayake, et al. (2009). CBR based workflow composition assistant. *World Congress on Services*. Los Angeles, California, USA, IEEE Computer Society, 352–355.

217. Bruno, G., F. Dengler, et al. (2011). "Key challenges for enabling agile BPM with social software." *Journal of Software Maintenance and Evolution: Research and Practice* **23** (4): 297–326.

218. Erol, S., M. Granitzer, et al. (2010). "Combining BPM and social software: contradiction or chance?" *Journal of Software Maintenance and Evolution: Research and Practice* **22** (6–7): 449–476.

219. Koschmider, A., M. Song, et al. (2010). "Social software for business process modeling." *Journal of Information Technology* **25** (3): 308–322.

220. Maamar, Z., H. Hacid, et al. (2011). "Why Web services need social networks." *IEEE Internet Computing* **15** (2): 90–94.

221. Maamar, Z., F. Noura, et al. (2011). "Using social networks for Web services discovery." *IEEE Internet Computing* **15**: 48–54.

222. Tan, W., J. Zhang, et al. (2010). "Network Analysis of Scientific Workflows: a Gateway to Reuse." *IEEE Computer* **43** (9): 54–61.

223. Nooy, W. d., A. Mrvar, et al. (2011). *Exploratory Social Network Analysis with Pajek*. New York, Cambridge University Press.

224. Tan, W., J. Zhang, et al. (2011). ServiceMap: providing map and GPS assistance to service composition in bioinformatics. IEEE International Conference on Services Computing (SCC). Washington, DC, 632–639.

225. Hall, M., E. Frank, et al. (2009). "The WEKA data mining software: an update." *ACM SIGKDD Explorations Newsletter* **11** (1): 10–18.

226. Salton, G. and C. Buckley (1988). "Term-weighting approaches in automatic text retrieval." *Information Processing and Management* **24** (5): 513–523.

227. He, H., H. Wang, et al. (2007). BLINKS: ranked keyword searches on graphs. *ACM International Conference on Management of Data (SIGMOD)*. ACM, 305–316.

228. Liu, Z., Q. Shao, et al. (2010). Searching workflows with hierarchical views. 36th International Conference on Very Large Data Bases. Singapore, 918–927.

229. The Economist (2010). The data deluge: Businesses, governments and society are only starting to tap its vast potential. As seen in http://www.economist.com/opinion/displaystory.cfm?story_id=15579717 (February 25, 2010).

230. Dean, J. and S. Ghemawat (2008). "MapReduce: simplified data processing on large clusters." *Communications of the ACM* **51** (1): 107–113.

231. Chen, C., D. Neal, et al. (2013). "Understanding the Evolution of a Disaster—A Framework for Assessing Crisis in a System Environment (FACSE)." *Natural Hazards* **65** (1): 407–422.

232. Du, Y., C. Jiang, et al. (2009). "Modeling and monitoring of E-commerce workflows." *Information Sciences* **179**: 995–1006.

233. Wang, J. (2012). "Emergency healthcare workflow modeling and timeliness analysis." *IEEE Transactions on Systems, Man and Cybernetics, Part A*, **42** (6): 1323–1331.

234. Wang, J., W. Tepfenhart, et al. (2009). "Emergency Response Workflow Resource Requirements Modeling and Analysis." *IEEE Transactions on Systems, Man and Cybernetics, Part C*, **39** (3): 270–283.

235. Wang, J., D. Rosca, et al. (2008). "Dynamic workflow modeling and analysis in incident command systems." *IEEE Transactions on Systems, Man and Cybernetics, Part A* **38**, (5): 1041–1055.

# Index

activity diagram, 134
  decision node, 138–139
  guard, 138
acyclic well-structured process (AWSP), 48
acyclic Petri net, 108
aggregation function, 105
Amazon EC2, 192
API, 121, *see also* Application Programming Interface
Application Programming Interface (API), 121
assembly Petri net, 108
association rule mining, 210–211
automatic service composition, 75, 100, 125
availability, 104–105

big data, 224
binary mutual exclusion (BME), 154
BioCatalogue, 197
BPEL, *see also* Business Process Execution Language
Business Process Execution Language (BPEL), 15–16
  CPN formalism for BPEL, 70, 74
  example, 17
business process management (BPM), 5
  business process improvement (BPI), 6
  business process reengineering (BPR), 6
  business process outsourcing (BPO), 222
Business Process Model and Notation (BPMN), 18
business rule management system (BRMS), 7

caBIG, *see also* cancer Biomedical Informatics Grid
cancer Biomedical Informatics Grid (caBIG), 166
caGrid, *see also* cancer Grid
cancer Grid (caGrid), 166
  caGrid Workflow Toolkit, 174
  example workflows, 183–187
choreography, 100
CIMFlow-System, 123
circuit, 108
cloud computing, 222
CodeBook, 198
colored Petri nets (CPN), *see also* Petri nets
communicating reachability graph (CRG), 68, 81–82
  method to construct CRG, 82–83
  example, 83–84
composite service, 133
computer-supported cooperative work (CSCW), 7
configuration process (CP), 111
cost, 104–105
CP, 111, *see also* configuration process
CPN, *see also* colored Petri nets

*Business and Scientific Workflows: A Web Service-Oriented Approach*, First Edition.
Edited by Wei Tan and MengChu Zhou.

data driven composition rules, 45
sequential, 46
parallel, 46
choice, 47
decision node, 138–139
disassembly Petri net, 107
leaf, 107
root, 107
initial marking, 108
final marking, 107
disaster, 225
domain preference, 136, 137
dual attribute optimization, 118
Dummy Web services, 105, 108

e-Science, 162
Emergency Workflow, 225
Enterprise resource planning (ERP), 7
Extensible Markup Language, *see also* XML
Examples
JavaScript Object Notation (JSON), 10
online appointment registration, 152
online drug purchase, 148
online shopping, 155

Facebook, 190
final marking, 107

global optimization, 125
Globus Toolkit, 165
Google, 190
guard, 138

IBM, International Business Machines, 18
IBM Business Process Manager, 18, 40, 93
initial marking, 108

JavaScript Object Notation (JSON), 9
example, 10

LinkedIn, 190
leaf, 107
local optimization, 125

MADM, 116, *see also* multi-attribute decision-making
matrix, 214
adjacent matrix, 214–215
reachability matrix, 215–216
transfer matrix, 216–217
mediation, *see also* mediator
mediator, 76
types of mediator, 88–89
generation, 90–92
MethodBox, 197
multi-attribute decision-making (MADM), 116
multiset, 35
myExperiment, 182, 191, 194–197
workflow network, 199–206
operation network, 212–219
myGrid, 195

non-dummy Web services, 104

orchestration, 100, 123
online appointment registration, 152
online drug purchase, 148
online shopping, 155
Ontology Web Language–Service (OWL-S), 18
optimization, 125
global optimization, 125
local optimization, 125
Oracle, 18
Oracle SOA Suite, 18

Pajek, 200
parallel structure, 153
Petri nets, 29–30
colored Petri nets, CPN, 36–37, 41
CPN formalism for BPEL, 70, 74
comparison with CPN, 38
execution rule, 30–31
properties: reachability, boundedness, and liveness, 31
reachability graph, 31
process mining, 198
processing preference with conditional expression (PPCE), 139, 142

processing preference with multiple cases (PPMC), 139, 145
processing preference with priority (PPP), 139, 147

Quality of Service (QoS), 99
QoS attributes, 104–105
  aggregation function, 104–105
  availability, 104–105
  cost, 104–105
  reliability, 104
  successful execution rate, 104
QoS modeling, 99
QoS specification, 99

realizable configuration process, 111
reliability, 104
Representational State Transfer (REST), 14
  example, 15
root, 107

SAP, 18
SCA, *see also* Service Component Architecture
SC-net, 103, *see also* service configuration net
scientific workflow, 26, 169
  systems, 170
SDG, 102, *see also* service dependency graph
service, *see also* Web service
service community, 139
Service Component Architecture (SCA), 18, 101
  Service Data Object (SDO), 18
service composition, 75, 100, 125
  compatibility of service composition, 77
Service composition planner (SCP), 139
service configuration manager, 121–122
service configuration net (SC-net), 103
service configuration planner, 121–122
service configuration optimizer, 121–122
service dependency graph (SDG), 102
service functional configuration (SFC), 102
ServiceMap, 182, 207
Service Net, 49
  Reduced Service Net (RSN), 51
  decomposition of RSN, 54–55
service-oriented architecture (SOA), 1
  eight principles of, 2
service-oriented science, 163
  examples, 166
Service request, *see also* user's request
Service set, 108
Service Workflow Net (SWF-net), 70–71
  example, 71–72
  composition of SWF-nets, 75
SFC, 102, *see also* service functional configuration
SSE, 112, *see also* solution of state-shift equation
Simple Object Access Protocol (SOAP), 2, 13, 122
  example, 13–14
Six Sigma, 7
SOA, *see also* service-oriented architecture
social computing, 190
  and workflows, 223
social network services (SNS), 190
  for scientists, 191–194
software as a service (SaaS), 222
Solution of State-shift Equation (SSE), 112, 114, 115
Spring Framework, 122
state-shift equation, 110, 112
successful execution rate, 104

Taverna workbench, 171
  comparison with BPEL, 173
TF–IDF: term frequency–inverse document frequency, 212
tModel, 124
total quality management (TQM), 7
Trident, the scientific workflow tool, 165
Twitter, 190

UML class diagram, 41
aggregation relation, 41
generalization relation, 41
generation relation, 41
realization relation, 42–43
CPN representation, 43–44
Universal Description, Discovery, and Integration (UDDI), 3, 10–11, 121–122
user preference, 134, 137
user's request, 139

W3C, 2
Web service, 2–3
related standards, 8
service client, registry, and provider, 3–4
WS-Policy, WS-Addressing, WS-Transfer, WS-Enumeration, 19
Web Services Choreography Description Language (WS-CDL), 17
Web service composition, 100, 125, *see also* service composition and automatic service composition
Web service configuration, 100, 116
example, 102, 117–118
Web Service Definition Language (WSDL), 3, 11, 121
example, 12
Web service discovery, 125–126
Web Services Resource Framework (WSRF), 166
Weka: the data mining software, 210
wisdom of crowds, 191
Workflow, 4, 137, 225
engine, 19
glossary, 4–5
reference model, 4, 19
scientific workflow, *see also* scientific workflow
workflow-as-a-service, 222
workflow management, 225
Workflow Net, 32
soundness, 34

XML, 3, 9, 122
example, 10
XML Process Definition Language (XPDL), 20

Yahoo Pipes, 192

Printed and bound by CPI Group (UK) Ltd, Croydon, CR0 4YY

27/10/2024

14580265-0003